Pillars and Shadows

Statebuilding as peacebuilding in Solomon Islands

Pillars and Shadows

Statebuilding as peacebuilding in Solomon Islands

John Braithwaite, Sinclair Dinnen, Matthew Allen,
Valerie Braithwaite and Hilary Charlesworth

ANU
THE AUSTRALIAN NATIONAL UNIVERSITY

E PRESS

ANU

E PRESS

Published by ANU E Press
The Australian National University
Canberra ACT 0200, Australia
Email: anuepress@anu.edu.au
This title is also available online at: http://epress.anu.edu.au/pillars_shadows_citation.html

---

National Library of Australia Cataloguing-in-Publication entry

Title: Pillars and shadows : statebuilding as peacebuilding in Solomon Islands / John
                Braithwaite ... [et al.]

ISBN: 9781921666780 (pbk.) 9781921666797 (pdf)

Notes: Includes bibliographical references.

Subjects: Ethnic conflict--Solomon Islands.
                Peace-building--Solomon Islands.
                Solomon Islands--History.
                Solomon Islands--Politics and government.

Other Authors/Contributors:
                Braithwaite, John.

Dewey Number: 305.80099593

Cover design and layout by ANU E Press

Cover photo: Deference and affection of young armed men of the Isatabu Freedom Movement
on the front line at Alligator Creek are palpable in this photo of sisters and women's leaders of
various churches as peacemakers — Simon Schluter, *The Age*

Contents

Acknowledgments

Thanks to our Advisory Panel for their sage advice on the fieldwork and comments on the book; they bear no responsibility for its deficiencies. Our deepest thanks go to many Solomon Islanders on all sides of the conflict who generously gave of their time and shared their insights and to Regional Assistance Mission to Solomon Islands (RAMSI) members and other internationals whom we interviewed in Australia, New Zealand, Fiji, Papua New Guinea, Vanuatu and in Solomon Islands between 2005 and 2010. The Appendix to this book describes the nature of the interviews conducted by John Braithwaite and all the other members of the team of co-authors for this book who spent time in Solomon Islands doing fieldwork for the research with him. Sinclair Dinnen and Matthew Allen have undertaken their own extensive research in Solomon Islands over many years in addition to these interviews. Matthew's PhD research on the Solomon Islands conflict will be published in future as a book. It will take much further some of the issues only touched on in this publication.

We are fortunate in having such an outstanding community of scholars of Solomon Islands at The Australian National University and beyond, whose work has enriched ours. Their work is cited at relevant points in our text. We especially acknowledge the formidable work in documenting the story of the conflict that has been done in the important books by Jon Fraenkel (2004a) and Clive Moore (2004). Our work would have been much more difficult if we did not have this scholarship to lean on.

Special thanks for all manner of support from our colleagues on the project Leah Dunn, Kate Macfarlane, Charlie Beauchamp-Wood and Nick Kitchin. Leah (2005–08) and Kate (2009–10) in turn provided outstanding administrative leadership for the considerable infrastructure of an undertaking as large as the Peacebuilding Compared project. We also thank the Australian Research Council for funding this research.

We acknowledge our ANU E Press series editor, Margaret Thornton, managers, Lorena Kanellopoulos and Duncan Beard, copyeditor, Jan Borrie, and anonymous referees for their thoughtful insights and guidance. Their wonderful publishing model means this book is available free on the Internet and also at a modest price as a handsome hardcopy. This is a special virtue for research of which the important readers are in developing countries.

Please feel encouraged to make comments on the book on the Peacebuilding Compared web site: <http://peacebuilding.anu.edu.au>

Advisory Panel, Solomon Islands case of Peacebuilding Compared

Dr Jon Fraenkel, The Australian National University

David Hegarty, The Australian National University

Dr John Roughan, Solomon Islands Development Trust

Professor Ted Wolfers, University of Wollongong

John Wood, Consultant to RAMSI Machinery of Government

Glossary

AFP	Australian Federal Police
ASPI	Australian Strategic Policy Institute
AusAID	Australian Agency for International Development
BRA	Bougainville Revolutionary Army
COC	Christian Outreach Centre
DPP	Director of Public Prosecutions
EU	European Union
GDP	gross domestic product
GLF	Guadalcanal Liberation Front
IFM	Isatabu Freedom Movement
IMF	International Monetary Fund
IPMT	International Peace Monitoring Team
kastom	custom or customary law
kiap	patrol officers in colonial Papua and New Guinea
MEF	Malaita Eagle Force
MP	Member of Parliament
nabe	placid or peaceful
NGO	non-governmental organisation
NPC	National Peace Council
NZAID	New Zealand's International Aid and Development Agency
OECD	Organisation for Economic Cooperation and Development
PMC	Peace Monitoring Council
PNG	Papua New Guinea
PPF	Participating Police Force (police component of RAMSI)
RAMSI	Regional Assistance Mission to Solomon Islands
SDA	Seventh-Day Adventist Church
SICA	Solomon Islands Christian Association
SSEC	South Sea Evangelical Church
TRC	Truth and Reconciliation Commission
UK	United Kingdom

UN	United Nations
UNDP	United Nations Development Programme
UNICEF	United Nations International Children's Emergency Fund
UNPOL	United Nations Police Force
US	United States of America
waku	Chinese/Asian person
wantok	People with whom one shares a set of mutual social obligations. Literally translated as 'speaking the same language'.
wantokism	the wantok system
WWF	World Wide Fund for Nature

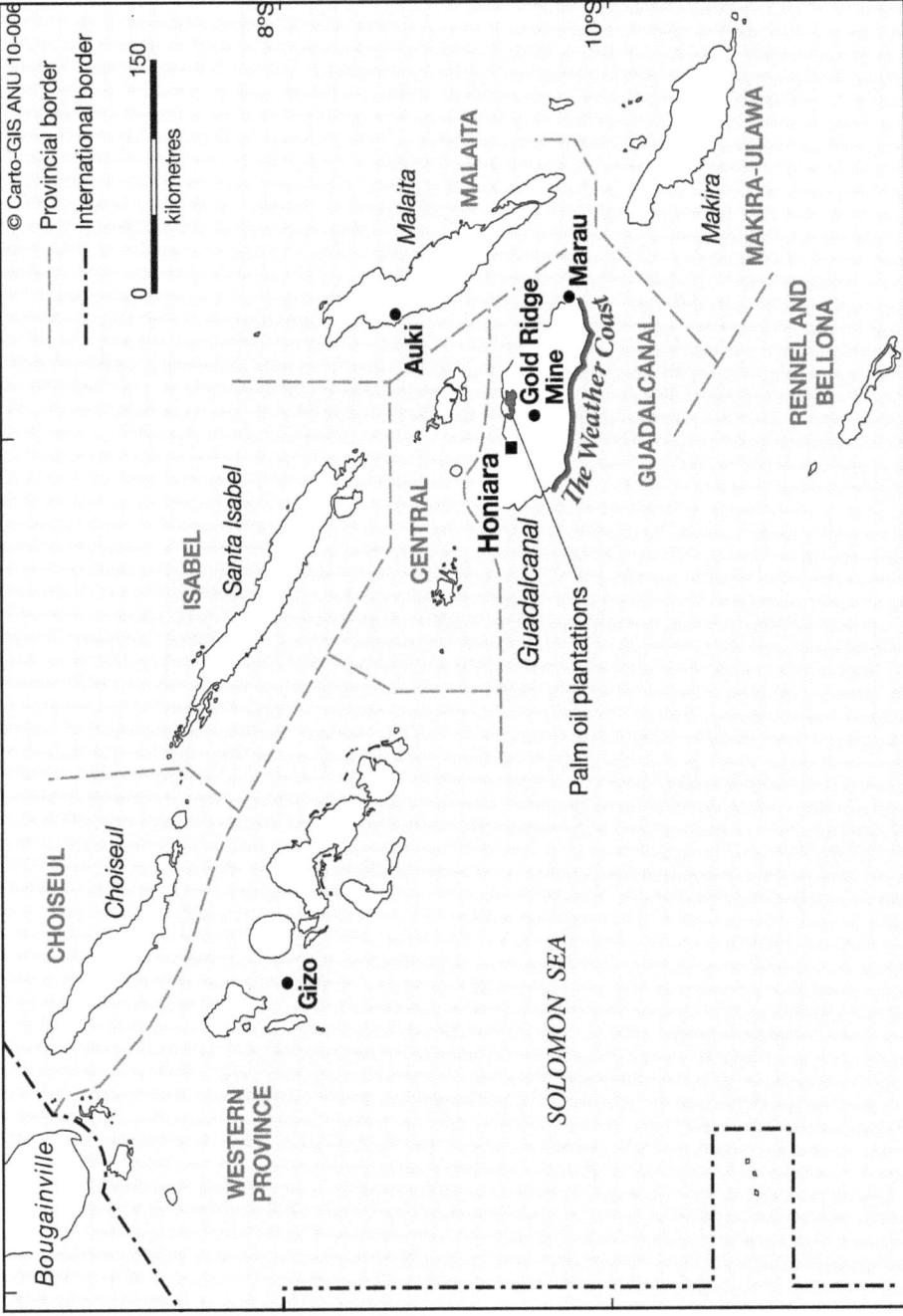

Map of Solomon Islands

Provincial border

International border

0   150

kilometres

8°S

10°S

CHOISEUL

Choiseul

WESTERN PROVINCE

Bougainville

Gizo

ISABEL

Santa Isabel

MALAITA

Malaita

Auki

CENTRAL

Honiara

Guadalcanal

Palm oil plantations

●Gold Ridge
  Mine

Marau

The Weather Coast

GUADALCANAL

MAKIRA-ULAWA

Makira

RENNEL AND
BELLONA

SOLOMON SEA

1. Peacebuilding Compared and the Solomons conflict

Statebuilding that neglects specific sources of conflict

The Solomon Islands conflict of 1998–2003 is often read simply as a story of a failed or fragile state. It was not a state that had been built and then failed. Rather it was a state that had never consolidated after decades since independence of taking at least as many steps back as steps forward. It was not a formed state; up to this point in its history, it has been a state in a process of formation. In this book, we conceive peacebuilding as the craft of supporting institutions, including non-state institutions, in a process of growing to provide human security. We do not conceive it as a process of following an outside architect's plan to erect core pillars of the state such as law, economic governance and public administration. We will argue that there is little that is generic about statebuilding in Solomon Islands and much that is shadowy in a distinctively Solomons way. There is a formal state defined by the nation's Constitution, but it is shadowed by economically, politically and diplomatically powerful figures who have shaped the nation's history, and particularly its history of conflict. In our text, we consider William Reno's (1995) metaphor of the shadow state and the earlier metaphor of the shadow (or underground) economy. And we ponder the possibility that when pillars of the state are driven into the sand of shadow governance that envelops the formal state to influence the outcome in moments of crisis, a false sense of security is created.

We read the Solomons conflict as occurring at the conjunction of a complex of fragilities—some in the Parliament, some in the police, some in a fragmented nation where the dignity of ethnic identities was exploited, some in the global political economy, others in institutions that regulate a scramble for key resources: land, forests, fish. Given this intricate knot of fragilities that is a legacy of Solomons history and culture, the peacebuilding[1] that has been done has been surprisingly successful. And in the event, this conflict that seemed forebodingly out of control did not spread to most villages of the nation, affecting

---

1 We use peacebuilding in the most general sense here to mean any peacemaking, peacekeeping, pre-conflict prevention of violence and post-conflict building of commitment to peace by any means, whether by local or international actors.

only Honiara and its surrounds, the Weather Coast, parts of North Malaita and pockets of Western Province. Perhaps 90 per cent of villages continued peacefully working at their village economies throughout, not dependent on the modern state and economy, and therefore also not greatly affected by the statebuilding intended to rebuild peace.

We conclude in the final chapter that while peacebuilding in Solomon Islands made many large and small mistakes, people learnt from these mistakes. This learning of greater humility in peacebuilding could be one reason why the Solomons peace has not failed so far. On the pessimistic side, we find it to be slow and costly learning. We wonder if there is not some inevitability about this. Nevertheless, we draw some lessons from the Solomon Islands intervention on how slow learning might be quickened somewhat by rethinking the peacebuilding craft. This rethinking involves overcoming fear of 'mission creep'. It means seeing 'peacebuilding creep' as about mission contraction as much as mandate expansion. The craft of peace as learned in Solomon Islands is about enabling spaces for dialogue that define where the mission should pull back to allow local actors to expand the horizons of their peacebuilding ambition. This leads us to compare the slow-learning approach of the 'heavy' Solomon Islands intervention initially aimed at rebuilding core pillars of the state with the 'slow-food' approach (Boege 2006; Bowden et al. 2009) of the Bougainville 'light intervention' (Regan 2010) next door.

Peacebuilding as launched in Honiara in 2003 has been lauded by the Organisation for Economic Cooperation and Development (OECD 2005:47) as an example of 'good practice' in a whole-of-government approach. Our analysis is more mixed. We see the intervention from 2003 to 2010 as involving a crude statebuilding agenda; it was not about unpicking the specificities of a knot of fragilities. For the most part, fragile strands in the web of Solomons society have been neither strengthened one by one nor rewoven into a more sturdy fabric of Solomons society. With such an important set of specific fragilities, we worry that there is considerable risk of Solomons society unravelling into violence again. Chapters 8 and 9 summarise the structural factors and proximate factors that led to armed violence and the peacebuilding weaknesses that were also ably identified in the National Peace Council (NPC 2004) strategic plan for 2004–09. The peacebuilding that has occurred has barely begun to tackle these specific weaknesses and sources of the original conflict (summarised in Table 8.1). Lise Howard's (2008) comparative study of completed UN multidimensional peacekeeping operations found an organisational learning culture in the peace operation to be the best predictor of its success:

> UN peacekeeping tends to be more successful when the peacekeepers are actively learning from the environment in which they are deployed. In other words, rather than seeking to impose preconceived notions

about how the missions should unfold, peacekeeping is at its best when the peacekeepers—both civilian and military—take their cues from the local population, and not UN headquarters, about how best to implement mandates. (Howard 2008:2)

The Solomons' experience is consistent with Howard's results. The intervention was a mix of success and failure that might have been more successful had it been adapting and learning earlier and more assiduously from indigenous organisations such as churches, women's groups and the National Peace Council. The peace almost unravelled completely on the streets of Honiara in 2006 at the hands of people who felt they were not listened to by the state or by the foreigners who were propping up its pillars. While recognising the limits that the narrower statebuilding strategy might place on the sustainability of the peace, we must acknowledge that strengthening the core of the state, especially its institutions of law and order, quickly re-established peace and mostly maintained it between 2003 and 2010. Or has it been the simple presence of peacekeepers for seven years that has maintained it?

This book tells the story of a country that might have had a much more calamitous conflict than it did. An international peace operation with an unusually strong rule-of-law agenda prevented a larger catastrophe. It is a case of a complex of structural grievances being exploited by men with political ambitions in a context in which holding power is a fragile accomplishment. These electoral conditions arose from a tragic interplay of social fragmentation, indigenous traditions of local politics (*wantokism*)[2] and global resource politics. Indigenous politicians were used by shadow governments of ethnic others (and vice versa). This book argues that the initial policy settings of the peace operation that saved Solomon Islands from deeper tragedy might not be settings that would work to create a secure future. Those settings might require a further shift of emphasis from statebuilding back to village building, from national policing to village policing, from incarceration to reconciliation in civil society, from an economics of short-term fiscal stabilisation to education for long-term leadership. This is even though statebuilding, police-led peacekeeping and fiscal stabilisation have saved the day up to a point.

If indigenous leadership is strong enough, island communities might seize back control of sustainable logging and sustainable fishing from foreign interests to fund the large investment to create a highly educated future generation who can develop new opportunities in tourism, agriculture and mining. A new generation of leaders might fix insecure land tenure and the host of other specific problems

---

2   *Wantok* is an adaptable and important concept in Solomon Islands, and Melanesia more generally, meaning in its broadest usage 'one's people with whom one shares a set of social obligations'. Literally, it is translated as people speaking the same language.

that led to this conflict. If they fail, the Solomons will be an interesting test in the decades ahead of whether generic statebuilding that for the most part neglects the specificities of a conflict can nevertheless secure continuing peace.

The Solomon Islands case differs from our Bougainville case in that indigenous leadership has so far (until 2010) been less effective in seizing a peacebuilding agenda. We will argue that an important reason for this is because it has been given less space to do so on a peacebuilding stage crowded with foreigners (Kabutaulaka 2006). As the resistance of the government of Manasseh Sogavare (2006–07) to the Australian-led intervention will illustrate, Solomons society has been more constrained by external forces from fully seizing that local control. To date, the Solomons shows much less resilience of reconciliation than Bougainville. We will see that when the National Peace Council showed promise as an enabler of participatory indigenous peacebuilding and reconciliation, it was snuffed out. Sustained reconciliation at many levels of society is important in conflicts such as Bougainville and the Solomons because both involve complex, multi-layered identity politics (see Chapter 7). In part, we read violence as a means to assert the dignity of different layers of identity that proponents believe have been treated with contempt by others and by the government. In the process, identity defenders have sought to heap indignity on the other, including on outside identities such as *waku* (Chinese/Asian). Healing indignity suffered at these multiple layers of identity is an unfinished reconciliation agenda. Like Morgan Brigg (2009), we see strengths and opportunities in harnessing *wantok* identities for peacebuilding, even as these identities have been factors in the conflict (Chapter 7).

External support for statebuilding has been much more intensive than in Bougainville or Timor-Leste or perhaps any other case known to us.[3] To a degree, we will conclude that statebuilding, including state prosecutions, has crowded off the political agenda the kind of iterative building of reconciliation we see in Bougainville (and to a lesser extent in Timor-Leste). Yet Solomon Islands is not like the Indonesian cases of Peacebuilding Compared, where there is both elite and grassroots support for what we called 'non-truth and reconciliation' (Braithwaite et al. 2010a). Especially today in Solomon Islands, there is formidable support for both truth and reconciliation. The absence has been of effective implementation of that commitment to reveal truths of the root

---

3 Iraq is the case that could be more expensive per capita if one is willing to call it a case of peacebuilding. Spending on statebuilding per capita in Afghanistan has been unfavourably compared as so much less than in Timor-Leste and the former Yugoslavia (for example, Maley 2009). The financial commitment to RAMSI from the two largest contributors, Australia and New Zealand, ranged between a low of A$232 million and a high of A$263 million per annum for the years 2003–09 (for a population of 500 000) (Parliamentary Inquiry 2009:101). Admittedly, most of this spending is on the security sector—a pattern of which we will be critical. Yet this RAMSI expenditure does not include bilateral aid from these two countries and from many other large donors such as the European Union, Japan, the United States and Taiwan, multilateral aid from UN agencies such as the UN Development Programme (UNDP) and from organisations such as Oxfam and World Vision.

causes of the conflict and to ground reconciliation in an acknowledgment of those truths. One of the problems here is that reconciliation has been gamed for cash compensation that was then embezzled by elites. This in turn was a result of the opportunities for extortion from and by powerbrokers of multiple shadow states that feast off the opportunities created by instability in the formal state.

As in Indonesia (Braithwaite et al. 2010a), in Solomon Islands, anomie—a breakdown of normative orders that previously secured peace—has been part of the problem. Breakdown of the sense of duty to the nation among police was a key part of this anomie; but so was a willingness of certain politicians to risk the future of the nation by playing the ethnic card in a forlorn effort to secure their personal political future; and so was the ambition of certain young militant leaders in certain parts of the country who cut their followers off from the traditional normative guidance of village elders. Anomie created conditions in which it was possible for the politicians and militants of 1998–2002 to loot the state, saddling the current generation with a crippling national debt. An intractable part of the problem so far has been the resilience of norms of Solomon Islands 'political culture' (Morgan 2005) that leave national politics available to the highest bidder, and therefore vulnerable to the kinds of crises and breakdowns in the confidence in institutions that we saw between 1998 and 2006.[4] Formidable resources have been pumped into rebuilding state institutions with inattention to Melanesian realities that compel politicians to be servants of networks of obligation and reciprocity with their *wantoks* much more than servants of the nation and its institutions (Allen and Dinnen 2010). We see the current Truth and Reconciliation Commission, the transformation of education, effective national regulation and ownership of fishing and logging and a 'raising-the-bar' approach to anti-corruption enforcement (as opposed to an across-the-board assault on corruption)[5] as gradualist opportunities for that nation building. We see elements of the strategic plan of the National Peace Council (NPC 2004) that, among other things, provided for nurturing national sporting, religious, artistic, indigenous, professional, business, youth and women's associations as another road to nation building via civil society not yet fully taken. While that plan was quickly superseded by other developments, many of these strands of civil society have been strengthening by dint of their own resilience and with support from donors.

---

4 'Melanesian political culture draws the attention of MPs away from their institutional responsibilities as lawmakers and overseers of government' (Morgan 2005:12). 'This is exemplified by increasing support for locally credible candidates whose major platforms are local development above all else…the political cultures of Melanesia lend themselves to patronage politics because of local peoples' needs for approachable political leaders. No Melanesian MP can afford to ignore local demands in favour of national or regional ones because unfulfilled promises to constituencies carry with them the threat of electoral defeat and a host of other negative social sanctions' (Morgan 2005:10).

5 We will argue in Chapter 5 that this raising-of-the-bar approach to tax evasion has indeed been progressively applied by Solomon Islands Inland Revenue with resultant progressive improvement in commitment to pay taxes to support the nation.

In the development of our comparative thinking about peacebuilding, we think the most instructive aspect of this case is in its lessons about the strengths and limitations of a strategy of strengthening the core pillars of the state. The Solomons is not quite statebuilding 'neat', but the focus has been on rebuilding the core pillars of the central state to the comparative neglect of the specific factors that fuelled conflict. Put in its best light, the Solomons intervention could be seen as succeeding by strengthening core pillars of a fragile state to the point where that state was then able to chart its own path to addressing the specificities of the conflict. Yet we will argue that not all aspects of the Solomons state were working badly compared with most developing countries finding their own path in the aftermath of colonialism. Moreover, village governance in Solomons society continued throughout the conflict years to do an outstanding job of caring for its most vulnerable and dependent members, as did the church. While the Solomons peacebuilding intervention has had some success, our conclusion will be that it might have been a more resilient success had it worked with Solomons civil society to identify the key peacebuilding risks and opportunities where civil society and the state most sought outside assistance. Some of those specific priorities would have included elements of statebuilding that might have been read off a generic World Bank good-governance template. Yet most of them, we will argue, would not have been about core pillars of the state. Most would have had a unique connection to Solomons history and to specific weaknesses and strengths of its social fabric.

The structure of this book is to first outline the historical context of the conflict in the next chapter, then the story of the descent into conflict and the climb back to peace. After attempting to understand the identity politics of the conflict, we then reach some conclusions about the drivers of the conflict and how well peacebuilding was attuned to those drivers. Finally, we draw some lessons on learning the craft of a contextual peace. The present chapter now outlines the ambitions—methodological and substantive—of the Peacebuilding Compared project, of which this Solomons volume is the third. Readers who have read the first chapter of previous volumes (Braithwaite et al. 2010a, 2010b) can skip to Chapter 2 without missing much.

Comparing conflict, comparing peacebuilding

The Peacebuilding Compared project hopes over more than 20 years to code 670 variables in relation to the major armed conflicts that have raged across the world since 1990. The first large volume covered seven different Indonesian armed conflicts (Braithwaite et al. 2010a), the second the Bougainville conflict. It is hoped the fourth volume will appear in quick succession to cover Timor-Leste. The project started with the region around the home country of the authors simply because it was easier to learn how to do it in the region with which the research team was most familiar. As it happens, this region experienced a great deal of armed conflict during the 1990s.

Peacebuilding Compared started in 2005. During the project's first five years, the senior author managed to do some serious fieldwork across each of the sites in the nations where these first 11 conflicts occurred.[6] In some cases, including Solomon Islands, he was joined by co-authors for that case with far greater knowledge of that site and its languages. Joint is better, more reflexive and reliable than solitary fieldwork, but often is not logistically possible. Thankfully in the Solomon Islands case, John Braithwaite was able to share two fieldwork trips with Sinclair Dinnen and one with each of the other authors in 2006 and 2009. Peacekeepers and other key international players were also interviewed in the United States, Australia, New Zealand, Papua New Guinea, Fiji and Vanuatu between 2005 and 2010. The Appendix summarises the types of people interviewed. Sinclair Dinnen and Matthew Allen have also conducted their own research on Solomon Islands over many years; where these data are relied on, this earlier work is cited. We encourage a participatory approach to the research and invite readers to check out the Peacebuilding Compared web site at <http:// peacebuilding.anu.edu.au>, where more information can be found. Please feel encouraged to post your ideas and information on that web site at any time throughout the 20-year life of the project.

For the project in general so far, we have been surprised by the level of access won to key players such as prime ministers (one current and six former prime ministers of Solomon Islands and one of Australia in this case), state and insurgent military commanders, foreign ministers, peace agreement negotiators and peacekeeping commanders. Yet, as is clear in the Appendix to this volume, in comparison with the appendices in our first two volumes that summarised the types of players in the conflict who were interviewed, there was always uneven coverage in the types of stakeholders accessed. In every case, there were regional specialists in the study of this conflict who had secured broader access to the key players and who had talked many times to decision makers we did not mange to tap. This means it is always more important to attend to the published fruits of the fieldwork of others than to one's own fieldwork notes.

---

6   John Braithwaite has been present for about 90 per cent of these interviews so far and he typed up the fieldwork notes or used voice-recognition software to record almost 90 per cent of them. The most common reason for occasionally not creating an electronic copy of fieldwork notes was that culpability for war crimes was discussed in the interview or other information was provided that might conceivably put someone in danger. The second most common reason was that there were some interviews that included little that was truthful or valuable! Handwritten notes taken during such interviews were still kept, in case a changed view of their truthfulness and value emerged later. No interviews were taped. Co-researchers had often done extensive fieldwork of their own for quite separate research projects. The latter fieldwork is not included in the interview statistics summarised in the appendix at the end of each book.

Yet this raises the question of what added value there could be in research of inferior coverage led by a team coordinator with an inferior background in the regions of conflict. One added value is that sometimes inferior researchers whose fieldwork engagement is thin are nevertheless lucky enough to gain superior access to some significant bits of information. So there is some value from our research in adding a little to the superior body of data and insights accumulated by the very best experts in each conflict. Yet this is not the main contribution of comparative research. Its main added value is in the comparison, and in the different ways of seeing that a comparative lens opens out. In each case study of Peacebuilding Compared, there tend to be a few scholars who have done the most insightful or thorough research on that case. The frequent citation of the work of these scholars makes it clear who they are. We are deeply grateful to them. Their work remains the scholarship to read on that case, but we do hope that by standing on their books, we might be able to peer over their shoulders to begin to see more clearly a comparative landscape of conflict patterns across the globe.

Peacebuilding Compared offers a different kind of comparativism than the dominant kind that is based on quantitative analysis of statistical information from databases maintained by organisations such as the World Bank, the United Nations Development Programme (UNDP), the US Central Intelligence Agency (CIA) and national statistics bureaus. Peacebuilding Compared uses these data sets as well to code one-third of its 670 variables in relation to each conflict. But most codes are of things not available in these databases, such as whether insurgents received training from a foreign power and whether significant numbers of the combatants were female, based on our interviews (and published fieldwork of others). Good examples of the kinds of variables never coded in the leading quantitative research are the dynamics and shape of reconciliation processes post-conflict. This is a particularly important gap according to some of the theoretical frameworks we address in this volume.

We also attempt to deal with two fundamental problems in the quantitative literature. One is that quantitative scholars are often interested only in data coded at the national level. The study of 'civil wars' dominated by the disciplines of political science and international relations is often, moreover, interested only in armed conflicts in which one of the combatants is a state.[7] Peacebuilding

---

7   Peacebuilding Compared studies armed conflicts in which one armed group with a command structure— even if its organisational auspices were episodic or non-institutionalised—engaged in group attacks with weapons on another armed group with a command structure. This means a clash of two warlord armies or two armed gangs can count as an armed conflict for Peacebuilding Compared if it passes certain other threshold conditions. For the moment, these are that two of the following three conditions are met: that at least 200 people were killed in the fighting within three years, at least 30 000 people were driven from their homes by the fighting and an internationally sanctioned peacekeeping mission was sent to make peace in the war-torn region. Including the last condition prevents us from excluding from consideration serious armed conflicts that started but were prevented from escalating into mass slaughter by peacekeepers (for example, the arrival

Compared seeks to maximise coding at the local or provincial level. Hence the code recorded for the separatist conflict in Aceh might be quite different from that of the separatist conflict in Papua at the other end of Indonesia. Another difference is that Peacebuilding Compared is content to code conflicts that are many things at once. Hence, for example, Peacebuilding Compared codes both Aceh and Papua as separatist conflicts and also as ethnic conflicts. This is different from the approach in the quantitative literature, which tends to force conflicts into one category or another. Third, as is clear from the summary in Table 8.1, we also enter certain codes as 'consensus' codes among scholars and other expert commentators on the case, others as 'contested but credible'.

A difference from the ethnographic/qualitative literature is that Peacebuilding Compared is much less engaged with adjudicating the most contested debates about the case. We just code them as contested interpretations and report the nature of the contestation in our narrative. What we are interested in doing is ruling out non-credible interpretations. Conflict zones are teeming with them— wild, unsubstantiated rumours, ridiculous theories propagated by people who spread lies to protect their culpability, clever pieces of misinformation planted by double agents, imagined histories concocted by supposed combatants with grandiose visions of their self-importance to saving their nation. A significant level of fieldwork on the ground and in the capitals of combatant and peacekeeping states (or at UN headquarters) is needed. The intent is not to get the research team to the point where it can settle the most contested debates among the experts, but to the point where it can rule out most (hopefully all) the myriad non-credible interpretations.

A distinctive comparativism

This renders Peacebuilding Compared a distinctive form of comparativism. The approach was motivated by reading most of the best research as falling into one of two camps. The first is a large number of wonderful studies of particular conflicts, or comparing a couple, written by scholars who have deep knowledge and long experience of that region. The second is the more recent quantitative tradition led by outstanding comparativists such as Ted Gurr, Jack Goldstone, Paul Collier, Anke Hoeffler, Virginia Page Fortna, James Fearon, David Laitin, Michael Doyle and Nicholas Sambanis, among others cited in the references. In choosing a method that aspires to significant fieldwork engagement that is inferior to the best ethnographic work, and is on a smaller number of cases to

---

of UN peacekeepers in Timor-Leste in 2006). This, however, is just a starting definition for our armed conflicts that could change as new wars occur. It sets a threshold that excludes a lot of conflicts that one might want to include. Solomon Islands perhaps only barely passes our threshold for the number of deaths, but more than satisfies the other two provisional thresholds we have set for inclusion.

the best quantitative work, we are simply filling a methodological niche that has been under-exploited in the literature. We do not have the view that it is necessarily a superior method to the dominant two.[8] One of its demands is that it requires one person to read very extensively on each case and to be in the room or under the tree for most of the fieldwork. Otherwise it would be impossible to code the 670 variables consistently across cases. The thematic unity of narrative volumes such as this might offer no advance on an edited collection of haphazard comparisons, insightful though such casual comparativism can be.

By 2030, we hope that some sort of cluster analysis or fuzzy-set analysis to the best quantitative standards of that time will reveal something new about types of conflicts. We would also hope to define which might be the most important of probably a long list of risk factors that conduce to the persistence of armed conflict—and which are the most important protective factors for preserving peace. Narrative and analytical books such as this lay an important foundation for this future quantitative work. They discover new variables that are worth coding for all cases, new complexities in the dynamics among these variables that might ultimately account for why certain quantitative models will not explain much and why others might do so.

A final part of the method was to invite the people who seemed to be producing some of the best insights on the case to be members of an advisory panel. We

---

8 One battleground between large-n quantitative methods and single case studies arises from the qualitative critique that quantitative methods freeze (into one code) dynamic phenomena that are one thing at one point in time and another thing at another point in an unfolding conflict. This means that case studies of single conflicts actually do not have an n of 1. Rather, they are studies of many separate episodes of violence, some of which might be more ethnic, others more religious, or involving attacks by different ethnic groups than the first episode. Hence, combining the results of X qualitative analyses of protracted conflicts is more like a qualitative meta-analysis than it is like combining X cases each with an n of 1. What we are attempting in Peacebuilding Compared is a unique kind of meta-analytical hybrid. John Braithwaite deploys his knowledge of the narratives of the set of episodes of violence that makes up a particular case to code most variables as 'High, Average or Low' on that variable. If there is some doubt about how to code (a common occurrence), it is coded 'Average'. So 'Average' is given the broad meaning of 'the range on this variable where most cases of armed conflict in Peacebuilding Compared lie'. If there is both doubt and thinness of data that make it very hard to code, it is also coded as 'Hard to code'. Imagine coding two variables on the extent to which greed and grievance are motivations for fighting. The first point to make is that they can both be high or low, or they can have different values. The second is that if greed is highly prominent in some episodes, moderately present in most and totally absent in some then the greed variable will be coded 'Average'. So these three-point codes are in fact crude summaries from a sometimes large number of data points within the single case. For some variables, such as the number of combatants on various sides and the number of refugees, we code a specific number (or estimate a midpoint of a best-guess range). But we code both a maximum number (the high-water mark of the number of combatants or refugees across all episodes of the conflict) and a separate variable, which is an estimated average number across the various episodes of the conflict. All this is perhaps only slightly less crude than a purported single quantitative estimate for a single conflict (as in the extant quantitative literature). However crude, it is an attempt to quantitatively summarise from qualitative cases that are more than narratives of an n of 1. Moreover, this approach to aggregating from a multiple-n sensibility for each conflict is combined with actually writing an episodic, dynamic narrative for that conflict. This is what we are doing in this book. The hope is that new kinds of insights will ultimately come from the interplay between multiple case study narratives and quantitative analysis of the codes with this multiple-n sensibility.

asked the advisory panel to suggest important people to interview, to read our first draft, comment on erroneous insights within it and on research and lines of inquiry that needed to be pursued before the next draft.

Our ethical obligations under The Australian National University's Research Ethics Committee approval were explained to all participants. These included an obligation to report quotes and insights from each informant anonymously unless they specifically indicated that they wanted to be quoted as the source of an insight. Wherever a quote appears without a citation to some other source in the literature, it is an anonymous quote from an informant interviewed for Peacebuilding Compared.

2. Historical background to the conflict

When human beings first arrived on the Solomon Islands of the south-west Pacific some 29 000 years ago, one large island joined the islands of Bougainville to the western islands of the Solomons, with some other large islands sitting to the south and east. As ice melted in subsequent millennia, the Solomon Islands physically fragmented into 900 islands and atolls that are now home to 500 000 people. Most of them still live in some 4000 village communities or hamlets. Cultural diversity was increased by Austronesian migrations to the Solomons from the north-west three or four millennia ago. Later Austronesian invasions swept backwards as Polynesian migrations from the south and east. The nation today is 94 per cent Melanesian and 4 per cent Polynesian (a majority on a number of the islands), with significant Chinese, European and Gilbert Islander (Micronesian) minorities. Racial differences are great—from the pitch-black people of the Western Province who are related to neighbours in Bougainville to much lighter-skinned Melanesians and Polynesians in the east. At least 64 living languages of many dialects are spoken in Solomon Islands (Tryon and Hackman 1983). Pidjin (English) is the widely spoken lingua franca. Solomon Islands, like Melanesia in general, is an extreme case of ethnic fractionalisation. Melanesia accounts for about one-thousandth (certainly less than two-thousandths) of the world's population, but one-quarter of its language stock (Fraenkel 2004a:20).

The state today is still not central to most of the day to day existence of the overwhelming majority of the population, who live in villages distant from towns. Most villagers continue to draw most of their needs for food, water, security, recovery from natural and human disasters and recreation from village, church and kinship-based social systems that are little buttressed by national and international markets or by state taxation and state service provision. Vulnerable villagers do not go without food and shelter for the want of state welfare. The systems that still care for them predate the state; few villagers fall through gaps in those systems of provision compared with the numbers that fall through gaps in Western state-based welfare systems. While there are urbanisation dynamics that are making all this less true, there have also been since the 1980s, and earlier, settlement dispersal dynamics whereby families start up new hamlets when villages become so large as to make access to gardens a challenge (Hviding 1996:77).

The focus of this book is on problems of violence and how institutions of land disputation, forestry, gender and many others were involved in its spread. As we diagnose all these problems, there is a tendency to lose sight of the basic strengths of a society. At various points in our text, we attempt to arrest the social problem narrative to take stock of various peacebuilding strengths that are also in play. In most villages most of the time, the experience of villagers is overwhelmingly one of egalitarian inclusion rather than exclusion (White 2007). Villagers enjoy multidimensional opportunities for participation in village cultural life, religious life, social life and political decision making. Finally, we indulge one sweeping observation of the extraordinary *joie de vivre*, especially among children of course, that is so much more palpable as one walks around Solomon Islands villages compared with wandering around towns in the West. There is a collaborative sociability of Solomon Islands villages and hamlets that is palpable most of the time.

Figure 2.1 Children of Chief Moro's village in the resource-poor Weather Coast region of Solomon Islands, August 2005

Photo: David Jones

Yet because of the diversity of Solomon Islands cultures, general statements about them are hazardous. Even within a single locale, Edvard Hviding's (1996:xiv) ethnography of Marovo Lagoon, which is organised around the trope of 'flow', evinces a 'strong element of fluidity in the ways that social life is organized in Marovo [New Georgia]'. For Hviding, this flow is partly about the continuous movement of the sea and of people on it in archipelagic societies. Roger Keesing

(1992:vii) cautions about oversimplification as an inevitable risk in writing long books about the inland Kwaio of Malaita, given their 'flexibly adaptive cultural tradition' (see also White 2007:2). Hviding's (1996) ethnography shows that much of the dynamism in Solomons society is driven by opening up new networks of inter-island travel that connect one set of interactions between coastal people and the 'bush' people of the interior of one island to those interactions on another island. The conflicts that are the topic of this book are very much about social change driven by such inter-island and coastal–interior interaction. The glimpses we give in this text of their inadequately documented complexity and flux are very partial.

Our methodological dilemma in writing a book like this is that one comes to realise that one knows enough about the diversity of Solomon Islands societies to see that one-size-fits-all policies will play very differently at different places and times. Yet one does not know enough about even one point in Solomons space-time to understand what would amount to successful mediation of peacebuilding efforts in that one context, let alone the others scattered across time among these 900 islands. Still, glimpses of diversity help us grasp the disparate character of local mediation of peacebuilding efforts that an international intervention might enable. Methodological humility requires us not to pretend that we are capable of summarising for the reader the nature of the diversity of Solomons social systems across time. Instead, our text is about giving enough glimpses of war making and peacebuilding at key points in Solomons space and time to inform an understanding of factors that have contributed to peace and war and to critique extant theories of peacebuilding in a way that leads to constructive alternatives. According to our approach, those alternatives must be grounded in greater methodological humility than current peacebuilding practice.

The first key moments in time on which we focus are that Solomon Islands became a British Protectorate in 1893 and gained independence in 1978. While Solomon Islands was never one of Britain's strategically prioritised colonies, in World War II it actually did become strategically important. Few places on Earth are more remote from the West and few places have been more attractive to anthropologists because of how culturally different Melanesian gift economies are from the West and from one another. Yet, like Bougainville, Solomon Islands today is far more consistently and committedly Christian than the population of any Western society. Christian traditions of forgiveness and their blending with indigenous practices of reconciliation have proved useful in transcending outbreaks of warfare that have been exacerbated by other centrifugal impulses of the global political economy. Christianity has been the one impact of globalisation on the Solomons that has been unifying. We will see that other global forces interacted with local schisms in the Solomons in ways that increased disintegration and inter-island and inter-communal violence. For all nations, a unified national identity is a historically recent accomplishment. Even in 1870, a decade after today's great power, the United States, had a massive civil war, the great power of that time, France, was a 'nation' where most country dwellers still did not consider themselves members of the French nation (Weber 1976). Nation building remains a continuing process, even in countries where national identity appears relatively well established. In 2009, there are nevertheless few countries that have travelled less distance down the road towards forging a unified national identity than Solomon Islands (Dinnen 2007a; Jourdan 1995b).

The first widespread contacts with Europeans were with whalers. These were the first of a sequence of disintegrative contacts with global forces. At the same time, we will see that there were integrative, pacifying contacts as well, starting with the church, and most recently with an international peacekeeping intervention. Commercially ruthless whaling by the early nineteenth century had decimated Atlantic stocks, attracting whalers finally to the far reaches of the south-west Pacific. The most valued things the whalers traded to Solomon Islanders were steel axes; the most valued trades in return were of women (Bennett 1987:30). Slavery seems to have long existed in many Solomon Islands societies. Women captured in warfare had been used as, among other things, prostitutes. When the demand for sex work from slaves increased—as it did from the whalers—we can speculate that this might have motivated increased warfare in hope of capturing more slaves. When traders started selling guns to both sides in such conflicts, the warfare could have become more bloody (Bennett 1987:43, 55, 81–2). Whether warfare, and the lives lost in it, increased significantly as a result, we know not. We do know that venereal diseases did increase, though this decimation was controlled in places like the New Georgia Group of islands, where the practice was to kill women infected by the whalers (Bennett 1987:70).

The prized axes that the whalers, and later the trading posts, sold to Melanesians have been estimated by rather credible early ethnography to have increased male productivity by more than one-third (Salisbury 1962:109–10, 220). Compared with the stone adzes they replaced, steel blades could more quickly clear grounds for planting, fell trees, hew canoes and construct houses and even shell money. This was an economy in which increased productivity did not expand accumulation of goods but rather was transformed into increased status (as by big-men giving gifts). Status was also acquired by ceremonial activity and headhunting. These activities did increase as a result of the reduced time required for subsistence cultivation enabled by steel (Fraenkel 2004a:22). Men not tempted to use their newly acquired spare time for headhunting nevertheless had to use it to defend against headhunting, pre-empt and avenge it. The globalisation of commercial whaling and of trading diasporas in its wake was the first European impact that motivated new wars in the Solomons.

Between 1870 and 1910, about 30 000 Solomon Islanders, mostly Malaitans, were taken, sometimes voluntarily, often not, to work as 'indentured labourers' on plantations in Queensland, but also in Fiji and other destinations (Corris 1973). The most cherished things returnees from Queensland and Fiji brought were muskets to strengthen their group's position in inter-communal conflicts. Communal divisions were opened up by indigenous 'passage masters' who in effect were entrepreneurs of slave entrapment. While we will see that the plantation economy led to pacification of inter-communal conflict, the plantations themselves were violent places, as Judith Bennett's (1993) research shows. Violence against masters and overseers who inflicted beatings was a common form of resistance by plantation workers—violence that Bennett interprets in the frame of James C. Scott's (1985) 'weapons of the weak'. These can be read as nascent forms of resistance to those in authority who control the money, the state and organised violence—resistance from below that becomes more organised and political in later periods of Solomons history.

The Australian colonies pressured Britain to annex Solomon Islands because of concern about Germany's presence and intentions in the region. A new global trade reality—increasing copra prices—also made the Solomons an attractive site for English investment, channelled through Australian trading firms such as Burns Philp, in a plantation economy. Pacification of what Fraenkel (2004a) called the headhunting era was necessary for security of this investment. A combination of the guns of the colonial administration and the sermons of missionaries preaching apology and forgiveness as an alternative to blood feud was promulgated with vigour and effectiveness in ending the headhunting era before the outbreak of World War II. It had ended 50 years earlier in parts of Guadalcanal and New Georgia. War canoes were smashed and guns surrendered to the colonial authorities.

Two great cataclysms of the mid-twentieth century decimated that peaceful side of the promise of the plantation era. The first was the depression that pushed copra prices down to 7 per cent of their 1926 peak by 1935 (Fraenkel 2004a:29). The second was savage fighting between Japanese and American imperial armies that destroyed plantation infrastructure, making it mostly uneconomic to re-establish after the war. This unusually intensive affliction of northern *Guns, Germs and Steel* (Diamond 1997) in the 1940s, especially in Guadalcanal, uprooted communities, disrupted subsistence agriculture and introduced epidemics, thereby contracting the Solomons' population as well as its economy. Collapse of the plantation economy is one major reason for the underdevelopment that saw Solomon Islands ranked 128 out of 177 countries on the United Nations'

Human Development Index in the late 2000s even after some years of impressive post-conflict growth. Nevertheless, between 1960 and 1965, copra still provided an average of 88 per cent of Solomon Islands' exports (Fraenkel 2004a:32) and most paid workers remained Malaitan plantation labourers.

In the 1970s, timber and fish were catching up to copra in importance as exports. In the 1980s, fish became the dominant export; in the 1990s, timber became dominant. This history of extreme underdevelopment and exploitation, by both foreigners and Solomon Islanders from other ethnic groups, was a root cause of the armed conflict that started in 1998. Another was a new wave of natural resource plunder in recent decades by Malaysian, Taiwanese and Korean timber multinationals. Mostly this involved zero value adding to the felled timber in the Solomons, soil erosion and decimation of environments and village livelihoods. Most decisively, corrupt payments by competing logging interests split open pre-existing political cleavages in Solomons society, as well as creating new ones, contributing to the armed violence we now describe. Large numbers of indigenous beneficiaries of logging—concentrated in elites, but not exclusively elites—supported unsustainable logging that gave away so much of the future of the nation to foreigners at bargain prices.

There are few contexts more remote than the Solomons from where we perceive the forces of global political economy to be dominant. Yet here we still find global capitalist dynamics pillaging environments and livelihoods, contributing to poverty, disintegration and warfare. And we see international institutions ranging from the church to the United Nations supporting peacebuilding efforts as well.

Roots of tension between Malaita and Guadalcanal

World War II attracted many Malaitans, whose agricultural land was overpopulated, to move to Guadalcanal to work for the US military; many stayed and more followed in the post-war decades. Subsequent British colonial policy increased incentives to stay by concentrating infrastructure investment where the export investment opportunities were—mainly Guadalcanal, but also Western Province. Malaita, by far the most populous province, was neglected by all forms of private and public investment, sometimes because of the obstacles Malaitan landowners put in the way of investors. So, increasing numbers of hardworking Malaitans moved to the opportunities in Honiara and environs (Guadalcanal), as well as to commercial nodes such as Gizo (Western Province). The problem was not only slow development, but resentment over uneven development. The people of Guadalcanal came to view Malaitans as disrespectful guests on their land. One of the Guadalcanal militia commanders, George Gray, explained the importance of this disrespect as a grievance that led to violence:

> The most important issue that inspired me to join the Guadalcanal militancy was what I perceived as the disrespect that settlers (especially Malaitans) had towards our people and our land. Since independence our people have been murdered, our cultural sites desecrated, our land settled without permission and our people have been treated as second class citizens in the capital city, which is located on our island. I had seen these things since I was a kid and they offended me. (Gray 2002, quoted in Fraenkel 2004a:50)

When marriage occurred between mostly patrilineal Malaitans and mostly matrilineal Guales (people of Guadalcanal), the result was a marriage in which a claim to land was inherited either through both partners or through neither. The latter is particularly likely to engender a sense of disenfranchisement and structural grievance. But also when patrilineal Malaitans[1] married women from matrilineal societies, indigenes often resented this as marriage to obtain their land. Guadalcanal male leaders were often tempted to take money for the 'sale' of land to Malaitan settlers. These were often deals for short-term gain for these men; the land was usually in no sense owned by them as individuals but was owned by a matrilineage of which the female leaders were the custodians.

> [M]any Guadalcanal people (predominantly males) from areas around Honiara were selling customary land to those from other provinces, even though Guadalcanal is a matrilineal society where females are regarded as the custodians of land. Many individuals were selling land without consulting other members of their line (*laen*, tribe), often causing arguments among landowners. What is important to note here is that many of those who purchased land did so legitimately either through customary procedures or through legal means. The sale of land has, over the years, been resented by a younger generation of Guadalcanal people who view the act as a sale of their 'birth right'. (Kabutaulaka 2001:15)

This was a source of profound cultural misunderstanding. When Guale militants started evicting Malaitans from Guadalcanal, Malaitans sometimes viewed this as uncompensated eviction from lands they had paid to share, while the militants saw it as termination of invitations to the Malaitans to be guests on their land. Young people rebelled against elders who took money for land that they did not own in any continuing sense because in much of Solomon Islands people do not own land, but rather the land owns people who are there to take care of it

---

1 Many parts of Malaita are actually cognatic with patriliny dominating.

(Moore 2007:189). Because Malaitans were believed to have been disrespectful guests, they had forfeited their right to stay. There were common cultural misunderstandings—for example, when Malaitans demanded compensation payment for seemingly innocent flirtation with Malaitan girls, for stepping over the legs of Malaitan women or for swearing. This fed into ethnic caricatures by one group of the other: Malaitans were violent and aggressive; Guales were lazy and unproductive (Allen 2007:186).

In Matthew Allen's (2007:130) interviews with Guadalcanal militants, it became clear that unfair treatment in employment and educational opportunities was another of the grievances that justified their violence. Allen found motives for Guale militancy to be varied, but to cluster into two groups: 'development equity' and 'cultural respect'.

The conflict and its stages

The Solomon Islands conflict from 1998 to 2003 is at the bottom end of armed conflicts in terms of people killed. Robert Muggah (2004:5) of the respected Small Arms Survey of the Graduate Institute of International Studies in Geneva concluded that the conflict resulted in the intentional deaths of 150–200 people and 430–60 non-fatal small arms-related injuries. A common underestimate of the number killed is 100. This number could have resulted from the work of the Missing Persons Committee of mid-1998 on which Archbishop Adrian Smith played a prominent role. It named 100 people who were known to be missing well before the end of 1998. But there were also large numbers of people known to have been killed (and not on this list of 100 missing). And far larger numbers of people were probably killed after the work of the Missing Persons Committee was complete. In the early stages of the conflict, there was political pressure to downplay the number of Malaitans killed in an effort to contain the risk of a Malaitan counterattack. So probably the estimate of 200 we have coded for this conflict is too low; Archbishop Smith thinks it is less than half a realistic estimate.

This was a conflict that was a source of regional instability precisely in the period when the political settlement to the war in neighbouring Bougainville was being negotiated. The violence triggered one of the longer international peacekeeping missions the world has seen—in its eighth year at the time of writing with no exit imminent—as well as one of the most substantial in terms of personnel and resources deployed in proportion to the size of the country. We conclude that without this intervention, a much larger death toll could have occurred.

There were two major stages to the conflict. The first was an indigenous uprising initially among young men from the impoverished Weather Coast region of Guadalcanal, with the active involvement of political leaders such as Guadalcanal Premier, Ezekiel Alebua. This was the insurgency of the Isatabu Freedom Movement (IFM), previously called the Guadalcanal Revolutionary Army. Its leaders had the objective of driving settlers from Malaita off the island of Guadalcanal. Late in 1999, the second phase began with the creation of the Malaita Eagle Force (MEF), initially to defend Malaitan interests against the Guale rebels—something the government of Bart Ulufa'alu appeared to be incapable of doing. In a joint operation with the Malaitan-dominated paramilitary wing of the Royal Solomon Islands Police, the MEF effectively staged a coup that resulted in the coerced resignation of the incumbent prime minister on 5 June 2000. The IFM, with the notable exception of Harold Keke and his followers, and the MEF signed a peace treaty in Townsville, Australia, in October 2000. But most arms were not surrendered and the two militias splintered into a variety of armed criminal groups who indulged in banditry, intimidation and payback against a backdrop of growing impunity facilitated by the effective collapse of the police force.

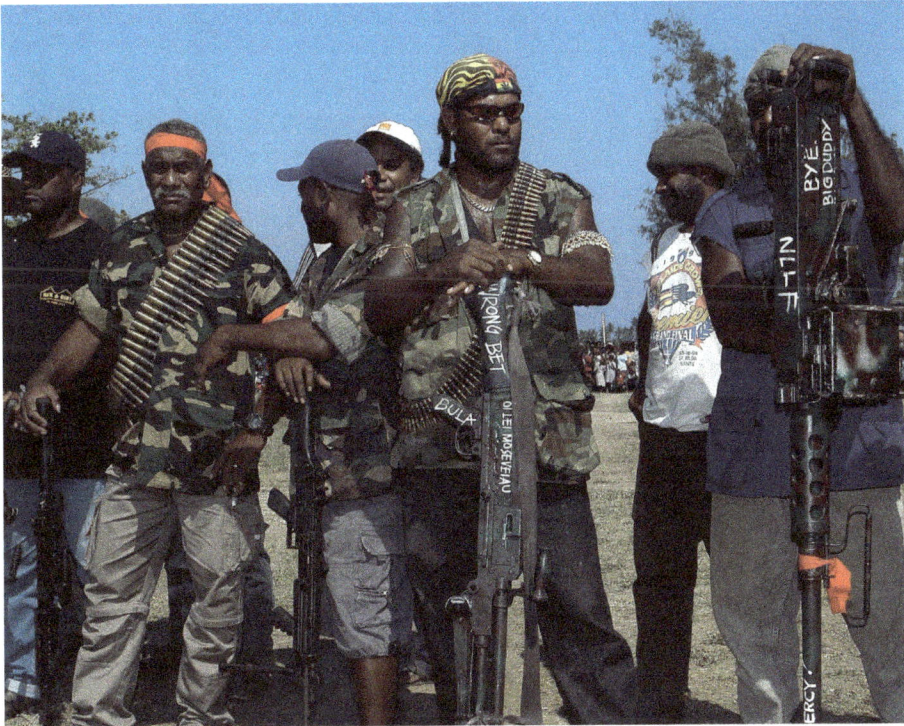

Figure 2.2 MEF commander Jimmy Rasta Lusibaea (centre) and other MEF members

Photo: Courtesy of David Hegarty

The militias bankrupted the state and left citizens in Honiara, the Weather Coast and in a small number of other pockets of conflict feeling no more secure from violence after the Townsville treaty than they had been before. Led by Australia, the Pacific Islands Forum finally yielded to pleas from the prime minister and the Parliament of Solomon Islands to send in troops to disarm the marauding militias. Peaceful conditions consolidated as soon as the Regional Assistance Mission to Solomon Islands (RAMSI) arrived. RAMSI quickly evolved into an ambitious statebuilding intervention, though hardly one targeted on the diagnosed drivers of the conflict. In Chapter 3, we describe step by step the unfolding of the fighting.

3. Descent into armed conflict

Fighting begins

In 1988, three Guadalcanal villagers were reportedly murdered in a payback killing by a group of men from Malaita. This led to the submission of a petition to the government from 'the indigenous people of Guadalcanal'. Among other things, it called for an end to impunity for the crimes of settlers and for the government to look for 'ways and means to repatriate all non-indigenous unemployed illegal squatters' (Fraenkel 2004a:47). The prime minister at the time was Ezekiel Alebua from Guadalcanal. He took no action on the petition. For this, he was much criticised by his own Guadalcanal people. By 30 November 1998, Alebua was the Premier of Guadalcanal, and indigenous grievances had built to the point that it was good politics for him to issue a demand for S$2.5 million compensation for 25 Guadalcanal people murdered by immigrants and for the building of Honiara as the national capital on indigenous land.[1] The Premier's speech was widely read as threatening violent reprisals if the demands were not met. They were not met at the time, so at this point a loose band of young Guadalcanal men—the 'Guadalcanal Revolutionary Army'—began to evict and harass Malaitan settlers in rural parts of the island.

We can interpret the evictions as partly a running out of patience with inaction over grievances that Guadalcanal had sought to assert by democratic means since 1978. But it was also in 1998 partly a political play of the ethnicity card by a premier who was vulnerable over inaction concerning longstanding

---

1   John Braithwaite interviewed Ezekiel Alebua in prison in 2009 about why he had not supported the Guadalcanal claims in 1988 when he was prime minister. He said, 'I was not prime minister of Guadalcanal, I was prime minister of the Solomon Islands [Harold Keke has scornfully confirmed, including in his trial, that this indeed is what Alebua said to the militants]. But maybe I should have responded more. And I had a little bit of regret about that but not too much. If I had granted what they requested there would have been uproar from the other side. My ministers would have left.' To the question of whether this meant he would have lost the government, he said: 'Yes I probably would have lost the government.' He went on to say that he was trying to be more responsive and to listen better in 1998. The irony as he sees it is that as a result of him doing that, he was blamed for leading and starting the conflict. Because Prime Minister Ulufa'alu in 1998 was also listening, Ulufa'alu was accused of being on the Guadalcanal side. They both asked Australia to become involved to secure the peace at that point. Premier Alebua went with the Prime Minister and met with the Australian and New Zealand high commissioners to ask Australia to send peacekeepers. Alebua did not think, as the Prime Minister himself did, that this was a campaign to destabilise the Prime Minister by the then opposition leader, Solomon Mamaloni. Or at least at the early stages Alebua did not believe it was a campaign against the Prime Minister led by his opponents. Mamaloni also worked with Premier Alebua and with the Prime Minister to try to settle the conflict and calm militants down. The three of them really worked together quite well, as Alebua saw it.

indigenous grievances—what the Guadalcanal Provincial Assembly in 1999 declared as 'Demands by the Bona Fide and Indigenous People of Guadalcanal' that included among many other demands state government for Guadalcanal under a federal system. Clive Moore (2004:104–6, 222) has identified some evidence for his conclusion that Premier Alebua could have been the mastermind of the violent expulsions and could have funded them, including purchase of weapons. Premier Alebua argued in our interview with him that he was just trying to stay close to the militants so he could steer them to peace. A context for the simmering grievance was a government that was captured much more by Malaitan interests than by Guadalcanal interests and that had given in to some quite large compensation demands from Malaitans who alleged insult and violence by non-Malaitans. The Guadalcanal Revolutionary Army secured some quality weapons through a raid on a Russell Islands police armoury. But most of their weapons were rehabilitated World War II 303s or homemade guns. During the Bougainville crisis, Honiara was home to a large Bougainville refugee population and the manufacture of homemade weapons was probably a legacy of this period. Guns had never previously been a big issue in Guadalacanal or elsewhere in the Solomons. As well as more than 100 people killed in this first phase of the fighting in 1998 and 1999, a number of Malaitan women were raped (Amnesty International 2004; Moore 2004:112). The IFM was a loose coalition of militant groups focused on different local grievances—some on the Gold Ridge mine, some on the large Guadalcanal oil-palm plantation,[2] some on specific land grievances and some were just criminal gangs exploiting the opportunity of the collapse of order. By November 1999, about 35 000 people were reported to have been displaced from their homes in Guadalcanal as a result of the violence (Fraenkel 2004a:55).

The militants seemed surprised, empowered and exhilarated by their early successes in driving terrified Malaitans off their lands. The response from the state was a strategy of vacillation. The Prime Minister, Bart Ulufa'alu, shifted regularly between a hard-edged 'law and order' response and his personal belief that the 'tensions' were a conspiracy on the part of his political opponents. The expatriate police commissioner responded aggressively at first with counterattacks directed at militants who resisted arrest. Some of his Malaitan senior officers at the time alleged that the commissioner's intent was to kill

---

2   Oil-palm was originally established on the Guadalcanal Plains in the 1970s by Solomon Islands Plantation Limited (SIPL), a company co-owned by the Solomon Islands Government (18 per cent), the Commonwealth Development Corporation (80 per cent) and local landowners (2 per cent). As part of the establishment of the plantation, some land was compulsorily acquired from the customary landowners, but most was formerly alienated land that had been converted to government ownership with perpetual estate title vested in the landowners (Fraenkel et al. 2010). SIPL took over vast tracts of land with a workforce that was more than 50 per cent Malaitan (Karle 2004:39).

the Guadalcanal militant leaders one by one.[3] Given the Malaitan-dominated character of the police, ruthless policing tactics were at great risk of being seen from the Guadalcanal side as ethnic politics by state means. Certain politicians felt a more Melanesian approach based on a great deal of dialogue and then offers of compensation was a better way to go. The effect of this contest was that the militants first experienced force, then a melting away of that force, which they attributed to their own strength, then offers of dialogue and compensation, which they interpreted as evidence of weakness of the state. The sequence of force, then dialogue, then vacillating back to more force when dialogue was shunned was the opposite strategy to responsive regulation. Responsive regulation counsels holding off on all use of force while dialogue is attempted again and again. Yet responsive regulatory dialogue implicitly signals a willingness to escalate to whatever degree of force is ultimately needed to protect citizens. Instead of projecting this posture of firm but fair listening, the state projected vacillation between vindictiveness and talk of capitulation. One reason for this is that it was difficult for the government to identify a clear militant organisation and leadership structure to negotiate with—the same problem the Indonesian state often confronted with its ethnic and religious conflicts of this period (Braithwaite et al. 2010a).

Failed early peacemaking efforts

Before the largest evictions of Malaitans began, on 23 May 1999, a government-organised traditional *kastom* feast was held with an exchange of traditional gifts to seek to reconcile representatives of the two ethnic groups, though none of the militants attended (Moore 2004:110). This set a pattern for most of the subsequent reconciliation initiatives right up to the time of our fieldwork in 2009; the key players were mostly politicians, chiefs and religious leaders, with the leading militants not being reconciled.

The next effort at brokering peace was more successful, however, in engaging the Guadalcanal militants. The Commonwealth, following a request from the Solomons Government, invited in 1987 Fijian coup leader, General Sitiveni Rabuka, as a special peacemaking envoy joined by another Commonwealth envoy, Ade Adefuye from Nigeria. They brokered the 28 June 1999 Honiara Peace Accord, in which all sides renounced violence, large compensation

---

3   An assassination policy had support from some members of the elite. John Braithwaite's notes from an interview with one prominent business leader record that he favoured assassinations targeted on the Malaitan side as well: 'He would assassinate Dausebea. He believes Commissioner had right idea on this. Compared Dausebea to Idi Amin or Hitler. Just have to go. He thinks RAMSI is too soft and would do better by country to kill those who would come back to haunt the country.' Mediator General Rabuka spoke on the record ('If what embarrasses me teaches the world that's fine') when we interviewed him in Fiji; he agreed with targeted killings of the militant leaders by the police to give Solomon Islands a better future.

payments were made to the people of Guadalcanal to respond to the militants' compensation claims and considerable compensation was also paid to develop Malaita, assisting Malaitans driven back to their island. The hope was that this might motivate the Malaitan refugees to stay in Malaita. Displaced families were given S$1000 a head. The money went to the provincial authorities for distribution, with the justice and integrity of this distribution becoming a new source of grievance in both Malaita and Guadalcanal. The rest of the nation, in turn, was deeply unimpressed with violence extorting a deal in which the largest and most powerful islands received large payments, in effect funded by the rest of the country. This was compounded by subsequent payments from the national government in May 2000 for chiefs who had been sworn at or insulted in both Malaita and Guadalcanal, though Premier Alebua seems to have purloined a good bit of the Guadalcanal chiefs' compensation and MEF leaders seem to have pocketed most of that intended for Malaitan chiefs (Moore 2004:135). While the IFM leaders attended the two days of peace talks convened by Rabuka and imbibed the spirit of the June 1999 Honiara Peace Accord, they did not sign it and continued to evict Malaitans after it.

A follow-up Panatina Agreement, on 12 August 1999, upheld the Honiara Accord after a shoot-out with the police in which three IFM members were killed. Panatina called on militants to give up their arms and on the police to moderate their violence, shifting back to community policing. The IFM saw the police as thuggish and Malaitan dominated. At the time of the coup, some 75 per cent of the police were Malaitan and only 3 per cent were from Guadalcanal (with most of the latter assigned to other provinces at the time of the coup) (Amnesty International 2000:7–8). Again, the Guadalcanal militants did not sign the Panatina Agreement. Church leaders were enrolled to run weapons-surrender centres, but few were surrendered. A succession of two foreign police commissioners came and went, powerless to manage the disorder within their force and without.

The first regional peace conferences occurred in August 1999 concerning mainly Malaitan evictions from Western Province. The Marau region of Guadalcanal was another unusually complex regional peacemaking process that proceeded much more slowly than the main Guadalcanal–Malaita process.

In October 1999, an unarmed Multinational Police Peace Monitoring Group of 20 arrived from Fiji and Vanuatu to monitor the surrender of weapons—with limited impact. By January 2000, some Guadalcanal militants were beginning to disarm. But on 17 January, the Malaita Eagle Force (MEF) captured 34 mainly high-powered weapons, a grenade launcher and ammunition from the main Auki Police Station on Malaita (Moore 2004:124)—almost certainly with the knowledge and tacit approval of police commanders. Surrendering their arms then seemed imprudent to the Guadalcanal militia leaders.

In May 2000, General Rabuka was back mediating a peace meeting of 100 delegates in Buala (Isabel Province). But militia leaders from the MEF and the IFM did not attend in the end, unimpressed that their organisations had been banned by the government and by the government's decision not to grant them amnesties as a condition of their participation. This banning seems another early mistake of the government in that it drove the militants underground, beyond the embrace of dialogue.

The coup

Prime Minister Ulufa'alu wrote to Australian Prime Minister, John Howard, in April 2000 asking for the intervention of Australian and multinational security forces. The request was denied. There was a rumour in subsequent weeks that Ulufa'alu then asked for Cuban mercenaries to prop up his government. Some people we interviewed saw this as a final trigger for the coup. But the main motivation was the determination of certain Malaitan leaders to resist further evictions from Guadalcanal (in particular, to protect Malaitans who dominated the national capital), extract larger compensation payments for insults they believed they had suffered and frustration at the failure of the Guadalcanal militants to surrender their arms pursuant to the Honiara and Panatina accords. In addition to widespread Malaitan frustration at the failure of the government to deliver security, there were powerful elements in the business community who wanted to unseat a reformist government. And there was a lot of resistance to the Ulufa'alu government from vested interests across the Public Service and the Parliament who had shared in the spoils of the patronage system of Solomon Mamaloni.

Successful lawyer and former finance minister Andrew Nori allegedly helped bankroll the coup and was the 'spokesman' for the MEF. He announced on 5 June 2000 that the MEF had captured the main police armoury in the capital at 4 am. Solomon Islands does not have an army, so the armoury of the paramilitary wing of the police was the most potent in the nation. Weapons were collected from other police stations and prisons, giving the MEF control of almost all the high-powered weapons in the country by the time the Prime Minister and the Governor-General woke that morning to find they were under a form of house arrest (Moore 2004:4). Three Australian-funded patrol boats were also seized, as was the state electronic media monopoly, the Solomon Islands Broadcasting Corporation, and the government Telekom Centre. A substantial proportion of the police joined the joint operation, with both neutral police who stood for the rule of law and Guale police who supported the IFM fleeing the capital or being stripped of their weapons and marginalised. Nori styled himself as a 'mediator' and opened up negotiations with heads of state and with the Australian and

New Zealand high commissioners on behalf of the MEF. As with the Fiji coup just a few weeks earlier, here the regional powers were persuaded not to go in. This was in accordance with a longstanding strategic preference of Australia and New Zealand for military non-interference in the internal affairs of neighbouring states—a policy that was displaced with a more muscular philosophy in 2003.

Nori was a clever lawyer who had a realistic fear of an international intervention that might see him rot in prison for leading the coup. So he insisted this was not a coup; *de facto* it was a coup, but *de jure* Nori was perhaps right. On Nori's account, it was a joint operation of the police and the MEF under his guidance to restore security to the capital, Honiara. Nori said he had no intention to install himself or anyone else as prime minister. The legislative and judicial branches of governance were still intact. All he was doing was demanding the resignation of the Prime Minister. Even though these demands were at times made at the point of the gun, the Prime Minister did not tender his resignation until 14 June. By this time, six members of his government had been persuaded, some with threats, to desert their prime minister. Amid much corruption and coercion, Opposition Leader, Manasseh Sogavare, became prime minister on 30 June 2000.

Nori asked for his interview to be on the record so that it could attribute his perspective on these events to him by name (contrary to our normal approach of guaranteeing anonymity). He said in his interview that the MEF was a spontaneous movement of mostly young men whose families had been evicted from their land. Far from recruiting them, the MEF came to him and sought to recruit him to declare a coup and be installed as prime minister. He said he declined this invitation and opted instead to be a mediator who sat down with the high commissioners of Australia, New Zealand and other nations to find an internationally acceptable way of getting around the house arrest of the Prime Minister to discover a parliamentary means for changing the government.[4] He claimed there was general agreement by the international players that the MEF should be persuaded by Nori to allow the Prime Minister to contest a parliamentary vote for his leadership. Nori said that the MEF wanted him to be prime minister, did not want Charles Dausebea, who was being touted by many Malaitans, and was not especially keen on Sogavare.

Other MEF leaders insisted that they did not go to Nori asking him to lead; rather Nori went to them offering to represent them in negotiations—an offer they accepted. Nori had been a senior minister in the former Mamaloni government. Most MEF leaders see the root cause of the tension more in terms

---

4 One prominent government official involved in negotiations with Nori during this period said: 'Nori was very clever. He would always steer the meetings, then go outside the meetings and say he was just the spokesman. He was always the cleverest person in the room.'

of an elite political conspiracy than in terms of land. While they tend to agree on this, they have very different views on who was the powerbroker at the root of the conflict; some say it was Mamaloni wanting to unseat Ulufa'alu, others say it was Alebua, others say it was Nori's pursuit of a dream to lead. One saw elements of political culpability in all three. Some informants believe Nori, like Alex Bartlett, was being used by the Opposition Leader, Solomon Mamaloni, initially to destabilise the government. But the MEF militants were a power unto themselves and only rather partially under the control of Nori or any Mamaloni-Nori-Bartlett axis, if that is what it was. It could be that when Mamaloni unexpectedly died in 2000, there was a political vacuum devoid of an alternative and Nori filled that vacuum in the critical period.

In the end, the MEF leaders felt stability would require a prime minister who was neither Malaitan nor Guale. That ruled out Nori. Sir Allan Kemakeza was one prominent non-Malaitan who was not liked by some MEF leaders. Manasseh Sogavare from Choiseul Province became the compromise choice in the event in 2000. Sogavare struggled to hold a majority together after he dismissed Kemakeza as deputy prime minister. This happened after evidence emerged that Kemakeza had paid huge compensation to himself as minister responsible for reconciliation and compensation payments. Kemakeza regrouped and bought the votes of Members of Parliament to have himself elected prime minister, following the national election of December 2001, replacing Sogavare. Solomon Islands government formation is not based on automatic assumption of power of the leader of the party with most members in the Parliament, or of the leader who can form a coalition of parties with the most members. Instead, MPs trade their individual vote, often for cash, in open ballots of members for the prime ministership, without great reference to any party allegiances they might have (Steeves' [1996] notion of 'unbounded politics', which we will discuss further). This system allows the kind of instability that saw Kemakeza replace Sogavare in 2001. A further destabilising feature of this system is that it is so opaque; it is impossible for anyone not right inside the process to predict a likely outcome.[5]

What other interviews confirm to be absolutely correct is that Nori did not recruit the MEF; he harnessed them to a bold political project. Our interviews with the most prominent militant leaders such as Jimmy Rasta Lusibaea and Alex Bartlett also do not suggest that they worked hard to recruit a militia. The on-the-record account of the most prominent MEF commander, Jimmy Rasta, makes this point. Once Rasta took a public stand in favour of resistance, fighters spontaneously flooded to him without any recruitment drive on his part. Malaitan young men were ripe by 2000 for a militarised response to defend and protect their people; there were so many who no longer fitted into the world

---

5   We saw this with the subsequent riots fuelled by surprise and anger at the election of Snyder Rini as prime minister in 2006.

of the modern village and felt excluded from opportunities in town (Hegarty et al. 2004b:11). Rastą simply provided the most important focal point they could rally around. This was a Melanesian leadership model of a big-man and his followers. Each of the many militia groups in both of the main entities (IFM and MEF) revolved around individual leaders and followers (often from the same area and sharing the same language).

Figure 3.1 MEF fighter, with 'Freedom for All' on his weapon

Photo: Courtesy of David Hegarty

The IFM found itself outgunned and outmanoeuvred by the audacity of the coup. Honiara had become almost completely a Malaitan enclave controlled by the MEF. The IFM fought back on behalf of the indigenous people of the island through some skirmishes with MEF forces. Nori urged restraint on hotheads within the MEF ranks who might have used their superior firepower to more aggressively go after the IFM. He and Henry Tobani (an IFM spokesman) organised a conference on the Australian Navy's *HMAS Tobruk* to discuss a cease-fire between the IFM and MEF, but the MEF refused to attend because not all IFM leaders were attending. A meeting was held chaired by church leaders on the *Tobruk* on 23 June with the premiers of Malaita and Guadalcanal, who did attend, calling on the militants to cease fire.

Churches and women leaders ameliorate escalation

The Anglican Melanesian Brothers (Carter 2006) and the Red Cross played significant roles as mediators when skirmishes broke out. For a year before the coup, women had organised themselves as peacemakers into a Reconciliation and Peace Committee and a Honiara Women for Peace group (Leslie 2002; Pollard 2000). The 'Malaita Women for Peace were the first to go to the MEF bunkers arguing for peace' (former Malaitan premier, 2006). Honiara had a besieged character, with MEF bunkers surrounding the town, facing outwards to defend against IFM attacks; beyond a 'no-man's land' lay IFM bunkers facing towards Honiara. The Catholic Daughters of Mary Immaculate Sisters were also very active. At the height of the coup, as illustrated on this book's cover, these women's groups took food to militants on both sides. 'Stories emerged of men from both sides in the conflict leaving their bunkers and meeting together with the brave women, hugging and crying, honestly showing fear of the conflict in which they were enmeshed' (Moore 2004:15). As leading regional women's activist (and Solomon Islander) Afu Billy put it, the contribution of women was especially important at the height of the conflict in demanding that their own young men stop fighting, as we saw in Bougainville: 'If it wasn't for the women of Solomon Islands the armed conflict wouldn't have ended. They went beyond their own safety and security to go out there to the camps to talk to their warring boys to stop fighting' (Oxfam 2003:17). In an even more direct parallel with Bougainville, a provincial premier said that much later women had a 'very big effect' in the peace talks that led to the Townsville Peace Agreement by telling their stories of how women were the worst affected by the tension. In contrast with Bougainville, however, here women were excluded from the process of actually crafting the peace agreement in Townsville (Corrin 2008:187).

As in Bougainville, in the Solomons, when the fighting finally did stop, women were quickly marginalised in peacebuilding decision making. Their contribution was also quickly excluded from a memory of how peace was accomplished, which was dominated by the RAMSI public relations machine. Australian memory gives central place to the top two RAMSI leaders—Nick Warner and Ben McDevitt—in persuading Harold Keke to surrender to them, even though local mediators had already persuaded Keke to do this before the RAMSI leaders landed, and one of these local mediators was with them when the final surrender was transacted. It gives no place at all in the view of Melanesian Brothers whom we interviewed to Melanesian Sisters (Sister Rosa's Christian Care Centre sisters), who in the process of nursing Keke's brother, Joe Sangu, persuaded him to lead his followers to join the peace.

We are jumping ahead of our narrative here as we seek to make the point that not just at this early stage of the conflict, but at every stage, it might have spiralled into something much worse without the restraining influences of church leaders and women leaders, and the efforts of many ordinary Solomon Islands villagers in general. The story of the intervention is one written by the interveners. The stories of local players remain largely unheard.

Economic collapse

Most foreign nationals were evacuated on Australian and New Zealand military ships and aircraft immediately after the 2000 coup. All the major export industries had also shut down by then; many hundreds of jobs had been lost at the Gold Ridge Mine; the Solomon Taiyo fish cannery closed at a cost of 2200 jobs (3000 at its peak); and Solomon Islands Plantations Limited closed at a cost of 1800 jobs (2500 at its peak) (Government of Solomon Islands 2002:63). Tourism and logging[6] collapsed to almost zero in export income (a silver lining in fact). International assistance to Solomon Islands fell from US$75 million in 1998 to US$28 million in 2001 (Plunkett 2003:43). The secretariats of many international non-governmental organisations (NGOs) also closed their doors. This could have been an overreaction. It certainly had a number of negative effects on prospects for peace. The evacuation of most expatriates was demoralising for many Solomon Islanders, who naturally felt abandoned. In Honiara, the evacuation was referred to as 'the chicken run' and T-shirts appeared bearing that inscription. It accelerated the utter collapse of the waged economy, though the informal economy remained resilient in villages, where most people lived. Locals lost their jobs both in businesses and as community workers and in other roles working for NGOs all over the country. Real gross domestic product (GDP)

---

6   Logging had started to collapse in 1997 due to the Asian financial crisis.

dropped 14 per cent in 2000 (18 per cent in GDP per capita) and another 9 per cent the next year (Department of Foreign Affairs and Trade 2004:5). Following a further fall in 2002, the Australian Prime Minister pointed out that in six years, per capita GDP had halved in the Solomons (Howard 2003:2).

The contraction increased the supply of unemployed urban youth who were angry and in the market for a rumble. Two-thirds of the nation's teachers found themselves on unpaid leave during the conflict (Moore 2004:14). This further increased the supply of young people on the streets with time on their hands. Solomon Islands has a formidable 'youth bulge', with a median age for the population of nineteen (Dinnen 2008a:60). The expatriate evacuation 'also removed the stabilising international presence that had held both militant groups back from all-out attack' (Moore 2004:11).

One businessman said that two prominent MEF leaders in Honiara during their period of control of the city cooperated in a hard-cop–soft-cop routine. One would shake down a businessman then the other would arrive to offer the business protection. With other businessmen, they would reverse roles.[7]

While the IFM militancy of 1998 and 1999 caused great harm for those displaced, GDP in fact grew slightly in these two years. It was the three years (2000–02) when the MEF controlled the capital and milked its economic institutions that economic collapse and default on interest payments on its bonds occurred. And as soon as control of Honiara business and government by the militants and their cronies ended with the arrival of RAMSI, growth returned to more than 5 per cent, for 2003 (Department of Foreign Affairs and Trade 2004:5) and the next three years, to 6.1 per cent in 2006 and 10.3 per cent in 2007, falling back to only 8.2 per cent with the onset of the global financial crisis in 2008. Much of this was a result of the resumption of unsustainable logging enabled by the restoration of security; logging accounts for 70 per cent of export earnings (Parliamentary Inquiry 2009:149). There was also a surge in post-conflict construction and in foreign aid pumping up GDP.

---

7 A prominent Chinese business leader suggested the MEF did not loot the country as effectively as it could have. It mostly shook down wealthy people and businesses for small amounts of cash, television sets, cars and the like. They 'could have made millions, hundreds of millions instead of thousands by doing a deal with' foreign logging interests to offer them armed protection to go into places such as Ringi Cove and cut all the timber there. Even though the MEF controlled most of the modern weapons in the country, it could be asked whether such an offer would have been credible given that MEF control did not extend to the areas where most logs were to be found.

Figure 3.2 An IFM checkpoint stops a vehicle on the outskirts of Honiara, mid-2000

Photo: Ben Bohane

Grievances unresolved

On 11 June 2000, a Commonwealth Ministerial Action Group arrived that included the foreign ministers of Australia, New Zealand and Botswana. Nothing concrete towards peaceful resolution was accomplished. The next day, the general state of disorder allowed conflict to spread to Western Province. Early June had seen a sign appear in the market of the Western Province capital, Gizo, advising the 200 Malaitans living there to leave within 21 days. Anti-Malaitan feeling was widespread in the west, as in many provinces.[8] Forty men associated with the Bougainville Revolutionary Army (BRA) arrived from Bougainville armed with M-16s on 12 June in support of locals who had provided their ethnic brethren in the BRA so much assistance during their war. It seems the BRA was invited in by provincial leaders to guarantee security. Without a police force, these leaders feared harassment by the MEF. Before arriving in Gizo, the BRA fighters looted a police armoury on the nearby island of Choiseul. Senior BRA commanders Ishmael Toroama and Thomas Tari were persuaded to go to Gizo

---

8   There had been clashes between Malaitans and the people of Rennell and Bellona in 1989 and between Malaitans and people from Temotu in 1996 (Parliamentary Inquiry 2009:197).

and convinced the BRA men to return to Bougainville without further incident. During what became known as 'the Tension', there were numerous incidents of violence associated with the BRA crossing into Western Province.

Like the IFM, the MEF was a loose coalition of separate militant groups—some motivated by grievance over the eviction of Malaitans and other insults, others footloose young men motivated by the pursuit of excitement, others criminals more concerned to inflict injustice than to correct it. Theoretically, camp commanders took orders from the MEF Supreme Council, but they acted as local gang leaders. There was an interesting symbiosis between the MEF with more political objectives and militants with more criminal objectives. The former taxed robbers 'as they passed through roadblocks with their loot' (Moore 2004:140). Most of the MEF leaders had been displaced from their homes on Guadalcanal. But we must be careful about simply saying that grievance over the expulsions was the most important motive for joining the MEF. Among Malaitans there was a surprising degree of acceptance of a right of the people of Guadalcanal to evict them as guests on their land even if land had been purchased on terms recognised by colonial or post-colonial land law or under customary law. There was a shared acceptance of the principle—even by an MEF lawyer such as Andrew Nori, who made a living from state law, and certainly by Jimmy Rasta—that guests on traditional land could be asked to leave. What Nori and Rasta resented was the way it was done—with violence and without assistance for repatriation back to Malaita and appropriate compensation for what had been paid for what was left behind.[9]

Nori spoke with anger at the way Prime Minister Ulufa'alu told 1000 Malaitans who marched on Parliament in December 1999 that it was their decision to come to Guadalcanal, not the government's; it was not the government who chased them out and the government had neither the responsibility nor the funds to compensate them. That dismissiveness engendered anger. Nori says it was that response from the Prime Minister that resolved Malaitans to respond militarily.

JB: 'What was the ultimate objective of the MEF?'

Andrew Nori: 'To get paid.'

---

9 Both 'sides' shared a common cultural understanding about the importance of land and identity, as well as a common resentment of 'government' (meaning generically all governments) for ineffectiveness and corruption. Indeed, they were probably more angry towards 'government' than towards each other. The mutual blaming of the 'government' for 'causing' the conflict is discussed in detail in Allen (2007:189–94).

4. Peace processes

Towards Townsville

Some more inclusive peace negotiations were held on the Australian Navy ship *Tobruk* in July 2000. Militant leaders from both the IFM and the MEF sat down with representatives of the government, the Solomon Islands Christian Association, NGOs, women's organisations, the Chamber of Commerce and the Chinese and Gilbertese communities (Moore 2004:143). But key IFM commanders Harold Keke, his brother, Joseph Sangu, and nephew, George Gray, did not attend. The MEF expressed great concern about the absence of their signatures on the IFM cease-fire proposal. Things fell apart when other IFM leaders said they could not sign because Keke would not sign the cease-fire. Keke in mid-2000 became the decisive spoiler of the peace. Fraenkel (2004a:96) says that the bloodiest engagements of the IFM–MEF conflict occurred in early July 2000. Nori alleges that Kemakeza then paid Keke and others large sums of money to buy their signatures. Nori also said (something others confirmed) that as late as 28 May 2002 Kemakeza asked the MEF not to give up their weapons until Keke did. Then a purchased cease-fire agreement was signed. This was a shaky foundation for negotiating the terms of an enduring peace agreement, which consequently stalled. Nevertheless, on 2 August, the MEF let women from Guadalcanal in to the Honiara markets for the first time. While this was a large gesture of progress, no disarmament occurred during August and considerable violence and looting continued.

An even more inclusive National Peace Conference was conducted on the New Zealand Navy ship *Te Kaha*, organised by the Civil Society Network, with 150 participants, on 25–27 August 2000. Militant leaders were, however, intentionally excluded, which resulted in its communiqué being ignored. The conference validated the grievances of both sides and called for a National Truth and Reconciliation Commission and amnesties, among other things. Further talks occurred on the *Te Kaha* during September. Keke continued to play the spoiler role in September, hijacking a Solomon Islands Airlines aircraft and demanding a ransom to hand it over with its pilot. One thing agreed in September was the holding of the meeting to settle a Townsville Peace Agreement. The MEF insisted the Townsville meeting exclude the civil society groups; the MEF was concerned about losing its control of the agenda based on its military superiority. This ended the one period of integrated engagement of both militants and civil society in the peace process of July–September 2000. It led to a brief moment in

Townsville when reconciliation for Solomon Islands was dominated by militants and their political accomplices, particularly Andrew Nori. This was followed by years up to the election of Jimmy Rasta to parliament in 2010 where militants were again excluded from peacemaking and treated simply as common criminals.

Nori led the MEF negotiating team; the IFM team was led by scholar Tarcisius Tara Kabutaulaka with assistance from Bougainville peace negotiations veteran and Brisbane lawyer Leo White. Some 143 people attended—approximately equal numbers of MEF/Joint Force, IFM and government delegates. Keke did not show—nor did delegates from the Marau region of Guadalcanal, who conducted a separate and more protracted peace process on the unique complexities of their local conflict. Australia imposed a decidedly un-Melanesian deadline of three days for the talks to be completed.

The Townsville agreement asked the Parliament to pass an Amnesty Act once all weapons and ammunition had been surrendered in 30 days under the supervision of an International Peace Monitoring Team and indigenous Peace Monitoring Council (PMC). In the event, the *Amnesty Act* was passed long before most weapons were handed in.[1] Only 800, mostly homemade weapons were surrendered within the 30-day deadline (Dinnen 2002:292). Other important issues such as the pursuit of greater ethnic equality in the composition of the security forces were agreed. Donor funds would be used to compensate all who had lost property and militants would receive a payment for demobilising and returning unarmed to their villages. Many returned and collected a payment, then went back to Honiara and collected a second and third time. A flaw of the Townsville agreement is that it assumed Solomon Islands government capacity to implement its provisions; the government had little such capacity and was compromised in its relationship with the MEF side in particular. Part of the agreement that created a monster was absorbing large numbers of militants onto the police payroll as 'special constables' or 'police reserves'. There were 2000 of them, mostly ex-MEF, by the end of 2001. They further criminalised the security sector. At Townsville, the understanding had been that only 200 ex-combatants from the MEF and IFM would be demobilised as special constables (UNDP 2004:25).

The Townsville agreement was greeted by scenes of jubilation in Honiara as combatants from both sides left their bunkers and walked across the lines to hug their enemies and chew betel-nut together. The euphoria did not last long. Some of the new spirit of cooperation was in organised crime; some former

---

1   There were in fact two *Amnesty Acts*. The *Amnesty Act (2000)* was passed on 18 December 2000 and assented to on 19 February 2001 (<http://www.paclii.org/sb/legis/num_act/aa2000111/>; <http://www.paclii.org/sb/legis/num_act/aa2000111/>). The *Amnesty Act (2001)*, covering the Marau Peace Agreement, was passed on 2 April 2001 and assented to on 23 May 2001 (<http://www.paclii.org/sb/legis/num_act/aa2001111/>; <http://www.paclii.org/sb/legis/num_act/aa2001111/>).

Guadalcanal militants took to growing marijuana; some former members of the police Joint Operation began to trade weapons and ammunition to them for the marijuana. Many militants gamed repatriation to their villages, returning home for a short period, collecting their repatriation payment and then returning to their militia groups. As in earlier peace negotiations, here there was concern, especially from conflict-affected Western Province, that the Townsville settlement was one between Guadalcanal and Malaita to have the rest of the country pay extortionate compensation for the damage they had inflicted on each other. Civil society groups, among others, saw it as a flawed document—'a militants' charter' (Fraenkel 2004a:101)—rushed and ridden with loopholes and premised on unrealistic assumptions as to the integrity and capabilities of the Solomon Islands Government.

The International Peace Monitoring Team

Australian diplomat and scholar David Hegarty (2003) was the first head of the International Peace Monitoring Team (IPMT) of 14 New Zealanders and 35 Australians, who were unarmed police, military and civil servants, with smaller representation from Vanuatu, Cook Islands, Tonga and other Pacific island states. By July 2002, 2043 weapons and 2.86 tonnes of explosives had been handed in to be held in IPMT containers—mostly World War II and homemade weapons—with only a small proportion of the high-powered weapons surrendered (Fraenkel 2004a:102, 142). While this was very partial success, it was more than modest. The real significance of the IPMT was in supporting confidence building. The Peace Monitoring Council organised a 'Walkabout for Peace' in March 2002 in which 10 000 people are estimated to have marched. Some MEF insisted on returning some weapons to the police rather than to the peace monitors, which was seen as tantamount to returning weapons to the control of their own side, as weapons continued to 'disappear' from police armouries. Nevertheless, at the hot-spot monitoring posts that the Peace Monitoring Council established, the council worked with the Melanesian Brothers and Sisters and other religious organisations to persuade villages to become weapon free.

Increasingly during the time of the IPMT, Harold Keke came to be seen as the big problem for the peace. He became increasingly mentally unstable and continued to be murderous, ultimately facing 24 murder charges (Allen 2007:237). Keke and those who joined him in refusing to sign the Townsville Peace Agreement split from the IFM to form the Guadalcanal Liberation Front (GLF). Even joint operations between the remnants of the IFM, the MEF and the police failed to kill or capture Keke and increased his defiant resistance to peace, as well as adding significantly to the suffering of Weather Coast communities (Kenilorea and Moore 2008:390). In his rugged Weather Coast homeland, he seemed impregnable. Seven Melanesian Brothers who went to the Weather Coast as peacemakers were kidnapped and all were eventually murdered by Keke and his men (Carter 2006). The division that opened up between a large group of Weather Coast militants under Keke and IFM militants mostly from the rest of Guadalcanal was one of a number of divisions that rendered the conflict increasingly complex. There were also divisions within groups from the same area, often within the same families and kinship groups—some longstanding (predating the conflict), some new. There was also division between MEF fighters from the north and those from the south of Malaita and even conflict played out between different factions of the Bougainville Revolutionary Army (BRA) in Western Province.

Figure 4.1 Harold Keke (centre, front) with Guadalcanal Liberation Front (GLF) fighters, Mbiti village, Weather Coast, July 2003, a month before his surrender

Photo: Ben Bohane

Keke had been arrested soon after his involvement in the raid on the Yandina armoury in December 1998. When Premier Alebua and a Catholic priest posted bail, Keke absconded to the Weather Coast and ratcheted up the conflict across Guadalcanal from that base in his home district. Absconding with these serious charges hanging over him, he had little to lose except his sanity, which progressively slipped from him. Some informants we interviewed rated the court's decision to grant bail to Keke one of the most tragic errors that escalated the conflict. While the IPMT and PMC laid a valuable foundation for peace, they were not viewed as successful because in their time the worst spoilers, notably Keke, became even more determined spoilers of the peace, and success in weapons surrender was very partial.

The IPMT departed in June 2002. In January 2003, the work of the PMC, which had provided the indigenous leadership for the peace process in civil society and an architecture of monitoring posts (Hegarty et al. 2004a)[2] was handed over to a National Peace Council led by Paul Tovua.

The work of the National Peace Council

Like the Peace Monitoring Council, the National Peace Council (NPC 2006) has not received the credit it deserves for contributing to the peace process. While the accomplishments of the NPC were also partial, RAMSI was inclined to take full credit for work that was overwhelmingly done by the NPC. Collecting weapons was a good example of this credit taking in RAMSI media statements, when 55 per cent were handed in to the NPC or to the Melanesian Brothers acting on its behalf and then passed to RAMSI (NPC 2004:15). One member of the NPC, the highly respected Sir Alfred Soaki, the retired first indigenous police commissioner of the nation, was assassinated while working for the council. Another councillor was lucky to escape with his life in the same attack.

It was a backward step for the Sogavare government to shut the NPC down in 2006 instead of building on its work and on the infrastructure of indigenous monitoring posts it had developed on the foundational efforts of the PMC. The government at the time was no fan of the leadership of the NPC and did not like the way it provided a platform for leaders who were not supporters of the government. The Australian Agency for International Development (AusAID, the lead NPC funder) provided technical assistance to the government for the production of reports that were hatchet jobs on the work of the NPC. One widespread criticism we heard in 2006 from senior people in both the government and RAMSI, sourced from these reports, was that the NPC did not even have a strategic plan. Indeed, it had a particularly sophisticated, self-critical strategic plan that was transparent about the limitations of what had been achieved in the peace process, visionary about what could be achieved and practical about steps for achieving this. It had been developed at a participatory one-week retreat (NPC 2004). When John Braithwaite pointed out this particular error in the hatchet job that was being done on the NPC at very senior levels of RAMSI and the government, there was no interest in correcting the error in a report that had not been finalised and no interest in taking up an offer to organise for a copy of the strategic plan to be delivered. The claim that the NPC should be dismantled because it had not even developed a strategic plan continued to be the currency of its execution.

---

2   The PMC was itself actually a continuation of the Ceasefire Monitoring Council of community leaders set up to monitor the 1999 Ceasefire Agreement between the Guadalcanal Liberation Front, the MEF and the government.

The greatest tragedy of the dismantling of the NPC was that it had dispersed networks on the ground, in the villages, encouraging traditional leaders to mediate conflicts (including all-important land disputes) locally, to support the local rebuilding of the legitimacy of the Solomon Islands police, to watch for weapons, to provide an early warning of rekindling hot-spots and to involve schoolteachers and churches in peace education and assisting children recovering from trauma. In other words, a strength of the NPC was that it was participatory, indigenously led and under the thumb of neither the government nor RAMSI. Those from Honiara and Australia who killed it off had an agenda of more centralised control of, and spin about, the peace process from the capital.

Worse than that, the dismantling of the NPC was done hastily in a way that created risks for the peace. One of the successful programs of the NPC, building on the work of the PMC, was the 'Weapons Free Village Campaign'. When the council certified a village as weapons free after passing through an audit process, it would receive a large sign from the council certifying that it was weapons free. This was important not only in allowing villagers to signify their pride in having created their own local peace. In many cases, two communities that were in conflict would agree together to go through the Weapons Free Village program, so that each community could give the other assurance that they were safe from them. When the budget was suddenly cut off in 2006 for production of the signs certifying the weapons-free status, there were communities complaining that they had played their part in meeting the requirements of certification, but because they had received no sign, neighbouring communities that distrusted them were alleging they had received no sign from the government because they had cheated on weapons disposal.

Central to the philosophy of the NPC was a praxis of unity through diversity:

> Kastom law leaders are beginning to:

- Sit down together to search for the common principles underlying all the kastoms of Solomon Islands
- Provide skilful and appropriate support for parents to pass on common norms to all Solomon Island children. (NPC 2006)

The NPC facilitated youth peace rallies to nurture youth leadership in the peace. The NPC worked with local organisations to resurrect the practice of all children and adults working one day a month on civic clean-up. Part of the council's school education priorities in terms of land disputes as a root cause of conflict were that 'All children know their genealogy' and 'All children know the land laws of the Solomon Islands' (NPC 2004:Appendix 4). National networking to support midwives to in turn better support new parents and encourage them to take responsibility for peace education for their new child was a support strategy attuned to the evidence from criminology on the importance of social support for parents and small children for reducing violence (Cullen 1994). This work included teaching families non-violent methods of resolving conflict within families. Probably the most important work of the council was simply facilitating reconciliations such as that described in Box 4.1.

Box 4.1 'Reconciliation makes good relationship even without the culprit of perpetrators of crime'

> ### *Story of Ronald Gugui, recorded by Dykes Angiki*
>
> This is a story relating to an incident which took place in 2002 on Guadalcanal.
>
> A family, a Malaitan husband and a Guadalcanal wife, were driving back from Tina village on their way back to town, when their vehicle was shot at by someone. One of their teenage daughters was hit and died almost instantly. Her sister also received injury but survived. It was dark as the journey was taken at night, that the family had any idea even to date, who the perpetrators were or are.
>
> Three weeks after the incident, a reconciliation was arranged to take place at White River in the West Honiara constituency. Councillor Ronald Fugui was involved in facilitating the reconciliation (as he is related to the family).
>
> Chiefs, grandparents and village elders all came down to White River bearing gifts of foods and traditional shell money. They met and exchanged gifts with family members and relatives of the husband's family in a reconciliation ceremony.
>
> This case represents an interesting, as well as a very important aspect of kastom reconciliation. For though the perpetrators of the fatal shooting incident had never been found or identified, reconciliation was still necessary in order to restore and maintain good relationships between the relatives and communities of the Malaita husband and his Guadalcanal wife.

Source: NPC (2004:36).

Out of the dialogues conducted by the NPC at the village level came a different analysis of the sources of governance failure from that prevalent in Honiara and Canberra. This analysis saw the problem as

- an independence in 1978 'based on educated leaders without strong support from villages'
- the 'Government centred in Honiara'
- 'Economic development centred in Guadalcanal'
- 'Ministry of Justice and Royal Solomon Islands Police failing to enforce decisions of traditional leaders'
- 'Chiefs and traditional leaders with responsibility for resolving land disputes having no place in emerging constitution of Solomon Islands' (NPC 2004:27).

In addition, this analysis saw a culture of centralised corruption in Honiara producing a culture of decentralised monetarisation of compensation in response, so that local actors could secure their share of the peace payout.

In the wide-ranging consultations of the recent Parliamentary Inquiry (2009) into RAMSI across the archipelago, the peacebuilding debate finally returned in a productive way to these NPC concerns. It was not only civil society actors from many islands who were responsible for this, it was also some of the most thoughtful and respected members of the Honiara elite. The Chief Justice, Sir Albert Palmer, in his testimony, 'acknowledged the lack of legislation recognising the role played by community chiefs' (Parliamentary Inquiry 2009:196). Several former prime ministers asserted that a peacebuilding priority was reversion of the erosion of the authority and support for the traditional justice system.[3] More broadly, the then Prime Minister, Dr Derek Sikua, said:

> When we adopted our form of government upon independence what we have done is putting our worthy customs and traditions outside government. We have put our laws, our traditions, our customs, our practices outside of government and we put a government in that doesn't link in very nicely to our worthy customs and traditions and practices, so there is no connection. (Parliamentary Inquiry 2009: 195)

The 2009 Parliamentary Inquiry hearings into RAMSI deeply engaged civil society again by being beamed from the islands where sittings occurred to the nation's television sets. Most specifically, much testimony saw a failure to support dispute-resolution mechanisms that might reconcile customary and formal land laws as a root cause of the conflict. The 'rule of law' as a core pillar of the state was seen as part of the problem:

> Much of the origin of the tension was based on outsiders, especially but not only Malaitans, who followed the 'rule of law', that is the written 'western-based' laws of Solomon Islands. They paid money for pieces of land to people of Guadalcanal and then claimed that they were owners in perpetuity according to 'western' customs and laws. The people of

---

3   The report also emphasised that the People's Surveys in 2007 and 2008 found, respectively, 93 per cent and 84 per cent of respondents favoured resolving disputes 'entirely within their own community through the chief, customary law, or through the Church' (Parliamentary Inquiry 2009:174). Picking this up, lawyer Andrew Nori testified: 'if we are talking about improving the capacity, capacity building of our justice administration system, of our law enforcement system, we should be building the capacity of those people who are dealing with 90 per cent of the disputes and grievances in Solomon Islands, and they are down in the villages, the chiefs and our church leaders. In other words, in that area we need to persuade RAMSI and ourselves to allocate more resources to the rural mass where the volume of disputes are great and where the population is located and where there is a need to ensure that leaders in the churches and in the chiefly tribes are placed in a position to manage disputes at a community level' (Parliamentary Inquiry 2009:174).

Guadalcanal, following Melanesian laws, said 'NO', this is still our land and we now want it returned, so you have to leave. (Julian Treadaway quoted in Parliamentary Inquiry 2009:196)

The NPC had a more networked vision of how to unify the nation as an alternative to the view that a nation would simply follow from the creation of a state. Its strategy was to:

Strengthen and increase the number of national bodies and groups that unite the Solomon Islands

- National business associations
- National sports associations
- National professional associations
- National youth associations
- National church associations
- Church women's groups
- Mother's Union
- CDOCAS
- National Council of Women. (NPC 2004:Appendix 8)

Dance, stories in Pidgin and music were also seen as forming a shared heritage that different ethnic groups participated in together. The Solomon Islands Broadcasting Corporation was seen as having an important national role here and also in broadcasting 'Story Bilong Solomons' and three-monthly NPC reports.

Compensation

The Solomon Islands case fits the common pattern of conflict initially driven more by grievance than greed being captured by opportunistic leaders who saw opportunities for personal enrichment. Dinnen (2002:285) sees this as an 'instrumentalisation of disorder' with elements in common with that phenomenon in Africa (Chabal and Daloz 1999). We saw criminalisation of the conflict: exploiting local monopolies of force to extort or just loot from businesses, to steal cars, stage armed robberies, occupy commercially attractive land and demand tax remissions. Another form of opportunism was demanding compensation payments, mostly from the government. In many other cases, perpetrators demanded compensation from the very victims they attacked— attacked with the intention of eliciting offensive behaviour in response that could justify a demand for compensation. Donors, particularly the Government of Taiwan, which bankrolled government compensation funds, were also attacked with the intention of setting up a justification for compensation claims against them. As Satish Chand (2002:158) points out, in circumstances of grievance being harnessed to personal greed, the availability of compensation funding can exacerbate the conflict. In the Solomons case, it not only did this by creating an economic incentive for gaming compensation demands, compensation also made things worse by bringing the integrity of customary reconciliation into disrepute, making meaningful reconciliation harder for the future. It also underwrote profoundly counterproductive philosophies of peacemaking such as Prime Minister Sogavare's 'justice before peace', discussed in the next paragraph.

There were many ways in which the events of June 2000 were not a conventional coup. One was that we can conceive the agenda of the MEF leadership less as running the state and more as using a temporary monopoly of force to demand financial compensation from the state for the loss of Malaitan lives and property. Security for Malaitans and positioning of men such as Andrew Nori, Alex Bartlett and Jimmy Rasta as kingmakers within a shadow state of sorts (Reno 1998, 2000)[4] were also part of the agenda. A paramount reason for the fall of the Ulufa'alu government was the Prime Minister's refusal to agree to the compensation payments demanded by evicted Malaitans. Hence, the Sogavare government of 2000–01 implemented a 'justice before peace' philosophy that it defended in terms of Melanesian *kastom*, in which justice meant financial compensation for both sides. This resonated with Guadalcanal Premier Alebua's earlier (1999) philosophy/demand of 'compensation before reconciliation' (Fraenkel 2004a:52). In the event, the militia leaders of both sides were allowed to capture the compensation payments, with most ordinary victims missing out. Jon Fraenkel's research does a fine job of documenting the detail of the development over two decades before the crisis of a politics of responding to genuine grievance against some ethnic other by extorting cash compensation from the state (as opposed to the ethnic other) and justifying this through *kastom*. The Ulufa'alu government made compensation payments of this kind as well, but it sought to reverse the trend towards meeting such demands as they became ever more fiscally unsustainable. And that is the main reason it fell.

Politicians who advocate cash compensation payments by the state can be sincere in believing that this is a Melanesian way of running the state. But of course traditional Melanesian societies did not pay compensation through the state; mostly it was paid collectively to the offended lineage of kin from the offending lineage. They also did not traditionally pay with money issued by the state's central bank. They paid with traditional shell money and in pigs primarily, but often other kinds of gifts such as root crops were also provided. Throughout Melanesian societies, there are many words that represent different kinds of

---

4 The applicability of the idea of the shadow state here is discussed in more detail in Chapter 9.

compensation. David Akin (1999) in his ethnographic work among the Kwaio of Malaita found the primary meaning of goods transferred in compensation was restoration of dignity and recognition of status. The restitution manifests recognition that offence has been given and seeks to repair that harm. That is, it is not compensation that pretends to be monetarily proportionate, as in the pretensions of Western law, to the losses actually suffered. Indeed, traditional payments after warfare on Malaita mostly seem to be unaffected by the number lost on each side (Fraenkel 2004a:110) (as opposed to much of Highlands New Guinea, where traditional fighting tends to continue until there is a moment of rough balance between lives lost on the two sides). Just as for the Kwaio, in many Melanesian societies, payment symbolises mainly restoration of dignity and status; the payments made symbolise how precious is the spilt blood of those who have been killed and injured. It does not put a monetary value on human life in the way Western law and economics do. Indeed that would be an insult to Melanesian sensibilities. This is not to deny that offers of traditional payment are often rejected in pre-reconciliation negotiations as so insufficient as to be an insult. Yet an unusually poor family might offer an extremely modest payment that would be accepted as appropriate recognition of the harm done because it would be seen that this payment is a big sacrifice for such a poor family. Therein lies the risk with grafting this form of *kastom* into the state. Because the state is seen as having the deepest of pockets, even payments that would be interpreted as massive in traditional lineage-to-lineage compensation can be interpreted as insultingly low when proffered by the state. In Solomon Islands, feverish attempts by politicians who wanted to avoid the fate that befell Ulufa'alu actually bankrupted the state.

A list of compensation payments that were made by the Ministry of National Unity, Reconciliation and Peace between October 2000 and May 2001 was leaked. There were 269 payments, costing S$18.8 million. Some were in effect bribes to militants to join the peace, such as a 'disarmament allowance' of S$123 840 to IFM commander Andrew Te'e (Moore 2004:163). An investigation by the Acting Auditor-General found that half the claims for compensation that had been paid were fraudulent (Fraenkel 2004a:122). There were considerable problems of kickbacks to civil servants and politicians to have compensation payments approved. In the 12 months from August 2000, the government also granted S$140 million in duty remissions—much of it to MEF commanders who had gone into business or acted for businesses (Moore 2004:168). MEF commander Jimmy Rasta, for example, ran a bottle shop and received S$280 000 remission on spirit and beverage imports. Logging companies and certain leading Chinese businessmen were also major beneficiaries. Sir Allan Kemakeza was the minister who was sacked for the corrupt administration of the compensation payments and Snyder Rini was the finance minister responsible for the corrupt administration of duty remissions. After the 2001 election, these leaders became prime minister and deputy prime minister, respectively. In 2006, Rini, with vote-buying support from Chinese business leaders coordinated by Sir Thomas Chan, was elected prime minister by the Parliament—a result that led to the 2006 riots at the Parliament and the razing of Chinatown.

When it became clear that Ulufa'alu was right—that the state could not afford to keep up the pace of the compensation payments without becoming insolvent— the Sogavare government turned to the Republic of Taiwan, to which it continued to grant diplomatic recognition while gesturing at a threatened shift of recognition to Beijing, for at least S$20 million in assistance. Most of the Taiwanese cash was for compensation payments.

Figure 4.2 IFM commander Andrew Te'e in June 2000 with his fighters at a checkpoint on the road into Honiara

Photo: Ben Bohane

5. Regional Assistance Mission to Solomon Islands

In September 2002, Prime Minister Kemakeza made two requests from his embattled and unpopular government to the United Nations for international assistance to stop the violence that persisted. The United Nations sent an inter-agency mission to investigate (Ponzio 2005:176), but by early 2003 it was clear that a consequence of the Solomons' diplomatic recognition of Taiwan would be that China would veto any Security Council resolution to step up assistance. Australia had not invited the United Nations to participate in the Townsville peace talks. At every stage from then on, the United Nations played a more marginal role than is normally the case with an international peace operation— even the previous regional one in Bougainville. Nevertheless, particularly the UNDP, but also UNICEF and a number of other UN agencies played important roles in post-conflict development and support for reconciliation.

Australia had declined multiple invitations to support international peacekeeping since 1998 to restore order in the Solomons. The 11 September 2001 attacks in New York, the 2002 Bali bombing and the 'war on terror' began to change Prime Minister Howard's thinking towards his region. He decided to become more activist in stabilising the 'arc of instability' around Australia and drew praise from the US Bush administration for this proactive approach. This new Australian interventionism was a sudden shift 'from a particularist and developmental lens to a global and security lens in viewing Pacific developments' (Fry and Kabutaulaka 2008:16). The Australian Strategic Policy Institute (ASPI) (Wainwright 2003:28) produced an influential paper that suggested Solomon Islands was at greatest risk of state failure in the region and was a potential haven for terrorist groups. The paper contained 'five references to possible terrorism and twelve references to a "failed state"' (Anderson 2008:6). Among other things, the ASPI paper set the initial tone for a 'muscular' law-enforcement approach to peacebuilding in Solomon Islands that was not even a Western community policing approach, let alone the more devolved *kiap* model of government by patrol that combined policing with other government functions (Gordon 1983), which once worked well in Melanesia, delivering a more dispersed community policing presence into rural areas than occurs today (Dinnen and Braithwaite 2009):

> The central requirement is for active, sustained and muscular policing. The force that undertakes the task will need to be well resourced and

effectively led. It will need to impose a policy of zero tolerance for violence and intimidation, and be prepared to use significant force, including lethal force, to do so. (Wainwright 2003:41)

Some 6300 Solomon Islanders were arrested, many on multiple charges, in the first three years of the Regional Assistance Mission to Solomon Islands (RAMSI). This was way more than 1 per cent of the population, and a much greater percentage of the population in Honiara, where the arrests were concentrated (Carroll and Hameiri 2007:421). There were many cases of defendants spending two, three or more than four years in prison on remand then being acquitted (Averre 2008:2).[1] Some RAMSI officers we interviewed saw it as a de facto policy in the early years of the intervention to charge leading militants with something reasonably plausible to get them locked up on remand while they more carefully sought to build evidence against them. When Prime Minister Howard announced the intervention, he referred to the risk of the Solomons becoming a safe haven for 'transnational criminals and even terrorists'. It seemed implausible to people who knew the Solomons well that it could be a hospitable safe haven for transnational criminals or terrorists. Howard dismissed in his interview with us any influence of 'war on terror' thinking in his actual decision to go in. He believed RAMSI was politically popular with the Australian people and his media people did promote the terror angle at times in seeking to generate interest in the electorate. Many who supported the intervention as a good thing for the people of the Solomons went along with a story that also allowed Howard to impress members of the Bush administration—for example, Secretary of State, Condoleezza Rice, with how he was cleaning up his regional badlands.

Our interview with then Australian Foreign Minister, Alexander Downer, who had launched the ASPI report, suggested that the sharp policy reversal to intervene with international peacekeepers in the Solomons—against the advice of his department and the Australian Public Service more widely—was a result of his conversation with Prime Minister Howard about Prime Minister Kemakeza's request for help. This conversation revealed that Howard's thinking was similar to Downer's. They decided to go in with a spirit of statebuilding until the job was done, without any exit timetable. Our interview notes say

---

1   In 2006, Solomon Islands boasted the second-highest remand population, as a proportion of the total prison population, in the Pacific region (International Centre for Prison Studies, cited in Averre 2006). Just less than 50 per cent of prisoners were on remand—second only to Timor-Leste, where 70 per cent of prisoners were on remand. According to the then Public Solicitor, Ken Averre, writing in 2006 (p. 16): 'The number of cases in the criminal justice system is without parallel and the infrastructure and personnel are simply not there to deal with it.' In relation to the length of pre-trial detention, the US-based Bureau of Democracy, Human Rights and Labor, in its annual *Country Report on Human Rights Practices in Solomon Islands* (published in March 2006), reported lengthy pre-trial detention as a 'human rights problem' and explicitly linked this state of affairs with the large number of arrests made by RAMSI (Bureau of Democracy, Human Rights and Labor 2006).

that his department's view was that 'you would have to completely redesign the place' to be effective and, because that would be very expensive and take a long time, it was unwise. Downer took this seriously, but concluded 'let's do that then even if it takes more than a decade. Howard agreed [according to Downer] "Let's reengineer it".' Howard told Kemakeza that the intervention would be 'all or nothing'; his government would have to agree to in-line expatriate personnel in the police and the Finance Ministry with full access to all financial records.

The New Zealand Foreign Minister, Phil Goff, likewise convinced his prime minister and cabinet to support what became RAMSI. Goff, like Downer, had 'nightmares of a Pacific version of Rwanda on their doorstep' (Moore 2004:206). The support of the Pacific Islands Forum and bipartisan support from the Solomon Islands Parliament were conditions of the intervention. These were unanimously delivered in July 2003. Some 1700 of the 2200 RAMSI personnel who landed in July 2003 were Australian, but there were small contingents from all 10 Pacific Island Forum states. Prime Minister Kemakeza announced a new, 21-day amnesty for handing in guns (31 July 2003 to 21 August 2003), after which 10-year prison sentences would be imposed on militants with weapons. Firearms flooded in immediately; 2500 weapons that included large numbers of high-powered weapons and light machine guns and 300 000 rounds of ammunition were surrendered. This allowed RAMSI to proliferate public spectacles of weapons destruction soon after they landed. After RAMSI had been in place for a year, this had risen to 3713 weapons—about 700 of them high-powered—which, when combined with the earlier surrenders, suggests a higher level of armament of militants than was the case in Bougainville. At least 300 of the weapons stolen from police armouries were never returned; how many were sold and exported and how many were buried are not known. RAMSI intelligence fears many are buried and pose a future threat.

The capture of Harold Keke

The size of the intervention was much more than was needed. RAMSI Special Coordinator Nick Warner has said this was an explicit policy of 'shock and awe'. It was a language of intervention that would impress Condoleezza Rice as much as Melanesian militants at a time when Australia was planning withdrawal of the troops it had committed to the initial invasion of Iraq. The landing on Guadalcanal under the gaze of the regional and international media was transacted with spectacle—helicopters dropping troops in visible locations, landing barges crashing onto the beach loaded with troops when the landing could have been more efficiently transacted at the wharf, and so on. It worked in immediately transforming the climate of security, so much so that one senior PNG military officer who was there felt their job would have been easier had something similar been done on Malaita at the same time as the Honiara landing. At the least, he thinks the navy vessels should have sailed around Malaita first with helicopters buzzing off them onto the island.[2]

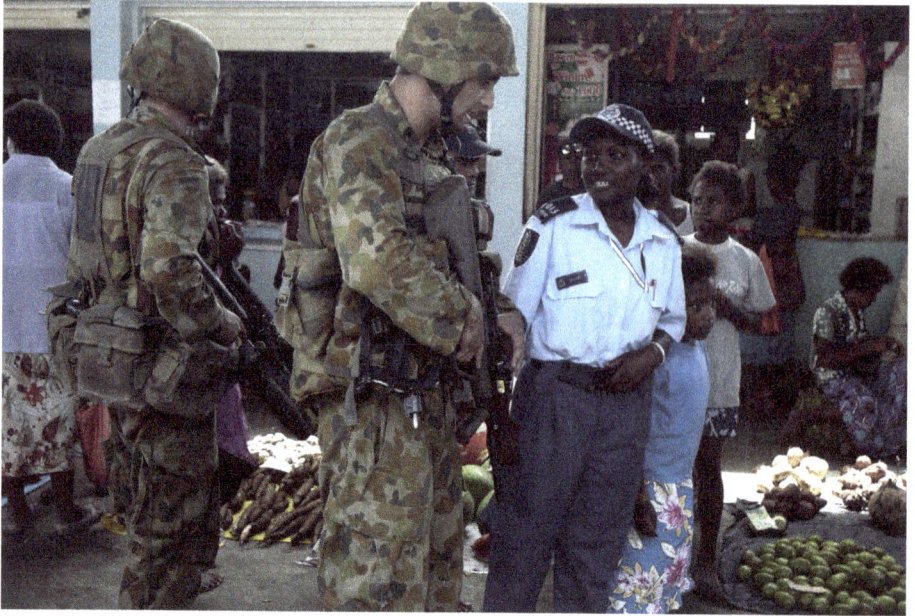

Figure 5.1 RAMSI soldiers and a Solomon Islands police officer exchange information as they patrol their different ways in the Central Market in Honiara

Photo: Courtesy of *Defence Magazine*

RAMSI replaced the rule of the gun with the rule of law very quickly. Immediately, there was a new feeling that 'you could be arrested again when you broke the law. Chiefs would not talk to boys [during the Tension]. They were afraid to open their mouths. It was rule of the gun. RAMSI's arrival gave chiefs and elders courage to speak up' (Malaitan premier).

It can be argued that most of the best work of RAMSI was done as an announcement effect even before it landed. Most of the weapons that were handed in were deposited with the National Peace Council before RAMSI arrived. There were cases of stolen cars returned furtively to their owners' driveways before the RAMSI landing. The corrupt Snyder Rini was removed as Minister for Finance and eight departmental heads were sacked in early August before the in-line finance staff from the treasuries and finance departments of Australia and New Zealand followed in the wake of the peacekeepers. Rini, who became finance minister again in Prime Minister Sikua's government from 2007,

---

2   Malaita is the province where support for a continued presence of RAMSI was lowest in 2008—76 per cent (McMurray 2008:58).

and many of these officers, were to make a comeback within a few years. All warlords, including Harold Keke, made up their minds that they would urge their fighters to surrender their weapons and renounce violence before RAMSI landed. One Member of Parliament, Yokio Sato, and a former member, Kamilo Teke, had been gradually persuading Keke to the point where he was willing to surrender (Kenilorea and Moore 2008:427). We have seen that Keke was the key spoiler who instilled fear and fomented a security dilemma well beyond his base on the Weather Coast. His holding out was the main justification provided by ex-MEF for retaining their weapons.

RAMSI's first priority was to disarm and arrest Keke. RAMSI police commander Ben McDevitt wrote to Keke on 25 July 2003 offering to guarantee Keke's safety in custody in return for surrendering weapons and submitting to justice. Keke replied in writing that he wanted peace and was willing to surrender 'as long as the first priority is to disarm the militants in Honiara and get rid of corrupt politicians' (Fraenkel 2004a:168). Keke's Guadalcanal Liberation Front had declared a unilateral cease-fire three weeks before McDevitt's letter, on 5 July 2003 (Plunkett 2003:12). A no-nonsense message was sent in a letter to all militants from Warner and McDevitt:

> In our talks with militia leaders, we have made it very clear that we are not here to negotiate or make deals...It is in your interest to hand in all guns. Anyone found with a gun after midnight 21 August will be breaking the law and will face up to 10 years in prison and a S$25,000 fine...We are able to deal with any situation and track down illegal weapons. We will not be stopped by threats or intimidation. (Fraenkel 2004a:168)

As in Bougainville, in Solomon Islands, the rumour was spread that RAMSI had technology that could see buried guns from the air. While our interviews with the key players make it very clear that McDevitt and Warner were not bluffing, had Keke decided to hide out in his remote Weather Coast, it would have been extremely difficult to capture him and likely that he would have killed many of those pursuing him into the mountains before they killed him. Moreover, he was a mentally unstable man who had convinced others of his mystical indestructibility. So he could well have also persuaded himself of that fiction. There was a fear that Keke was beyond being appealed to in terms of either his grievances or his greed.

> In regards to the activities of Harold Keke and his men on the Weather Coast, transcripts, judgements and other documents associated with the Tension Trials paint a picture of unbridled criminality: extortion,

theft, kidnapping, arson, torture and murder.[3] Keke's reign of terror was characterised by a dark, grim, and self-serving dynamic of criminal gratification, bordering on criminal insanity, which clearly had little, if nothing, to do with the causes which he and some of his men claimed to be fighting for. (Allen 2007:131)

Keke was initially charged only with skipping bail in March 1999 and believed he was returning to a hearing in Honiara that would give him an opportunity to address the people on the bona fide grievances of the people of Guadalcanal. To some extent, he did that in the trial in which he was convicted of the murder of cabinet minister Father Geve.

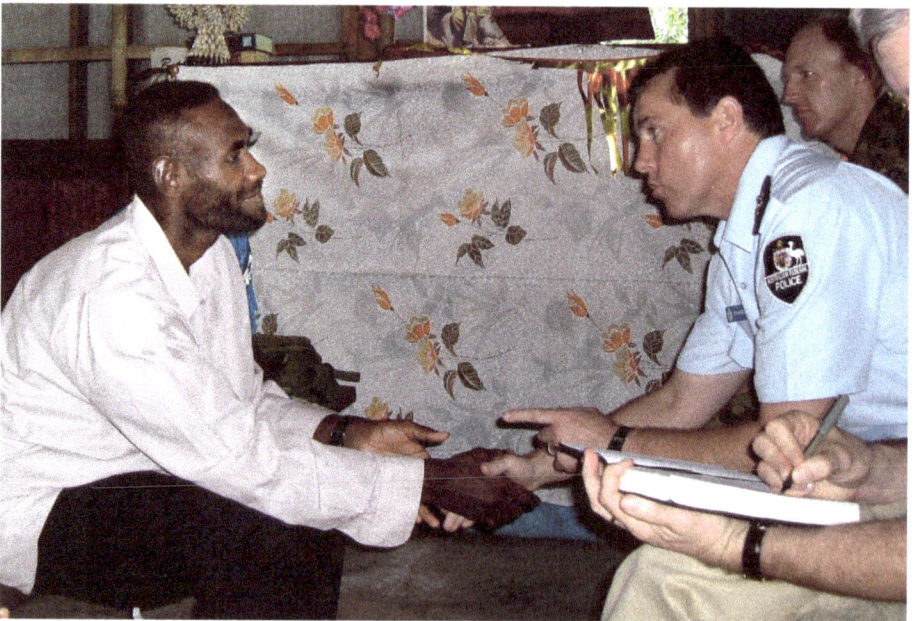

Figure 5.2 RAMSI leaders Ben McDevitt (right foreground) and Nick Warner negotiate the surrender of Harold Keke (left) in 2003 at a meeting in which he admits to murdering six Melanesian Brothers

Photo: AAP/AFP

By Christmas of the year of the landing most of the militant leaders were under arrest, including Joe Sangu, Harold Keke, Stanley 'Satan' Kaoni and Andrew Te'e on the IFM side and Jimmy Rasta Lusibaea on the MEF side as well as all the leaders of the Joint Operation within the police. At the time Moore (2004:18) was writing, he was able to say 'the entire supreme council of the MEF is now in prison or facing charges'. By May 2006, it was reported that a remarkable

---

3   And one might add rape and sexual assault, which were frequently reported on both sides. Peochakuri village on the Weather Coast has reported that 15 per cent of its women and girls were raped by ex-militants that included Harold Keke (Allen 2007:248).

160 former police officers had been arrested (Butler 2006:4) and ultimately more than 400 lost their jobs. Notwithstanding the amnesty signed at Townsville, in its first two years, RAMSI made 611 arrests on 'very serious charges'; these seemed mostly to comply with the letter of the poorly drafted *Amnesty Acts* of 2000 and 2001, but often not their spirit. Total RAMSI arrests even by 1 November 2003 had reached 1340, including 25 police officers.

In mid-2006, Allen (2007:38) concluded that on the Guadalcanal side alone, there were 47 Guadalcanal ex-militants still in custody at Rove prison. Only one cabinet minister was put behind bars in 2003: Daniel Fa'afunua was arrested for assaulting his wife and then assaulting the New Zealand policewoman who responded to the complaint. The next year (2004), MEF leader, Minister for Agriculture and Livestock and former foreign minister, Alex Bartlett, was imprisoned for demanding money with menace and other offences in 2000.

Fortunately, the overloaded Honiara courts were among the more resilient institutions in Solomon Islands, though it became necessary for RAMSI to invest heavily in expatriate lawyers and court administration reform. What was true of the Honiara courts was not true of the rest of the country; the working of local magistrate's courts had completely broken down by 2009 when 80 per cent of cases sent to a magistrate for a hearing were not happening.[4] While it is reported that there have been only 55 Tension trials (some with multiple defendants) (Parliamentary Inquiry 2009:135), actually many militant leaders were imprisoned on charges other than Tension killings, including domestic violence, robbery, extortion with threats, corruption and embezzlement. Andrew Nori was never put behind bars—nor were Kemakeza or Rini, among other leaders, to face corruption or embezzlement charges while they remained in power. Kemakeza was charged after he left office in 2006 and ultimately imprisoned. There seems to have been a conscious RAMSI decision to delay his arrest while he was prime minister in the interests of political stability, according to statements by a former Solomon Islands director of public prosecutions (Dinnen 2007b). Without RAMSI, Kemakeza would not have survived as long as he did; without Kemakeza fearing for his life as well as his political future, RAMSI would never have been welcomed in and given the free hand to run the show (in a way Kemakeza's successors were unwilling to allow).

The effect was a pact for three years with 'a grand council of thieves' (Plunkett 2003:37). It was not a totally unprincipled engagement with Kemakeza; it delivered peace and stability, and ultimately RAMSI turned on the kleptocrats. Another former prime minister, Alebua, was also imprisoned for corruption

---

4 In a 2006 interview, one leading Western Province business leader said in an interview in Gizo that 'RAMSI is not here to police, just here to arrest'. He went on to say that convictions rarely resulted from the arrests.

concerning compensation payments. Until these convictions occurred, there was a widespread feeling among ordinary Solomon Islanders that RAMSI was letting the 'big fish' swim away with their ill-gotten gains.

Cleaning up the finances

Treasury and finance department officers from Australia and New Zealand who moved into hands-on roles in the Ministry of Finance transformed the fiscal situation within months of RAMSI arriving.[5] Taxation revenue collected in December 2003 was 40 per cent higher than for the previous highest month of the year and total revenue collections (including customs) for the whole of 2003 doubled 2002 collections, while 2004 revenue collections were treble those of 2002 (Batten and Chand 2008:130). The revenue continued to rise sharply up to and including 2008, until the global financial crisis belatedly hit in 2009. In 2009, senior tax and customs officers said that trust in the tax system had increased. Voluntary compliance was up because people no longer felt that tax they paid would be stolen by militants and crooked politicians.

The fiscal recklessness of the past continues to place a heavy burden on the present, with the Honiara Club Agreement requiring the Solomon Islands Government to devote 10 per cent of all revenue to debt repayment and to take no new loans. By 2006, debt fell to 100 per cent of GDP and to 53 per cent by 2008 (Parliamentary Inquiry 2009:144–5).

Replacing the paper customs system with a computerised one made some kinds of corruption more difficult: the electronic architecture makes it impossible for most officers to make changes within certain fields; it leaves a trace of the identity of an officer who changes a number; and it forces non-compliance into areas where it is easier for an audit to pick up. Customs revenue has not accelerated nearly as rapidly as tax because top-down assaults on the revenue from the Minister for Finance are still possible (see also Allen forthcoming). Against advice on prevailing international market prices for logs, ministers for finance have repeatedly issued instructions to customs to reduce the valuation of logs below these prices. Ministerial tax exemptions have been repeatedly given to multinational loggers. For the most part, more sophisticated transfer pricing is hardly needed. The *Customs Act* penalty as of 2009 for failing to report the export of logs is $S200—about US$30. Allen (forthcoming) shows that simple capacity constraints on getting out to inspect logs to check physical correspondence with declaration are also a big part of the problem. With

---

5   In fact, tax administration capacity building has for some time been transferred from RAMSI to a five-year bilateral NZAID program in which seconded New Zealand tax officials have been doing a magnificent job of enhancing capacity.

logging a domain beyond the rule of law, other crime has flourished under the wing of protected loggers. Sexual abuse of indigenous children by Asian logging contractors has been widespread (Herbert 2007). In three interviews with senior RAMSI personnel, it was alleged that guns have been shipped in and out on logging vessels that enjoy political protection.

At the big end of town, the largest income earners in the economy also pay almost no tax. In the five years to 2009, a total of only S$5 million in tax was collected from the multinational logging companies (Inland Revenue interview). This is one of many less important aspects of the tax system where non-compliance is almost universal. These challenges of turning around the compliance culture can be tackled one at a time over a period of years and basically this is happening in Solomon Islands thanks to a productive partnership between indigenous and in-line expatriate revenue officials.

The rhetoric of partnership and capacity building was strong in RAMSI. Often it was not matched by the reality of in-line officers, who quickly found capacity building frustrating and found it easier to 'do it yourself' and 'get on with the job'.

> In the early years the government almost stood back and wanted RAMSI to do things. It has been difficult to pull back from this. RAMSI's instincts had become that if someone was going to get something done, we would be the ones to get it done. (RAMSI officer from AusAID, 2009)

It is a familiar dilemma that international interventions instead of building local capacity actually 'suck it out', as Michael Ignatieff (2003:162) puts it, by marginalising indigenous actors in their haste to get things done. Fraenkel (2004a:173) reports that feathers were ruffled early by a notorious sign on a toilet door in the Finance Ministry: 'RAMSI Personnel Only.' The Economic Reform Unit remained in 2009 an office that was a sea of expatriate faces. The confidence to hand over the reins was still wanting after six years. One minister was scathing:

> They are kids.[6] There's too many of them. They turn over too fast. Some only come for three months. Their minister does not know what they are doing, does not know the name of many of them. They are very weak on the training of local staff and all these years on there are only three of them. They don't understand the conditions of the country in

---

6   While many advisors are young and it can be a problem—for example, with a young police officer of limited experience in Australia telling an experienced indigenous police officer how to police his own society (McLeod 2009)—many police advisors, like advisors in all pillars, were over-fifty-fives seeking a new challenge.

which they are working…the Australian Treasury is using the Economic Reform Unit in the Solomon Islands as a training ground for its new graduates. (2009 interview)

One expatriate in that ministry put it this way: 'The Solomons suffers from lack of basic administrative capacity. How to fill out a form to release funds…We were policy people and we were not used to capacity building and management. We found these things tiresome to be honest.'[7]

Little recovery in micro-finance

The Solomon Islands Credit Union League received considerable donor assistance in the 1990s and much collegial support and capacity building from Australian credit unions. Most were located on Guadalcanal and these were all looted by militants during the conflict. Most were emptied out then burnt to the ground. The treasurer of the largest one was killed. As of late 2003, only 20 of 164 credit unions formerly operating in the country were still open (Department of Foreign Affairs and Trade 2004:82).

Post-conflict in Solomon Islands, as in Bougainville, the nation was awash with pyramid schemes that promised fast money and demolished many families' savings (Kabutaulaka 2004:395). One of them was Noah Musingku's Bougainvillean 'bank' that signed a memorandum of understanding with the Solomon Islands Cabinet in 2003 to lend it US$2.6 billion! Sadly, in the early years of this decade, more Solomon Islanders were 'saving' with the pyramid schemes than with members of the Solomon Islands Credit Union League. It says something about the relentless focus of RAMSI on statebuilding that rebuilding micro-finance in civil society was not a priority. In fact, it was a higher priority for Australian development assistance pre-conflict than post-conflict!

Police building

One factor that has made peacebuilding in Solomon Islands easier than in Bougainville, Timor-Leste and various Indonesian conflicts such as Aceh and Papua is that Solomon Islands does not have a military. So, unlike these other conflicts of the region, at least the problems to be managed did not include

---

7   Concerns surrounding capacity building and counterparting in the Ministry of Finance were highlighted in a Pacific Islands Forum Secretariat social impact assessment conducted in October 2003: 'A repeating concern has been raised about the effectiveness of current counterparting arrangements between RAMSI personnel and local DOF [Department of Finance] staff. Local staff members feel excluded and RAMSI personnel are not coaching/mentoring or transferring skills to national counterparts' (Pacific Islands Forum 2004:19).

elements of the military and the police shooting at each other. At the same time, the Solomons case shows that the absence of a military is no guarantee against a coup in which the best-armed organisations in the society participate—the police in the case of the Solomons, more specifically the Police Field Force (paramilitary border police).

Our interviews with police revealed that divisions within the police between those who participated in the coup and those who did not were still a huge problem. The Melanesian Brothers conducted a reconciliation service within the police in April 2002 (Moore 2004:217). Yet our interviews revealed that this was seen as a rather set-piece reconciliation, albeit with some emotion, tears and hugging, that touched the hearts of only some police. The reconciliations within the Bougainville police between factions who fought on different sides in their war secured a much more meaningful, deeper unification of the Bougainville police service. The Solomon Islands Police Force was purged of most of the Malaitans who played important roles in joining forces with the MEF. The resentments of expelled police are still carried in important ways by their *wantoks* still in the police. Police who refused to participate in the 2000 coup reported to us resentment at being disciplined or ordered around by more senior police who did participate (and who remain in the police today). 'Who are you to talk about discipline?' was the spirit of this feeling.

As has happened in the Ministry of Finance, in the early years of RAMSI's Participating Police Force (PPF), there was a major problem in the quality of the capacity building of foreign police who might have been well trained as police officers, but not as trainers. The logic of flawed capacity building in this regard could be inexorable. The PPF arrive at a police post in an area that has been racked by ethnic conflict to work with the Solomon Islands Police Force. For a variety of reasons, which include the good work the PPF does at community policing during their patrols, their arrival is associated both as a matter of fact and in the minds of locals with a dramatic improvement in security. Solomon Islanders heap praise on the PPF for this accomplishment much more than they do on the Solomon Islands police who patrol with the PPF (because local police are still tainted with blame for the violence and chaos of the Tension). It was only human that the PPF and their leaders accepted these accolades. And it is to the credit of their leaders that they eventually realised it was a mistake that the PPF used its superior public relations machine (compared with that of the local police) to take credit for things that should have been shared or even fully attributed to the Solomon Islands Police Force. The PPF realised that in the long run, RAMSI disappears and becomes irrelevant, while confidence in the local police will persist as a foundation that matters for future security. So the PPF became better at giving credit to Solomon Islanders when things were done well.

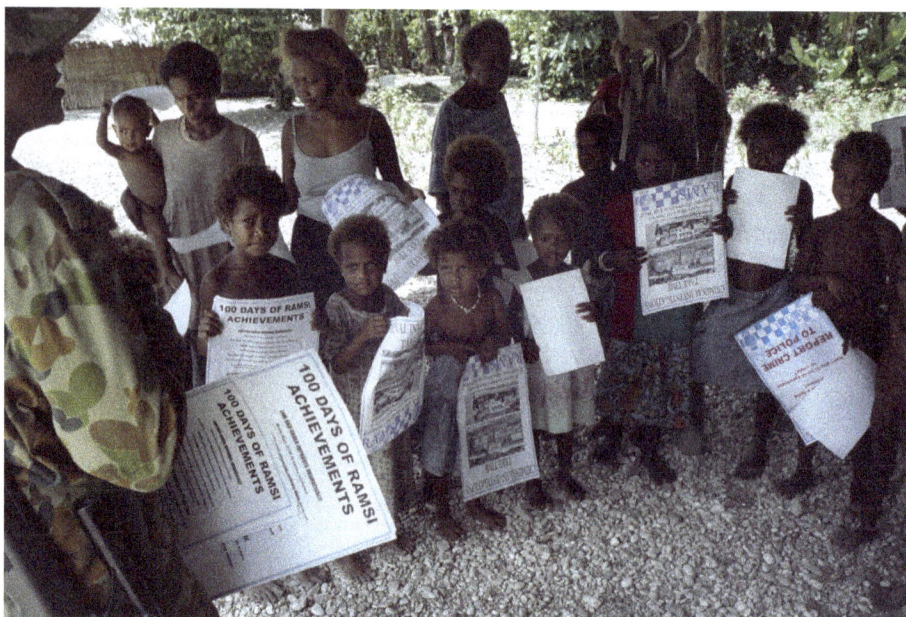

Figure 5.3 Children pose with posters handed out by an Australian intelligence officer that read, '100 Days of RAMSI Achievements', 5 November 2003, Malaita

Photo: Acquired through Australian War Memorial official commission, 2003

The second part of the inexorable logic of flawed capacity building arises from the following trap that foreign police advisors who are not experienced trainers fall into. They see a mistake that their local police partner makes because they have never been trained not to make it. The RAMSI officer explains the mistake and shows how to respond to or record an incident in the right way. Weeks later, the same situation arises and the same mistake is made. The RAMSI officer patiently explains again the right way to do it and why it is important to do it this way. On the third occasion when the mistake is made, the RAMSI officer simply takes over the handling and recording of the incident, telling themselves that it is 'easier to just do it myself', especially when the improved police efficiency is being appreciated by the community. But then when RAMSI withdraws and hands back all the policing to local officers, these officers have not learnt to implement the superior policing method.

This difficulty is compounded by the fact that in the case of RAMSI—as is generally the case with police building—the 330 foreign police initially assumed primarily operational roles to secure previously unsafe streets backed up by military peacekeepers. Police whom we interviewed emphasised that while they did most of the front-line work in the early days of RAMSI, militants feared and respected the khaki uniforms and 'long guns' of the military more than they did the blue uniforms of the police. An irony of community policing also arose because the PPF mostly patrolled in cars (especially after the murder of Australian Constable Dunning on 22 December 2004). The RAMSI military was more popular with locals than its police 'because they walk the streets and talk to people. The PPF, on the other hand, are rarely seen outside of their ubiquitous police vehicles' (Allen 2006:197).

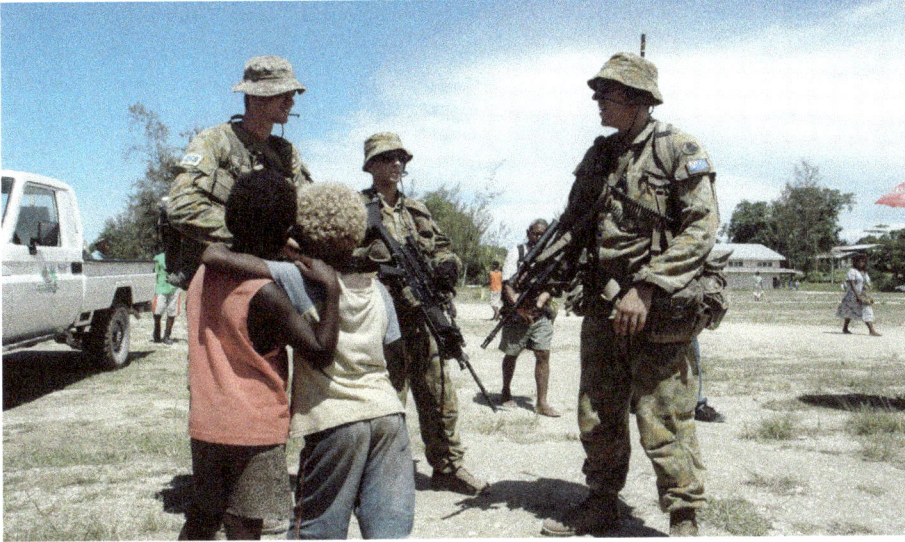

Figure 5.4 RAMSI military captures the attention of two young Solomon Islanders

Photo: AAP/Lloyd Jones

RAMSI police gradually pulled back from operational roles to capacity building (Goldsmith and Dinnen 2007)—a shift that can be hard for police whose only past experience has been operational. Moreover, the PPF continued to do the highest-profile operational work, such as major investigations, intelligence and controlling major outbreaks of disorder, and this was naturally the work foreign police sought to do as opposed to the less glamorous grind of capacity building in routine policing. There was also a more general problem of trust in the Solomon Islands police on the part of RAMSI. They were viewed as a broken and corrupted force that had contributed greatly to the Solomons conflict. Given that background, many in the PPF regarded local police who were not new recruits as potential suspects. This was not a great basis for effective capacity-development work.

A more fundamental problem continues to be the trust and confidence of the Solomons people in their police. People often prefer going to RAMSI police with their problems than to the Solomon Islands police and often complain that the latter act to enforce the law only when the RAMSI police are present (Parliamentary Inquiry 2009:172–3).

Lessons for the police from the 2006 riots

The worst moment in the history of the PPF was the riots of April 2006 that destroyed most of Chinatown in the capital and injured 36 Australian police, one very seriously. It is hard to judge whether the riots are better viewed as mostly spontaneous or as highly organised. Violence was fomented by criminal elements, among others (Commission of Inquiry 2009), who were likely organised by political opponents of the Rini government, which most people felt they had voted against. These riot organisers set out to 'cause such trouble so as to force a regime-change' (Commission of Inquiry 2009:47). This regime change was indeed accomplished by the rule of the mob. Police alleged that a named Member of Parliament made a statement in mid-2006 to the effect that 'if anything goes wrong, proceed with lawlessness' (Commission of Inquiry 2007:11). While there was an element of manipulation on the part of certain leaders, there was also a lot of spontaneity and opportunism in the riots and quite a bit of anti-RAMSI sentiment (Allen 2008, 2009b). There had been riots in Honiara before and they all followed the same broad pattern and had usually been responded to effectively by police. Viewing the April 2006 riots as manipulated by shadowy masterminds helped to cover for the mis-judgments and total lack of preparation on the part of the PPF.

> The looting and burning of shops in Chinatown after a demonstration of some kind, is a known scenario. It has been attempted on many occasions in the past and, each time, successfully blocked by Solomon Islands disciplinary forces. (Former Royal Solomon Islands Police Assistant Commissioner Mike Wheatley, *Solomon Star*, 26 May 2006:2)

There was clearly an intelligence failure by both the PPF and the Solomon Islands Police Force. Many in the latter organisation are believed to have had wind of the impending riots, but passed this intelligence neither to RAMSI nor to their own leadership. The intelligence function was no longer working communicatively within the Solomon Islands Police Force. This relates to a larger dilemma inherent in post-conflict police-building missions. In clearing out the 'bad apples', the interveners necessarily hollow out the institution, reducing its capacity in the short term in order to build it in the longer term. This was the point reached in 2006 with a Solomon Islands police force that had limited capacity of its own, including intelligence capacity. Allen (2006:199) connects the surprising failure of the PPF to hear of plans for a possible riot to an architecture of their presence that locked the PPF away in remote, airconditioned bases and patrol cars, rotations that were too short to build relationships and limited efforts to learn Pidgin. Terrorist-style arrest and search tactics directed at the most disaffected families and communities—the communities where the relevant intelligence was to be found—had also put up barriers to sharing secrets with the PPF (Allen 2006:199).

While the evidence of organisation for rioting was strong, as Christopher Waiwori (2006:7) pointed out, the politically driven organisers of the 2006 riots were a small group in comparison with the much larger crowd of looters who 'took advantage of the unstable security situation…to help themselves to anything they want'. Emulatory rioting broke out in Auki, the provincial capital of Malaita, soon after the Honiara riots. These were totally managed by the Solomon Islands Police Force and were much more successfully and quickly contained than was the case in Honiara, albeit in an unconventional way! Supporters of the police (who became a larger group than the rioters) began pelting rocks at the rioters, who were pelting rocks at the police. The counter-rioters were not discouraged by the police and prevailed in supporting the police to drive the rioters away from Chinese stores they were planning to loot! We were able to attend the trials of some of the ringleaders of the Auki riots in the local open-sided magistrate's court in 2006. It was an impressive example of community justice; about 100 people watched (a contrast with the tiny attendance at the Tension trials we frequented in Honiara). Offenders apologised for their wrongdoing and the magistrate gave quite long sentencing homilies about how the rioting was something that should never happen again because it 'reversim direction of country'.

In Honiara, the initial outbreak of violence in the form of stone throwing at Australian police and burning of PPF vehicles at the Parliament building after the Rini prime ministership was announced was certainly not a copybook riot-control performance by police with little experience in Australia of managing large stone-throwing crowds. The PPF Operations Response Team had only 13 people trained in riot control and the Solomon Islands police had no riot-control capability by April 2006 (Commission of Inquiry 2007:1). There was criticism that there was a failure by the police to cut off the bridge connecting the city to Chinatown—something former police commanders pointed out had been done in past times of unrest.

These problems point to some dilemmas of post-conflict police building. The Commission of Inquiry (2007:6) connected the intelligence failure to the standing down of the National Intelligence Unit as part of the project of depoliticising a police force that used its intelligence capability in the service of collecting dirt on enemies of the government of the day. And it connected the weak riot-control performance (for example, the use of tear gas in a way that blew back on the police)[8] to dismantling the former riot-control capability of the Solomon Islands Police Force as part of a complete disarmament of the Solomon Islands police in 2003. Without intelligence and capability to project force, police are hamstrung in their effectiveness at core policing tasks; yet when these areas play a part in a coup and a descent into violent chaos, there can be a need to temporarily dismantle them. This dilemma can be bridged only by peacekeepers stepping into these functions for a period; between 2003 and 2006, this policing gap was not effectively closed.

Several prominent political figures were charged with intimidation, arson, inciting violence and like charges related to organising the riots—including two men who were appointed as ministers in the successor Sogavare government, Charles Dausabea and Nelson Ne'e, and former minister and MEF leader Alex Bartlett. Some defendants argued that RAMSI arranged for school fees and other benefits to be paid to witnesses (see Averre 2008);[9] some RAMSI informants alleged that threats and inducements were made to persuade witnesses to retract their evidence. Amid the inappropriate pressure that probably was put on

---

8 'You tok, tok, tok until you calm crowd, have a peaceful manner and you stop anger. You cannot do this as you shoot tear gas at them' (Former Solomons police officer on Melanesian crowd management). The Speaker of the Parliament, Sir Peter Kenilorea, appealed to the PPF not to use tear gas and to allow more dialogue with the crowd by people like himself, but was ignored. A delegation from the National Council of Women, led by Hilda Kari, a National Peace Councillor, also asked the Australian police officers in charge at the Parliament to allow them to speak to and calm the agitated crowd—a role female leaders have traditionally performed at times of anger. The PPF decided it was dangerous to allow the women leaders to put themselves at risk in this way. But actually, no Solomon Islanders were injured by the mob, including the Solomon Islands police who stood at the front without protective equipment. Only the Australian PPF police who stood at the back with protective shields and helmets were injured because they were the ones seen as provoking the crowd and only PPF number-plated vehicles were destroyed during the unrest (Allen 2006:199).

9 There is now a legitimate worry that there could be an acceptance by the Australian Federal Police of paying cash to witnesses against priority Solomon Islands targets. Justice Mullins of the Supreme Court of Queensland, in finding that proceedings in former Solomon Islands attorney-general Julian Moti's indictment for child sex abuse offences (which were dismissed by a Vanuatu court in 1999) should be stayed for abuse of process, concluded: 'I am satisfied that the purpose that the financial support has been given to the complainant's family members in Vanuatu is to ensure that those witnesses and the complainant remain willing to give evidence against the applicant. The level of the financial support is of great concern and the expectation it has created on the part of the complainant's family in Vanuatu that the support remains ongoing whilst the prosecution continues. What would the complainant's parents and brother have done to support themselves since February 2008, if the AFP had not provided full financial support of them and their dependants? It raises questions about the integrity of the administration of the Australian justice system, when witnesses who live in a foreign country, where it is alleged an Australian citizen committed acts of child sex abuse, expect to be fully supported by the Australian Government, until they give evidence at the trial in Australia of the Australian citizen. The conduct of the AFP in taking over the financial support of these witnesses who live in Vanuatu is an affront to the public conscience. It squarely raises whether the court can countenance the means used to achieve the end of keeping the prosecution of the charges against the applicant on foot' (R v Moti [2009] QSC 407). In addition to large payments to the alleged victim herself, her parents and brother living in Vanuatu received payment of more than A$81 000—living expenses that go a long way in Vanuatu! Considerable additional payments have been made since then. As this book was going to press, the Queensland Court of Appeal overturned Justice Mullins' stay against prosecution, finding that the judge failed to 'recognise that the questioned payments were not designed to, and did not, procure evidence from the prosecution witness; and the failure to pay sufficient regard to the fact that the payments made, while beyond existing guidelines, were not illegal' (R v Moti [2010] QCA 178).

witnesses by both sides, all the prosecutions for conspiracy to organise the riots failed. In part, the problem here was a wider one of the politicisation of justice under RAMSI (Averre 2008; Goldsmith and Dinnen 2007; O'Connor 2007b, 2009a, 2009b).

The Commission of Inquiry (2009:6–7, 31) into the riots expressed concern that 'there still has been no in-house rigorous ("warts and all") lessons-learned policing evaluation of what happened'. The commission found the RAMSI policing function to be underfunded. Yet the ratio of a number of PPF that has ranged between 200 and 330 at its peak to about 1000 Solomon Islands police is a ratio that could never be dreamed of in a UN peace operation in Africa or anywhere else. Yet not everything that happened was negative. Many PPF and Solomon Islands police showed admirable restraint. Had an indigenous protestor been shot by an Australian police officer, a much more violent dynamic might have unfolded. As it was, no-one was killed and not a shot was fired from any side.[10] April 2006 was a litmus test of whether the disarming of Solomons civil society was working; the society passed the test. Indeed, in July 2006, the RAMSI chief, James Batley, reported that there had not been a single crime of any kind with a gun reported to the police in the previous 12 months (*Islands Business*, July 2006, p. 22). There have been only a few gun crimes in the seven years of RAMSI—a remarkable accomplishment for a society whose capital had been ruled by the gun. As we go to press in August 2010 a new prime minister, Danny Philip, was elected amid the kind of allegations of money changing hands that had been made of past elections, but this time without significant violence.

Police-building exit

Senior PPF officers with experience from the disastrous policing disintegration in Timor-Leste that culminated in the 2006 fire-fights recall that when the United Nations, and therefore the UN Police Force (UNPOL), decided to leave, the international police took everything with them. Overnight, police stations that had been equipped with computers, vehicles, GPS, riot-control equipment and vehicles suddenly were lucky to be left with the odd chair and desk. In contrast, the PPF has developed a sophisticated strategy of graduated exit.

The first step towards exit we have already described. It involves a shift in emphasis from in-line policing to international advisors stepping back to allow locals to execute the policing. The second step is an audit of which police posts where the PPF are located will be ready first for complete withdrawal of advisors. That is, the decision is not *when* to withdraw all advisors; it is *where*

---

10   'Destruction of property, then, is a constant feature of the pre-industrial crowd; but not the destruction of human lives' (Rudé 1981:255).

to withdraw advisors first. In the Solomons case, the contexts from which the PPF have been completely withdrawn first are islands without serious crime problems, where domestic violence is being addressed,[11] without major risks of re-ignition of ethnic conflict and where traditional reconciliation by elders of theft and violence works well. Before withdrawal occurs, an audit of police post needs is conducted to assess what equipment the internationals should leave behind, or add. After withdrawal, monitoring protocols are followed to check that the diagnosis was correct that this was a police post that could manage well (or better) without being propped up by outsiders. If the follow-up auditing indicates that certain problems have spun out of control as a result of the withdrawal, a decision may be made to return. If audit reveals the whole program of progressive exit to be going well then it may be accelerated.

One prominent Chinese business leader had an interesting perspective on the broader policy framework for thinking about RAMSI's exit:

> What is needed for RAMSI is not an exit strategy but for RAMSI to say to Solomon Islanders: 'What is your strategy to take over? What is your vision for your country. You must tell us. We must not tell you.' It's about the leadership of politicians—the masses follow.

Returning to lessons of colonial policing

There is currently a debate about whether a contemporary Western model of policing is the best one for Solomon Islands. Initially, this was another matter on which RAMSI was insufficiently sensitive to the limitations of the predominantly Australian policing model it was seeking to transfer to Honiara. We say Honiara because, even though a lot of fine policing was done by the PPF in more remote locations, the overwhelming majority of both PPF and Solomon Islands police have been located in Honiara and the majority of the remaining police are located in Auki or Gizo. Eighty-five per cent of the largely Australian-funded police cars supplied to the Solomon Islands Police Force are located in Honiara. Solomons Deputy Police Commissioner Sikua is leading a trial in three communities of a part-time community officer scheme using as a consultant a Bougainvillean police officer with experience of this kind of scheme. The plan is for the first 20 community officers to be in place in mid-2010. This has the support of the PPF and seconded New Zealand commissioner Marshall as an effort to return policing to the villages.

---

11   Domestic violence prevalence rates are high by international standards in Solomon Islands (Government of Solomon Islands 2002:40) and there is some evidence suggesting they increased during the Tension (AusAID 2008; Pacific Islands Forum 2004:36).

Beyond leaders within the Solomon Islands Police Force itself, former prime minister and the current Speaker, Sir Peter Kenilorea (Kenilorea and Moore 2008:155–7), is one leading advocate of a rethink of the current policing model as one insufficiently focused on the villages of a village society. In British colonial times, Sir Peter served as a district officer. Among his responsibilities in that role was supervising the local police (village constables, *ples men*) (Kabutaulaka 2008:98; Wolfers 1983) and serving as a travelling lay magistrate under the Solomon Islands version of governance by patrol.

Another leader, Manasseh Sogavare, was cynical about RAMSI's concentration of resources on punishing the crimes of the past during the time when he was prime minister:

> It is worrying that the strategy so far has been very heavily focused on punishing those who have been forced by the environment created during the crisis to commit crime. This is a backward look to addressing our problems. In fact one is fully justified to ask whether the huge investment in this program, that will only financially benefit foreign companies that run our prisons, will address the deep rooted problems of this country. (Solomon Star 2006)

Elsewhere (Dinnen and Braithwaite 2009), it has been argued that while Western models of urban policing could be an apt option for policing cities such as Honiara in developing countries, something more akin to colonial models of decentralised, indirect policing might better serve the villages of village societies. Mahmood Mamdani (1996, 1999) conceives of the typical African state as 'bifurcated'. On the one hand there is a 'civilised' urban society spawned by a history of direct rule and now practising a form of constitutional democracy. But most of the society is in fact a patchwork quilt of societies beyond the reach of the Constitution and profoundly ethnicised by a history of indirect rule and resentment of the predations of the capital. It could be that the Solomon Islands of the late 2000s is an even more bifurcated society than it was pre-RAMSI, making a bifurcated policing model even more relevant.[12]

Many share Sir Peter Kenilorea's view that if policing had been working effectively, the violence would have been calmed early in 1998 and there would have been no crisis. This would not have been accomplished by riot police or by an armed police field force. On Sir Peter's analysis, the problems started in rural Guadalcanal, not in the city. What failed was rural policing. He believes that in the rural colonial plantation economy intolerance and anger between different

---

12　For Mamdani, indirect rule through village constables and headmen was part of a fabric of oppressive colonial clientalism. It was 'decentralized despotism' (Berman 1998:316). But that of course does not preclude a post-colonial leader such as Sir Peter Kenilorea harnessing colonial technologies of policing to projects of contemporary emancipation from violence and commercial exploitation.

ethnic groups from different islands were rife. Village constables, headmen and district officers above them became sophisticated at reconciling these tensions, and particularly at nipping in the bud any rabble-rousing towards violence. That was their job and they had failed at their job if conflict spun out of control on their patch. They became skilled at homilies of 'when in Rome, do as the Romans do' and at admonishing one group to practise more tolerance towards another group. Sir Peter's view was also that colonial village courts were adept at assisting the police with give and take on inter-cultural clashes over land and other differences.

The village constable system collapsed soon after the demise of colonialism because part of the deal to placate separatists in Western Province was to hand over some important responsibilities to the provincial level of government. Rural policing was one of these. But because no revenue was transferred to go with the responsibility, village constables withered away for the want of allowances or any other support from their provincial capital. Ironically, one Western Province parliamentarian said that after the police presence in Western Province collapsed during the Tension (when there were threats from Bougainville Revolutionary Army militants staging armed sorties in and out of the province), 'a citizen community watch was set up…which while it was running was more effective than the police had been before or since'.

Police and logs

Dinnen and Braithwaite (2009) argue that the revolution in Western policing started by Sir Robert Peel in establishing the London Metropolitan Police in 1829 was a good thing for the policing of Western cities. But it was a bad model for the policing of rural England and the rural spaces of white settler colonies such as Australia. One reason why was that the London Metropolitan Police model was of a paramilitary police concentrating on crime (and quelling riots and urban disorder).[13] The older model of English village constables was not militarised, consisted mostly of part-timers and was not myopically focused on crime control. The English (and colonial American) village constables, like their counterparts on continental Europe, were regulatory generalists. They took care of consumer protection regulation, weights and measures regulation, early forms of environmental regulation such as pollution of rivers, regulation

---

13   It is often argued with some justification that it was the Irish colonial model of policing more than the London model that was exported across the British Empire. This was an even more militarised model than that of the London Police and more oriented to terrorising dangers to the state and suppressing political agitation (Ellison and O'Reilly 2008:398). But it was also a Peelian model in that it was forged during the time of three chief secretaries of Ireland: the Duke of Wellington, Sir Robert Peel and Sir Henry Goulburn, the lifelong friend and deputy of Peel. These three all became parliamentarians who played prominent roles in the formation of the London Metropolitan Police (Ellison and O'Reilly 2008:399).

of liquor licences, workplace safety laws and all forms of regulation up to and including the criminal law's regulation of theft and violence. One of the sad things about the demise of this generalist policing model for rural citizens of the West is that when it was replaced by Peelian police focused on crime control, no-one took an interest in consumer rip-offs and other regulatory offences that afflicted rural people. In Western cities, a knock-on effect of the police becoming specialists in crime control was the creation from the mid-nineteenth century of further specialist regulatory agencies to deal with other urban problems such as factory inspectorates, consumer protection agencies, health inspectorates to inspect places that served food, and so on. But these other specialist regulatory agencies—all much smaller than the police—had offices only in large cities. Their inspectors almost never visited rural villages. In early modern England and America, villagers complained about a regulatory abuse to the village constable; in late modern England and America, they learned to lump it.

Our Solomon Islands fieldwork reveals the same sad consequences for village people of Peelian policing modernity. Villagers said to us that they complained to the police about regulatory abuses by logging companies. The reply of the police was that this was not their responsibility; that was a matter for an inspector from the Forestry Department. But the Forestry Department inspectors were in an office in far-away Honiara. And they had no budget for travel to a distant island to respond to a complaint such as our villager made. As with pre-Peelian English village policing, in the days of colonial policing, the Solomon Islands villager could take a complaint about misuse of her/his land, forests or rivers to chiefs, then to the village constable, and if no satisfaction was obtained, then to the headman, and if none was obtained there, to a district officer like young Sir Peter Kenilorea sitting as a magistrate. That was a world of more practical, on-the-ground checks and balances against natural resource rip-offs.

Hence, one of the reasons we see the current Solomon Islands Police Force experiment with a dispersed, part-time community officer scheme as a promising development is that it holds out some hope of a law enforcement system that might return to doing something to respond to villagers' grievances about abuses by loggers. Village constables can receive some basic training on something as important to the nation as forestry law; they can provide the evidence to withdraw licences from lawless loggers and can arrest unlicensed loggers.

Saving the tropical forest is not the only desperate need for which this Solomon Islands Police Force policy shift might be an apt response. Foreign loggers so economically dominate locales where they log that they become a law unto themselves. Police intelligence suggests they use being above the law to traffic weapons and other illicit goods such as pornography on logging ships. Not only do they traffic pornography; they produce it by exploiting indigenous children, according to the systematic research of the Church of Melanesia on the large island of Makira, which is believed to reflect a more widespread problem (Herbert 2007). It was found that village children were raped, sold into marriage and used for pornography on a remarkably wide scale by Malaysian loggers. Child prostitution was found in every village visited on Makira.

> Last year I worked at the camp. There were seven Malaysian men there, and every one was married to a young girl—13 or 14. They are not interested in the older girls—once they are 18. (Solomon Islander former logger quoted in Herbert 2007:25)

This was happening at a place where the nearest police officer was three hours away by boat.

Corruption

When RAMSI issued a pamphlet to explain its mandate, on the list of things 'RAMSI has come to help with', the second item was 'Corruption: making the system more open and honest' (first on the list was 'Restoring law and order' and the third priority was 'Sorting out the government finances') (Office of the Special Coordinator 2004). For RAMSI's first four years, corruption was in fact well down on its list of priorities. A dilemma was that '[h]ad all the allegations [of corruption] been acted on, there would have been few leaders left to run the government' (Dinnen 2008b:15). We must recognise that Melanesian officials and Members of Parliament, 'like all Melanesians, are enmeshed in networks of social and financial obligation, and that this often influences their actions as elected officials' (Morgan 2005:5). There is a lot of corruption in Solomon Islands because there is a lot of indigenous demand for it that must be satisfied if politicians are to survive in a Melanesian political culture; and there have been spikes in the supply of foreign cash for corruption since the logging boom started in the 1990s and since the conflict from 1998 created temptations for foreign interests, notably Taiwan, to curry favour with embattled leaders by helping out with slush funds for development.

It seems possible to recognise these realities while being openly committed to raising the bar on corruption control over time. This could mean that at any point of time, the worst few abusers of conflicts of interest would be in the process of being tackled. Consequently, the worst abuses would over time become progressively less corrupt.[14] So the journey of reaching Western-style conflict-of-interest standards would take many decades, rather than the centuries it took

---

14 For a more detailed discussion of how this raising-the-bar strategy involves announcements that from certain dates targeted forms of law breaking will no longer be tolerated, see Braithwaite (2005:186–8). Solomon Islands Inland Revenue is an example of an agency that has progressively lifted the bar on what forms of tax compliance will be turned around next.

in the West. Ordinary Solomon Islanders who we spoke with saw the Prime Minister at the time of the RAMSI intervention, Sir Allan Kemakeza, Finance Minister, Snyder Rini, Premier, Ezekiel Alebua, leading businessman Robert Goh, Andrew Nori and some others as 'big fish' whom RAMSI was letting off for corruption and embezzlement while it targeted enforcement on militants whom they saw as 'used' by such big-men. In many cases, locals saw those imprisoned as guilty of little more than defending their *wantoks*.

RAMSI did make locking up militants its priority during its first four years. Since 2007, however, much of the prosecutorial focus has shifted and two former prime ministers who were central players in the drama of this conflict, Kemakeza and Alebua, did go to prison for financial crimes concerning reintegration and reconciliation funds. A number of corrupt former and serving cabinet ministers were also convicted of various crimes and it is believed at the time of writing that further high-profile corruption prosecutions are possible. All the prosecutions have been of indigenous officials who served in official government positions; there have been none of non-indigenous business leaders in the foreign 'shadow governments' we will discuss below, who activated the movement towards a kleptocratic state they could influence (Moore 2008:65).

It is noteworthy that only a long-term peace operation such as RAMSI could have succeeded in the complex investigations required for locking up powerful politicians such as former prime ministers. Had RAMSI left after three years, it would have left with the people feeling it had gone aggressively only after militants; it would have left a large pile of unfinished investigations into the corruption of the 'big fish' behind them. Other nations that have tackled cultures of loyalty to lineages trumping ethical duties to national institutions on the demand side, and foreign resources corruption making the supply side easier, have not managed across-the-board transformations in just a few years. It follows that commitment to tackle corruption must be indigenous and long term.

These realities also mean that education that instils a sense of obligation to the nation among elites whose education is funded by the nation is an important ingredient of corruption control (see Fukuyama 2008). Large sections of educated elites in many developing countries have managed to cultivate multiple identities in which on the one hand they hold to a strict moral code of duty to the institution in which they serve the nation and on the other hand they find alternative ways of sustaining their fidelity to networks of obligation and reciprocity with their lineage or village. A high quality of values dialogue within an outstanding indigenous education system is a more important solution to this problem than educating elites in the West. Developing-country elites educated in the West can easily dismiss anti-corruption values imbued within those Western institutions as relevant only to life in the West.[15]

The realities of a supply of foreign funds that has fuelled corruption go to the potential benefits of denying logging and fishing licences to foreign interests, reserving them for more cash-strapped indigenous entrepreneurs. This policy option will be discussed further below. There are in fact many strands to the web of controls that can be put in place to prevent corruption—from engaging civil society through organisations such as Transparency International and the anti-corruption pledges promoted during the 2006 election by local church-backed NGO Winds of Change to the state anti-corruption institutions discussed in the next paragraphs. To RAMSI's credit, today it is promoting a multidimensional approach to corruption control where each strand in the fabric of control is liable to snap, while the whole fabric develops some potential resilience over time. The difficulty is whether an anti-corruption fabric woven on a foreign loom will unravel when the short history of foreign presence ends.

Until the 1990s, discussion of corruption in Solomon Islands focused on politicians and civil servants using public funds to favour their *wantoks*. In the 1990s, elite corruption tied to the governance of a shadow economy of logging, tax and customs evasion, licences and contracts for big investments such as casinos and bribery of politicians to elect the prime minister[16] progressively transformed the corruption debate. Some contemporary commentary can be myopically preoccupied with this 'big fish' side of the problem. Our argument is that control strategies must attend to both demand and supply-side realities. Since independence, elections have become progressively more corrupt (Aqorau 2008:264). Civil servants in departments such as Forestry, Environment and Conservation[17] gradually became part of a corruption machine—by no means all of them; some struggle bravely against the culture. Like fish, these departments rotted from the head down—from the minister down. Fisheries was another department that rotted from the head down at the behest of foreign fishing interests who captured political leaders and the civil servants who served them, getting licences on favourable terms, underreporting catches and paying little revenue on the nation's second-largest export (after logs).

When civil servants who were honest or uninvolved in corruption (beyond doing the odd favour for *wantoks*) left or were pushed, they were replaced by

---

15   Also see below the discussion of Morgan Brigg's (2009) interesting thinking on *wantokism* as a potential resource for fighting corruption by securing checks and balances in a Melanesian way.

16   In the 2006 elections only five politicians signed the Winds of Change pledge that they would not accept bribes in relation to the vote for prime minister and it is believed bribes of S$20 000–60 000 were paid to persuade members to change sides in the vote for the prime ministership (Alasia 2008:128–9).

17   Another part of the wilful politics of neutering its regulatory effectiveness was that its regulatory function was starved of resources for monitoring and enforcement (Allen forthcoming; Bennett 2000:253).

loyalists to corrupt civil servants who in turn were loyal to corrupt politicians. A culture of corruption having been created from the top down by generations of corrupt ministers, it then became difficult for an honest minister to assume power and control a culture of corruption that permeated a department. Perhaps the most important forms of corruption in terms of millions of dollars in the past decade have been by ministers for finance issuing remissions of customs duties or reducing the determined value of log exports for customs assessment (see Allen forthcoming). Allocation of prime Honiara land to commercial interests has been another area of formidable corruption.

The Public Service Commission is an institution that once had an important role in corruption prevention, setting professional standards and discipline for civil servants, and especially education for integrity and efficiency (along with the public service training school, which was closed in the 1980s). By the time of RAMSI's arrival, the Public Service Commission was colluding in corrupt government (Roughan 2004). The Leadership Code Commission has been responsible since 1986 for investigating corruption and other forms of official misconduct by politicians. In practice, it became an institution tamed by corrupt politicians long before it had a chance to mature into an effective anti-corruption institution. A deeply defective statute is one of many problems that beset it (Wood Report 2005). It is a body whose chairman says it is responsive to complaints, yet we found during 2006 that no-one ever answered the phone! The only way to get attention was to physically arrive at their office—hard to do for a villager remote from the capital. The Chairman of the Leadership Code Commission could not tell the Commission of Inquiry (2009:42, 43) into the 2006 Honiara riots 'how many leaders had been dealt with over the past three years'—not even the most basic information on how many cases his commission had investigated. It also could not produce for the Commission of Inquiry any annual report to Parliament.[18]

One year after independence (1979),[19] the Auditor-General had a professional staff of 23 auditors and accountants; by 2004, it had only one professional staff member (Roughan 2004:19). In that year, the Ombudsman had only two investigators, neither with specialist ombudsman investigative training, and also went three years in a row without producing an annual report (Roughan 2004:24; see also Rawlings 2006). Even after considerable rebuilding of the Ombudsman's office, in 2008, fewer than 2 per cent of respondents to the

---

18 John Wood commented here: 'Not that it is an excuse, but there is no provision in their legislation for them to do so!'
19 The Auditor-General, the Leadership Code Commission and the Ombudsman were all accountability institutions established under the 1978 independence Constitution.

People's Survey mentioned the Ombudsman in response to the question of 'who should be informed if a Solomon Islands Police Force officer is not doing their job properly?' (up to three responses could be given) (McMurray 2008:51).

Since 2005, the Auditor-General's office has greatly increased its capacity and integrity. It has caught up on the backlog of uncompleted reports left by its quiescent predecessors. It produced 10 biting special audits in 2005 and 2006 exposing S$433 million in corrupt or fraudulent disbursements by the government (Office of the Auditor-General 2007:4). Unfortunately, in 2009, those reports were being received by a Public Accounts Committee of the Parliament chaired by a member sentenced to 22 months' prison for his actions when finance minister of corruptly approving a custom duties exemption for his wife. An appeal court overturned his conviction on the grounds that, as a minister, he was not an 'officer' in the terms of the Penal Code's provisions prohibiting official corruption in the Public Service. For the moment, reports of the Auditor-General exposing corruption in government are going nowhere after they are tabled in the Parliament.

The Solomon Islands media, 'while free, has been highly docile in its coverage and treatment of the corruption problem' because of its 'close relations with the establishment' (Roughan 2004:11). While there was considerable intimidation of the media between 1998 and 2003 by militants aligned with corrupt political leaders, the main problem has always been one of self-censorship. Nevertheless, the media is one of the essential strands in a web of controls against corruption that is in more resilient shape than in many developing countries and this resilience comes from indigenous journalists. The idea of a web of controls against corruption is that when state strands of the web snap, civil society strands such as the media and anti-corruption NGOs will step into the gap by exposing, and proposing repairs to, the rent in the fabric. In the difficult history of unravelling and repairing anti-corruption fabric, progress and regress are ever-present possibilities. Leaders committed to a multidimensional long-term struggle to raise the bar are what count; nihilists who believe corruption can never change because it is irredeemably cultural are the problem.

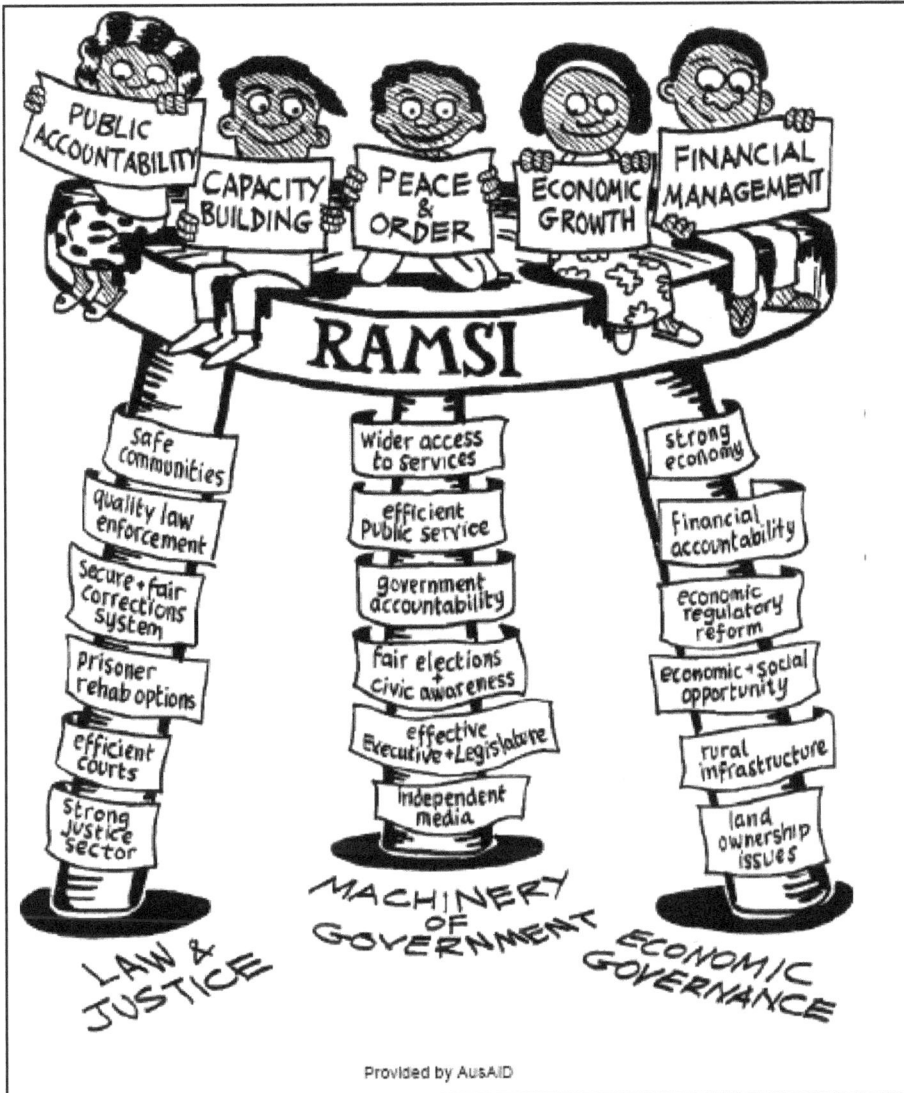

Figure 5.5 The three pillars of RAMSI's whole-of-government approach

Machinery of government: RAMSI's priority for statebuilding

RAMSI has three pillars: 'law and justice', 'economic governance and growth' and 'machinery of government' (see Figure 5.5). We have discussed the work of the first two pillars in the preceding sections, but only some of the dimensions of the machinery of government work. Much of the machinery of government pillar of RAMSI was about strengthening the accountability institutions that were vital to corruption control: the Ombudsman, the Leadership Code Commission and the Office of the Auditor-General. But there were also elements of the pillar concerned with electoral assistance, strengthening Parliament and parliamentary committees (undertaken through the UNDP) and strengthening provincial governance (which was in fact very focused on Honiara and Guadalcanal). But the biggest aspect of the machinery of government pillar was 'public service repair and reform', which covered areas as diverse as staff development, information technology support, refurbishment of offices, corporate planning, annual reporting, cabinet processes, government housing and recruitment. The machinery of government pillar completed RAMSI's whole-of-government approach (Patrick and Brown 2007; Wielders 2008:139).

Execution within each pillar was by a hybrid of expatriates working in-line within departments until it was felt that an indigenous counterpart was trained to do the job. At that point—which varied from department to department and job to job—the expatriate moved from an in-line position to being an advisor (and sometimes back again, as we saw with the police). Coordination among the pillars has been a rocky road. Yet coordination is a strength of RAMSI compared with other peace operations. The three leaders of the RAMSI pillars meet weekly under the Chairmanship of the Special Coordinator, a senior Australian diplomat, and at times go out into the community together to work with civil society to diagnose problems holistically and seek holistic solutions.[20] International peace operations before RAMSI tended to be thought of as having a peacekeeping phase in which the priority was security, followed by a post-conflict reconstruction phase that occurred mostly after peacekeepers had departed. RAMSI integrated these from the outset.

---

20 There are also consultative mechanisms that brought RAMSI, the Solomon Islands Government and the Pacific Islands Forum together regularly in Honiara; these newer mechanisms were a response to longstanding complaints about Australian dominance of the mission. See the discussion of the Enhanced Consultative Mechanism among these partners online, viewed 19 June 2010, <http://www.encyclopedia.com/doc/1G1-165067373.html>

Whole-of-government versus whole-of-society strategies

Integration with an armed peace operation dramatically changed the Australian-led development strategy for the Solomons. Before RAMSI, the AusAID country strategy had been that since the government was not functioning well because of corruption and rule of the gun, it was best for donors to work through civil society with a bottom-up development model rather than through the state: 'If you can't work with the government, then work beside the government' (AusAID official, 2006). Indeed, most international donors had that strategy—Taiwan being an important exception. The hope of this strategy was that a strengthened civil society would gradually make demands on the government for a more effective democracy; and meanwhile donors would get on with development at village level through civil society. While it was a credible strategy in the circumstances pre-RAMSI, the new analysis at the time of planning the intervention in early 2003 became that rapid progress would become possible only with an armed intervention that made the streets safe and then moved on to tackle corruption. That was a credible strategy, too, even though it was strong on the detail of how to create safety (and achieved it quickly) and weak on detail of how to tackle corruption (and had barely begun to tackle this in 2009).

With RAMSI assuming the monopoly on the use of force, it became the quintessence of government under the new strategy. Its in-line staff in government positions only slowly stepped back from being a parallel government to the elected one. So the new strategy was not only muscular in terms of the security pillar, it was also muscular in re-engineering the 'machinery of government'. Such in-line muscularity in rebuilding the state was possible only because RAMSI had assumed the core legitimacy associated with the monopoly over the use of force and guaranteeing the safety of citizens, not least of a prime minister who feared assassination. The three-pillared whole-of-government approach also changed the AusAID model of intervention from government by contract (managing contractors and paying by results) to return to a model of direct command and control in which AusAID staff and Australian and New Zealand public servants seconded to Solomon Islands government departments, rather than contractors, were in key meetings with Solomon Islands officials. This was better for whole-of-government coordination. But it also created a 'crowded stage' (Kabutaulaka 2006) that sometimes pushed off indigenous actors; or, as Ignatieff (2003:162) put it, 'sucked out' capacity rather than built it. Contractors resumed importance in other ways as RAMSI aged and a small cadre of contractors remained the only ones who had experience of the Solomons over many years, as the public servants left after one or two brief secondments.

The AusAID management model also moved from Canberra-centred management to in-country management, though Canberra bureaucracies varied in their willingness to devolve. For the most part, the real power was with the three leaders of the RAMSI pillars who were coordinating in Honiara and not with the folk they theoretically answered to in three Canberra departments. Such a bold shift from a bottom-up model that had been regarded internationally as quite sophisticated to a top-down whole-of-government model attracted some international acclaim in statebuilding circles.

A criticism of the shift could be that it involved too much of a rejection of the former civil society model as 'not working'. The 'Winds of Change', to use the name of one of the local movements demanding a non-corrupt democracy, were blowing, albeit feebly compared with the wounds of change inflicted by militias. The old civil society strategy required patience and might better have been viewed as something AusAID would encourage to bubble along in the background. This would have meant that instead of shifting from a civil society strategy to a *whole-of-government* strategy (Hameiri 2009b), RAMSI would have seen itself as shifting to a *whole-of-society* strategy that in 2003 slanted spending priority to the security sector first, then to economic ministries' reform, then to other institutions of the state, then back to bottom-up development that prioritised village society. Instead, there was a sense that statebuilding had transcended support for villages and the participatory empowerment of village citizens. The police constable, for example, was not to be thought of as an important part of the village-level development leadership; he or she was part of a whole-of-government team that was fixing problems of urban-centred government.

We are perhaps not being totally fair to AusAID in the previous paragraph, as the Community Sector Program that it funded pre-RAMSI (when it was called the Community Peace and Restoration Fund) continued to be bilaterally funded post-RAMSI, albeit as a poor sister of the intervention. Because village-level development was so neglected under RAMSI, one Western Province parliamentarian was concerned that 'rural people are losing confidence'. People were discouraged when the promise of earlier work such as the 1997–99 UNDP Participatory Planning Program was dropped. That program developed village-level needs assessments in an impressively collaborative way; during the Tension, it was cut without ever doing anything to follow through with implementation of the plans.

It might be said that RAMSI arrived with a set of templates for rebuilding the state and this priority was steadfast. Participatory bottom-up alternatives that came, for example, from the work of the National Peace Council that RAMSI discredited, were viewed as distractions from implementing the statist templates. One debate that RAMSI and the donor community more generally sought to choke off was over federalism. There was widespread post-conflict popularity among political leaders from most provinces for replacing the centralised political system with a federal model (Allen and Dinnen 2010), albeit with considerable resistance from Malaitan elites. There are reasons to be wary of federalism as a quick fix to excessive centralism. Where part of the problem to be fixed is that centralism has enabled waste by national elites, provincial governments can proliferate opportunities for waste and corruption by new provincial elites who monopolise power to the exclusion of village needs just as much as the old national elites. The Parliamentary Inquiry (2009:218–19) into RAMSI took up both the advocacy of federalism and opposition to it by quoting Andrew Nori:

> Mr Andrew Nori, former Member of Parliament...argued that the desire for federalism is based on an assumption that Solomon Islands' current economic, social and political problems are constitutional problems. This, however, is inaccurate because what the people normally complain about is poor every day services. Mr Nori subsequently blamed politicians for this misplaced assumption. He argued that when people complain about poor services, politicians take these complaints and translate them into constitutional problems, the solution to which is supposedly constitutional reform in the form of federalism. He explained...

> In a small nation like Solomon Islands, with due respect, I believe a well run national government, well resourced with good linkage and a sound delivery system to our people, can serve the interest of Solomon Islanders, because political structures only serve politicians. It is economic structures and commercial structures that benefit people in rural areas. (Parliamentary Inquiry 2009:218–19)

Yet a debate over decentralisation was one the Solomons had to have in the aftermath of the conflict. It is a debate that could indeed have led to the conclusion that village levels of governance more than provincial levels are the priority for enhanced support. On the other hand, it could have led to bolder locally initiated constitutional architectures that could not be predicted in advance of having the debate (Allen and Dinnen 2010). Building to standard templates imported from the West is statebuilding on shaky foundations, which, as in this case, can reflect international more than local priorities. RAMSI has kept the lid on debates for constitutional reform that enjoy strong currents of local support. For many years, a review of federalism has been stuck in the Constitutional Reform Unit in the Prime Minister's Office, with little sign of engaging the community with its work.

6. Reconciliation and reintegration

Many of the Solomon Islanders and RAMSI members we interviewed did not see reconciliation as part of RAMSI's job, particularly in its first few years. Rather this was seen as something Solomon Islanders must demand, initiate and lead. On the other hand, some informants, including Andrew Nori, Jimmy Rasta and former IFM leaders, felt RAMSI had crowded reconciliation off the policy agenda. The arrival of RAMSI was seen as putting the policy focus on everything but reconciliation, especially law and order (Allen and Dinnen 2010). MEF spokesman Andrew Nori told John Braithwaite that 'you can't reconcile by demand'. But a combination of RAMSI not demanding it, crowding it off the policy agenda with other important matters of statebuilding and Melanesian patience about getting around to reconciliation meant that reconciliation languished for years with little attention. Reconciliation is certainly a notable absence from the whole-of-government approach in Figure 5.5. We have seen that closure of the National Peace Council was a setback for reconciliation; the council's network of 80 mediators, mainly in Guadalcanal and Malaita, was slowly but progressively bringing conflicting parties back together in a spirit of forgiveness by sharing their stories.

A final obstacle to reconciliation was the philosophy that many parties to the conflict adopted—including RAMSI, the MEF, Premier Alebua and prime ministers Sogavare and Kemakeza—that justice should precede reconciliation, or compensation should precede reconciliation. Contrast this with Bougainville. There would certainly be negotiation of what payments (traditional or in kina) would be made before the scheduling of the formal reconciliation meeting. But in Bougainville this was viewed simply as a step towards the important thing, which was the reconciliation. Usually gifts were given in a spirit of symbolising how precious was the spilt blood, rather than in a spirit of compensation. There was rarely in Bougainville a philosophy of compensation before reconciliation.

Nori indicated to John Braithwaite how fundamental this difference was by saying if he took John's pen from him, John then hit him, and Andrew hit John back, they could reconcile. But the reconciliation could not occur without Andrew giving John his pen back first. What he saw as following from this was there could be no reconciliation until land taken from Malaitans was compensated. He claimed that expelled Malaitans were compensated only for their lost property (livestock, houses), not for land they had paid for. He thought a Truth and Reconciliation Commission could be a good idea when interviewed in 2006, but only if truth led to repair and then to reconciliation. In any case, he did not see a national commission as the most important form of reconciliation.

He had seen many examples of both sides praying together in church as groups of individuals and viewed this as much more important. Ultimately, Nori felt reconciliation must deal with 'real harms against real individuals' as opposed to 'unreal group harms against "Guadalcanal" or "Malaitans"'. For this reason, he favoured a government repository of individual complaints—'this was taken from or done to me'—as a foundation for real reconciliation.

There were many bottom-up reconciliations led by women. For example, a group of Guadalcanal women visited Malaita for a reconciliation ceremony at the Takwa Catholic Parish in September 2003 (Kabutaulaka 2004:396). Earlier still in the struggle for peace, Women for Peace regularly plied the airwaves of the Solomon Islands Broadcasting Corporation with pleas for reconciliation nationally, and locally used churches as peace platforms (Corrin 2008:188; Pollard 2000). Women became important in the training in restorative justice methods delivered by Solomon Islanders employed by international aid NGO World Vision (see Box 6.1). World Vision trained hundreds on the Weather Coast in restorative justice methods and established Bougainville-style Peace and Good Order Committees in eight villages there. These committees have led many family-to-family and village-to-village reconciliations over killings, arson and theft. These committees have also energised some EU micro-project initiatives through establishing village plans for development that involve tackling the micro-projects.

Box 6.1 Two Weather Coast peacebuilding stories from World Vision files

My name is Jacquelyn Tova and I am a Mother's Union member of Haliatu Anglican Church. I am very interested in this Peace Building Training as it gives me more idea on how to talk with other people. Also, I see it as a chance to increase my knowledge and moreover the knowledge of other women who are not well educated. I see this training fit to our culture and so it is simple to understand. In addition to that, I am also traumatised from this ethnic tension because my husband was killed during this crisis and all these years I have been searching for ways to heal the wound in my heart and also the hearts of my three children. Now this training had change[d] my life, I want to look for the men who did the killing and mediate for reconciliation with them in a restorative justice method...

* * *

My name is Rebecca Tova and I [am] just a housewife. I am thankful indeed for this kind of training to be held in our community and also it recognises not only the educated but also the uneducated like me. I am please[d] to train in this training as I will also share with other women like me who are uneducated about this training. It will really help my personal life because my husband is also a participant in this training. At the time of the ethnic tension the people here are so submissive but this course has encouraged us to be assertive, to come out with our feelings in a way that I won't hurt you and won't hurt myself also. Moreover, during this course I have seen that those people that are always submissive now are starting to come out from their nut-shells and sharing their experiences in front of the class during the training. I see this as a stepping stone towards coming out and making our way forward to finding the real true peace that we once experience[d] during the past but this is not a time to look back but to look forward to true peace.

Much of the church reconciliation was also led by men, with the Melanesian Brothers particularly important, as we have seen. The Solomon Islands Christian Association was the network that lobbied most persistently for a policy emphasis on reconciliation, specifically for a Truth and Reconciliation Commission. The commission proposal first emerged in the *Civil Society Peace Conference Communiqué* in 2000. Civil society programs that had an impact also always had a lot of church involvement, even being led by pastors. An example was the restorative justice training and reconciliation work between Malaita and the Weather Coast led by an indigenous pastor working for World Vision. The first phase of that work involved the training in restorative justice largely organised through churches in conflict areas. The second stage brought church leaders from the two areas together for more than a week of shared training, sharing of stories, apology, reconciliation and forgiveness. Then in June 2009, 30 Malaitan chiefs sailed to Marau for a reconciliation meeting with 30 chiefs from across the Weather Coast for the third stage of the project. The final stage—yet to occur at the time of writing—involves the militants who did the killing coming together to reconcile. For many programs, it has been getting onto this final stage of actually engaging the ex-militants to reconcile directly with one another that has proven too difficult.

By far the most important site where meaningful reconciliation has occurred between militants from both sides has been Rove prison. This was not initiated by the prison administration,[1] but substantially by the prisoners themselves. On one famous occasion, a Guadalcanal Liberation Front (GLF) prisoner was mistakenly put on the MEF side of Rove prison. When the police rushed to the prison to correct the mistake, he was found with his arm around Jimmy Rasta, with whom he had reconciled. Prison Fellowship International's Sycamore Tree Program (a Christian restorative justice approach) has been taken up by the Bible Way Church's ministry to the prison. It is led by a released former militant, Elton Kenasi. Welfare officers and the pastor at Rove prison got behind Sycamore Tree and the ex-combatants who lead its work. The Bible Way Church also runs a halfway house where militants from all sides have stayed, often for many months, often with their families, after release from prison until they are ready to build a new life. Families who have travelled from afar for reconciliations at the prison also stay at the halfway house. The church also

---

1 Hopefully, the thought given to rehabilitation in the prison is not well captured by AusAID's (2007:18) Solomon Islands Transitional Country Strategy—Performance Framework. Its 'Transitional strategy outcome' 1.4 is 'Rehabilitative programs established to reduce recidivism'. The '[s]ources for reviewing [that] transitional strategy outcome' are the '[n]umber of probation orders made and implemented'. Outcome 1.4.2 is '[c]ontinued monitoring of the extent to which probation is used as an alternative to custodial sentencing' and the associated source for reviewing this outcome circles back to '[r]ehabilitative programs established and used'! Not only is the strategy circular; 'probation' and 'rehabilitation programs' are limited options and outcomes in the circle in terms of their specificity and innovation. It reads as a fit to some sort of international template that bears no relationship to the ideas about rehabilitation that circulate in the local context.

does community mediation in former conflict areas, especially on Malaita. They have a philosophy of keeping the government out of their reconciliation work as they feel when the government gets involved it brings in victim demands for compensation from the government. The Bible Way reconciliation is very much about a personal religious journey to bring Jesus into the militant's life. For this reason, it has not engaged the 10 or so prisoners who have converted to an anti-Western Islam while in Rove prison. Many of these are ex-combatants. Note the irony that a RAMSI sent to guard against non-existent Muslim fundamentalists in Solomon Islands villages miraculously managed to create some in the prison it built.

The Bible Way reconciliation work has had little donor support. Much of the funding has come from former militants who participated in the program while inside and, as of 2009, were supporting it from outside. Leaders of the church and prison staff told us that Jimmy Rasta had provided formidable funding to transport families (by boat from Malaita, for example) to join reconciliations inside the prison and for other needs of the program. Jimmy's wife, Vika Koto, we were told, always cooks and brings the food for the reconciliations; she served two years in prison herself on remand awaiting a murder trial in which she was acquitted. We were struck that in our conversations with the Rasta family, they did not mention this generosity; it was others, including their former enemies, who reported their generosity. Rasta did, however, tell us that all 43 employees in his brick-making, plant hire and roadwork business are ex-combatants. He claimed the business existed for the purpose of serving their reintegration, rather than his accumulation of wealth. Rasta won a landslide victory to enter Parliament in 2010 and became a minister in the new government alongside another former prisoner from the Tension, ex-policeman Manasseh Maelanga, who became Deputy Prime Minister. Alex Bartlett is another militant leader who has donated many thousands of dollars worth of support to the work of the Bible Way Church with prisoners.

One reconciliation, between former prime minister Alebua and Ronnie Cawa, was discussed in a Sycamore Tree Program meeting at Rove prison. We also discussed it in a long interview with Alebua and a very brief one with Cawa. It was seen as a difficult reconciliation involving a number of stages. Cawa and Harold Keke are widely seen as the least reconciled individuals in Rove prison and the most volatile and violent; the worst incidents of violence between militants inside the prison have actually been between these two. Cawa was Keke's right-hand man who did much of his killing. Alebua, who was Premier of Guadalcanal at the time, was shot in the head, losing an eye, and through the elbow. He says he forgave all those who were responsible for doing that to him while he was in prison. Because of restrictions by the prison authorities on the number of relatives who could attend the reconciliation in the prison between Alebua and Cawa, Alebua said: 'There is peace in my heart after the reconciliation, but not peace in the heart of my tribe.' Like everyone else who had tried to reconcile with Harold Keke, his attempts would fall apart when Keke would lapse into imagining he was a different person. Alebua claims—as did other senior players on the Guadalcanal side—that he prayed with the many MEF militants in Rove prison and reconciled with them all.

Figure 6.1 Jimmy Rasta Lusibaea (second from right, in sunglasses) with ex-combatants who work in his brick-making, plant hire and roadwork business

Photo: John Braithwaite

Jimmy Rasta, Alex Bartlett, Andrew Te'e and Joe Sangu are other militant leaders who have been touched by the Sycamore Tree Program. Prison staff report amazement at observing the ex-combatants living together in a small prison for years and never observing unpleasant interactions, let alone violence, between the MEF and IFM inmates. Interestingly, Alebua liked being in prison very much. Rove to him was like 'a monastery' where he could 'develop his spiritual side' with time for contemplation without the constant pressure a big-man faces of demands from *wantoks* for help with this or that. Reconciliation with his enemies had been a big part of that monastic experience. But in a letter Ezekiel Alebua showed us in prison that he had written from there to the Minister for Peace, Unity and Reconciliation on 4 July 2008, he warned this is not enough:

Reconciliation will never achieve any changes if we hold ceremonies merely for the sake of fulfilling a spiritual or a traditional norm. To simply express an apology and recompensate [sic] for wrongs inflicted won't be enough. There must be changes in our strategies and approach to political, economic and social developments.

The new Truth and Reconciliation Commission debate

Until 2006, a widespread feeling among Solomons leaders was that theirs was a small nation where everyone in the elite knew everyone else, so a Truth and Reconciliation Commission might open up new conflicts that would be hard to manage. A common feeling was that while such a commission would be a good thing, the nation was not ready for it, not yet mature enough in its spirit of apology and forgiveness to learn from the past. From 2006, that changed, with both the Sogavare and the Sikua governments moving to a policy of support for a Truth and Reconciliation Commission. The Solomon Islands Christian Association (SICA) lobbied for it from 2000. Oxfam was a supporter of the churches in the campaign. But the Kemakeza government of 2001–06 feared truth and in these years RAMSI preferred prison to reconciliation, seeing reconciliation as something the people of Solomon Islands needed to sort out themselves.[2] SICA claims that an Australian high commissioner had in the past dismissed their analogy with South Africa by asserting that South Africa might have needed a Truth and Reconciliation Commission because it did not have a functioning multi-ethnic judiciary, whereas the Solomons had that. For its part, the Kemakeza government told SICA a commission might 'open up a can of worms'. Because of the history of dishonouring the spirit of the amnesty in the Townsville Peace Agreement, combatant leaders such as Jimmy Rasta, Alex Bartlett and Andrew Te'e were in 2009 openly hostile to the Truth and Reconciliation Commission, though 2010 reports indicated some softening of opposition from some militant leaders. They feared what they said would be

---

2   There is no direct partnership between RAMSI and the Ministry of National Unity, Reconciliation and Peace. The ministry does not come under any of the RAMSI pillars. The Permanent Secretary of the Ministry, Joy Kere, has argued that there would be great benefit from logistical support from RAMSI for the ministry's work and '[t]hat meaningful reconciliation and law and order [should] be considered as conditions for RAMSI's phase down'. In her evidence to the Parliamentary Inquiry (2009:204) into RAMSI, Kere said: 'If RAMSI's role is to assist in the long term stability of Solomon Islands then some effort and assistance is required to enable the Solomon Islands Government and its people to address and reconcile grievances in a manner that is meaningful to Solomon Islanders. As we are all aware, if grievances are not addressed appropriately and avenues for reconciliation are not provided then all the good work that has been presented by RAMSI might unravel.'

used against them in further prosecutions. The visit of Archbishop Desmond Tutu from South Africa in May 2009 began a process of turning around those fears.

The Solomon Islands context for mounting a Truth and Reconciliation Commission is very different from any previous commission. In the seven years since the conflict ended, the number of arrests and incarcerations per capita, more so per conflict death, exceeds that in any case of post-conflict justice the authors know of. The big question for Truth and Reconciliation Commissions in other nations has been: which will be the cases for which we will use the truth established to launch prosecutions and where will we allow amnesty? The Solomons already has an amnesty law (see Chapter 4, Footnote 1), albeit one whose spirit, as articulated in speeches in the Parliament that enacted it, has hardly been honoured. RAMSI, the Solomon Islands Police Force and the DPP no longer had great interest in launching new Tension cases at the time of our 2009 fieldwork, and a declining interest in cleaning out the old ones. As of June 2009, the DPP had a list of 13 pending Tension cases involving 30 defendants still to be tried. But some of these defendants were militants such as Harold Keke, who were already in prison or had already been convicted on other charges. In September 2010, within days of Jimmy Rasta Lusibaea being appointed Minister for Fisheries and Marine Resources, it was announced he would stand trial for attempted murder in November 2010. Along with Patterson Saeni, already in prison on a life sentence, Rasta is charged with firing shots at a senior police executive's home in 2002.

In a context in which most of the post-conflict justice work is done, the key policy question is no longer 'how willing are we to trade away justice to get to the truth and to reconciliation?' More of the emphasis can be on the nation-building opportunity that truth about the past and reconciliation for the future can deliver in a post-conflict environment. South Africa is the best-known example of seizing that nation-building opportunity thanks to the grace of leaders such as Nelson Mandela and Desmond Tutu, who were able to rewrite the national story of South Africa as a coming together of peoples—black, white and coloured—who were all victims of an institution called apartheid. Abraham Lincoln had likewise been able to re-narrate what it meant to be an American 160 years ago at the end of that country's Civil War: black or white, North or South, to be an American was to be a victim of slavery as an institution; an American is a person who is part of a national struggle to transcend the terrible legacy of slavery (Meister 1999). The truth and reconciliation process in Solomon Islands provides an opportunity for citizens to tell their stories and to hear those of others, to discover what it means to be a Solomon Islander. It provides an important vehicle for linking people in different parts of the archipelago through shared storytelling and the understanding and empathy this is likely to generate. These local stories could, in turn, contribute to a national narrative that will attempt to make sense of the conflict years and identify what is needed to ensure the same mistakes are not repeated. The process of storytelling began with the first hearings in March 2010 'featuring a procession by school children and victims' and an opening by the chair 'saying the hearings would disperse shame but also that the perpetrators would have a chance to regain their humanity' (Harris Rimmer 2010:7).

Jimmy Rasta says he wants a 'Forgiveness Bill'; Alex Bartlett wants a 'Pardon Bill'. The Sikua government's National Policy Statement included to '[t]able a Pardon/Forgiveness Bill in Parliament for enactment' (Parliamentary Inquiry 2009:200). On his election in August 2010, the incoming Prime Minister, Danny Philip, announced he would introduce a Forgiveness Bill to cover all ex-militants. Like most leaders of the Tension, Rasta and Bartlett have already served prison sentences. It is an option for the Solomon Islands Government to apologise to militants through the Truth and Reconciliation Commission for failing to honour the spirit of the amnesty agreement it signed in Townsville in 2000, to commit to an end to all new Tension trials and for the Governor-General to pardon all of those currently in prison who are rehabilitated and stand ready to apologise for their wrongdoing. Possibly only two of them would likely be a danger to the community and these happen to be the two most serious offenders. A Truth and Reconciliation Commission report recommendation in 2011 for a Forgiveness Bill would doubtless not be passed by the Parliament before 2012. By then, the ex-combatants remaining in prison would have been there a long time. Almost all have been model prisoners. Most had no prior criminal record of any kind and come from loving families that stand ready to support them on release. From inside prison, they have shown leadership to the rest of the nation in how to bring the killers from the two sides together in reconciliation. The Truth and Reconciliation Commission could acknowledge this leadership. Most of these ex-combatants are profoundly committed to non-violence as a result of their reconciliation experience with Sycamore Tree; most are respected, energetic leaders from communities that need more hard-working leaders. When Rasta was in prison, he organised a work group to fix the many examples of defective plumbing and drainage in the prison, to repair decaying buildings and paint them. A joint ex-IFM–MEF work team in the prison when we visited in 2009 was completely rebuilding and refurbishing the prison chapel, crafting fine pews for their services.

Rove prison is overcrowded, so there is a case that the nation would be well served by emptying out combatants who have paid their dues when so many other killers and masterminds of violence have gone free, when many more serious criminals than those locked up were released in return for testifying against those on the RAMSI target list. Of course, the argument against Rasta's

'Forgiveness Bill' is that it would do injustice and compromise the rule of law. But it also does violence to the rule of law to offer immunity to more serious criminals who testify against less serious ones because the latter happened to hold an office in the MEF command structure. It also does violence to the rule of law to turn a blind eye to the corruption of multinational logging companies and the ministers they paid as root causes of the Tension. It also does violence to the rule of law to fail to prosecute RAMSI officers who offered financial inducements to witnesses to testify against those on their target list. If it is an acceptable deviation from the rule of law to legislate for these RAMSI officers to enjoy immunity from prosecution in respect of any crimes they commit in responding to the conflict (Hameiri 2009b:566), why is it unacceptable to grant such immunity to former militants? A counter to the rule-of-law objection to a Rasta Forgiveness Bill is therefore that there was selective injustice in who served time in prison.

One interesting question is whether this debate might change if Andrew Nori were to be prosecuted. Nori is a wealthy man who secured impunity while so many of the poor men he influenced went to prison. Many Solomon Islanders wish to see him in jail. But perhaps even the launching of a Nori prosecution would not change the debate now, as Nori has been a loser, not a winner from the Tension. He has lost his professional and personal reputation and his family has suffered tragically as a result of the choices he made to stand with the militants. If he is ready to apologise in a deep and genuine way, perhaps the nation might now be ready to forgive him through a Truth and Reconciliation Commission.

Jimmy Rasta believes that without a Forgiveness Bill, the Gold Ridge mine will never be allowed to reopen safely because locals around the mine feel such a deep sense of injustice over the selective incarceration of their relatives. Some of them are keen to exact payback for this against the mine.[3] Rasta argues that emptying out the prisons of ex-militants would 'let RAMSI deal with corruption. Arrest all corrupt leaders and put them behind bars.' John Braithwaite replied that it seemed inconsistent to want a Forgiveness Bill for the Tension trials but then to want to fill the jails with corrupt leaders. No, he retorted, jails are expensive for a poor nation and must be reserved to help solve the nation's current problems, and no current problem is a bigger threat to the nation's future than corruption. Punishing crimes of a previous period of history is a luxury, an injustice the nation can no longer afford, in Rasta's view, as long as impunity remains for the crimes of logging that, more importantly than causing the last conflict, will cause the next one. He sees his Forgiveness Bill as bounded in time to crimes of the distant past, freeing up criminal enforcement for crimes that will endanger the nation's future.

---

3   Rasta worked at Gold Ridge before the Tension.

Another truth a commission could reveal is the location of perhaps 300 weapons stolen from police armouries that remain unaccounted for. That is a truth that the Rastas and the Bartletts who are calling for a Forgiveness Bill are in the strongest position to draw out. Another who could contribute greatly to answering that question is the man who is number one on RAMSI's fugitive list, Edmund Sae, the former police armourer accused of assassinating his former police commissioner. No-one would have more to gain from a Forgiveness Bill than Sae and, if he could promise to account for the missing weapons as part of the price for his pardon, that would be a truth that would greatly increase prospects for future peace.

Figure 6.2 Community spectacle to consummate weapons disposal

Photo: Courtesy of David Hegarty

At the time of our 2009 fieldwork, Father Sam Ata had recently been appointed as chairman and the Truth and Reconciliation Commission was recruiting only 30 staff. This of course will not be sufficient for the kind of historical analysis that was done by the Timor-Leste Truth and Reception Commission and the South African commission on the root causes of the conflict. These staff resources would also not be sufficient for the investigative work to turn over all the rocks on who were the key perpetrators and corruptors behind the conflict. The legislative model for the commission is influenced by Sierra Leone—another country whose commission was thinly funded. The timeline for the Solomon Islands commission is just one year, with an option for extension through a second year. It will not be able to award compensation or grant amnesties. Testimony of witnesses before the commission will not be able to be used against them in subsequent prosecutions. According to the *Truth and Reconciliation Commission Act 2008*, statements before the commission, as well as its findings and any other facts or information disclosed in relation to its work, cannot be used as evidence in any proceedings before a court of law. This provision has attracted criticism from human rights groups, notably Amnesty International (2009), on the grounds that it provides impunity to wrongdoers. The International Centre for Transitional Justice and the UNDP have been assisting the commission with advisors. But as one of them said, a difference from the Timor-Leste commission is that here most of the work will not be done by Australian advisors; it will be completed by Solomon Islander staff.

As in Bougainville, in the Solomons, genuine Melanesian reconciliation cannot be done in two years—the proposed maximum life of the Solomon Islands Truth and Reconciliation Commission. It will also not be done mainly at the national level. It will take decades of step-by-step local reconciliation work in villages and in churches. For problems whose roots are rural, long-term reconciliation work connected to bottom-up development that can deliver 'justice as a better future' (Shearing and Johnson 2005) is the reconciliation work that matters most. But just as the National Peace Council was, and World Vision is, pushing that slow process forward, so might the Truth and Reconciliation Commission do that in 2010 and beyond.

Refugee reintegration

One thing that has made reconciliation difficult is that most of the refugees fled rural Guadalcanal and most of them never returned to their former homes. If they returned from Malaita at all, it was mostly to the poverty of squatter settlements around Honiara. Malaitans who fled Western Province mostly did return and enjoy warm relationships with locals today. Public provision of payments for refugees to resettle increased anger because so many missed out as a consequence of militant leaders and politicians embezzling the money. NGOs such as Caritas and World Vision assisted with trauma counselling that was delivered through churches.

One of the important dilemmas of peacekeeping revealed by the Solomons experience was the effect on traumatised communities of continued armed patrols once the streets had been made safe. The importance of especially military peacekeepers' display of weapons in motivating militants to surrender theirs in mid-2003 was repeatedly emphasised in our interviews. In subsequent years, however, there was considerable local questioning of whether a move to the Bougainville policy of both police and military peacekeepers being unarmed was a better policy:

> [M]any women and children are still traumatised by the mere sight of firearms because the ethnic tension is still fresh in their minds. Another impact is that carriage of firearms openly in public has the potential to give the wrong impression that Solomon Islands can only have peace and stability through armed law enforcement. It is in the long term interests of Solomon Islanders that they regain their confidence in the police and the judiciary carrying out their functions without the use of firearms. On this basis, therefore, Rev Riti suggested that perhaps RAMSI should…slowly phase out the practice. (Parliamentary Inquiry 2009:179)

Many Malaitans evicted from rural Guadalcanal and from jobs at Gold Ridge and the oil-palm plantations returned to squatter settlements on the outskirts of Honiara such as Burns Creek, which have become hot-spots of youth crime and alcohol abuse. The Honiara City Council does not wish to encourage this squatting by non-ratepayers, so services are exceptionally poor there. At least 2000 and possibly 5000 people are believed to live at Burns Creek in an area relying on just two water taps. One foreign ambassador lamented that her country would like to help these displaced people, but the Honiara City Council, the Guadalcanal Provincial Government and the national government did not 'want us putting in running water'. There are a number of squatter settlements dominated by refugees from the violence of more than a decade ago that are almost as poorly serviced and as afflicted by violence and alcohol as Burns Creek. Most of the population of Honiara post-conflict are squatters.

Combatant reintegration

The attempt to reintegrate former combatants into the police as special constables was a disaster that cloaked many criminals as police, opening up a whole new world of criminal opportunities for them. This failure and the widespread embezzlement of reintegration funds for combatants created an environment at the time of RAMSI's arrival of resistance to any more government handouts to militants. So the Solomon Islands case did not see the widespread investment in support for ex-combatants to start up businesses that was seen in other regional conflicts in Bougainville, Aceh and elsewhere. More than 1000 special constables were dismissed and demobilised under a UNDP combatant reintegration program that included reconciliation ceremonies in the villages of the demobilised special constables followed by weapons surrender (UNDP 2005).

In the analysis of a former Malaitan premier, the reintegration assistance that did flow to combatants who handed in their weapons flowed too early. Militants wasted much of it on alcohol and wild living instead of investing it in income generation for their family's future. It was poorly used—first, because ex-combatants needed trauma counselling and assistance with reintegration with their families and villages as the starting priority. Second, the former premier argued, the rule of law needed to be re-established before it would be safe for ex-combatants to invest reintegration payments in businesses that had a chance of surviving. The interesting timing argument of the premier here is that combatants should not receive cash when they hand their guns in. Instead they should receive an IOU that promises a reintegration payment after they are reconciled and resettled in their community and after the business environment re-stabilises to one in which business start-ups can flourish.

This chapter shows reintegration occurring from the bottom up rather than the top down. Churches and villages provided the most striking examples. The important reconciliations that occurred in prison were also of the bottom-up type. Refugee and combatant reintegration has been mismanaged and misappropriated by national and provincial governments. Top-down command and control became a priority with the arrival of RAMSI, but not reconciliation and reintegration. In most places, refugees wanting to return to their homes have not received support to do so, and when they returned to squatter settlements instead, many basic services there were wilfully denied to them. While the top-down policy priorities did not help, divided local communities and churches often did manage to weave the fabric of their societies back together.

7. What layers of identity were involved in the conflict?

Identity multiplexity

Our colleague Ron May is fond of saying that ethnicity is a 'notoriously slippery concept in Melanesia'. Both Guadalcanal and Malaita comprise numerous linguistic and tribal groups, and there are few physical differences between the peoples of the two islands—far fewer than between Bougainvilleans and PNG Highlanders, for example. Moreover, island-wide identities such as 'Malaitan' and 'Guale' are relatively recent phenomena, doubtless reinforced by recent conflict, with their origins in the colonial and early contact periods. For most people in the Solomons, and indeed across Melanesia, primary identities and loyalties continue to reside with what can be variously described as kin groups, clans and tribes.

For these reasons, it is useful to visualise ethnicity in Solomon Islands in terms of Anthony Smith's (1991:24) 'concentric circles of allegiance'. For example, a young man's primary loyalty is usually to his clan on, say, northern Malaita. Under certain conditions, however, such as those that prevailed during the ethnic tension, that loyalty becomes refocused on the wider circle of 'Malaita' and its 'leaders'. Solomon Islanders can navigate between these wider and narrower circles of identity with considerable dexterity and alacrity. The fluidity and mutability of ethnic identity in Solomon Islands render it prone to manipulation. There are always those who seek to manipulate identity discourses purely for personal, political and economic ambition, and this was certainly evident during the conflict in Solomon Islands.

Among the multiplexity of identities that matter in the Solomons conflict, we will consider in turn kinship and island identities, big-man identities, youth identities such as *Masta Liu* and multiplex Chinese identities. We then consider the paradoxes of *wantokism* as obstacle and resource in national identity formation and national reconciliation.

Resistance as a font of identity

Allen (2007:90), following Bennett (1987), argues that colonial patterns of economic development created regional haves and have-nots. The people of Malaita and the Weather Coast, Allen continues, fell into the have-not category. They sold their labour to the blackbirders, then to the Solomons plantation economy away from their homes, then to the Honiara urban economy and on to the adjacent north-eastern plains after World War II, to compensate for their extremely limited opportunities at home. In the case of Malaitans, this has forged a sense of themselves as a people who have made the most of government neglect of their island to work their way up the class structure of Solomon Islands society.

Furthermore, Allen argues that identity was forged out of resistance to external sources of power—to traders and blackbirders, to the church, the colonial administration and the post-colonial state. On both the Weather Coast and Malaita, fidelity to *kastom* law as opposed to government law was a font of this identity of resistance. In colonial times, there were social movements such as the Maasina Rule Movement, of which Andrew Nori's father was one of the two founders, which helped forge a pan-Malaitan identity of resistance to colonial rule. On the Weather Coast, the Moro Movement mobilised a return to *kastom* across southern Guadalcanal against the church as well as the state. The IFM enrolled and re-energised the Moro Movement to its militant projects. When he was alive, Chief Moro kept his distance from the IFM, which adopted the ideas and practices of Moro selectively and only by some.

Figure 7.1 Isatabu Freedom Movement guerrilla, a son of Chief Moro, whose Moro Movement renounces modern ways, with foliage as camouflage, patrols with a homemade rifle in 2000 to protect a Moro Movement village on the Weather Coast

Figure 7.2 IFM fighters who are members of the Moro Movement, renouncing modern clothing, at a waterfall on a break from patrolling the Weather Coast, 2000

Photos: Ben Bohane

Big-men and identity

While hereditary male chiefs are not uncommon in Solomon Islands and female leadership, especially through the church, is also important, the dominant form of leadership identity is a big-man identity.[1] An effective big-man could widen the scope of identity by linking lineages that inherit different areas of land into a communal alliance. Big-man identities infuse contemporary parliamentary

---

1   The dominant form of political organisation in pre-contact times was the big-man system, though chiefly systems also existed, and in some places hereditary title and achieved status were 'intertwined or complementary' (Keesing 1985:237). In some areas, including much of Malaita, a clear distinction was maintained between three different types of leaders (discussed in Keesing 1985). There were the 'classic' big-men whose success lay in their ability to organise and mobilise resources, particularly pigs and root crops, in order to generate and distribute wealth. There were warrior-leaders, chosen for their strength, aggressiveness and skill in warfare. These men were also expert at raising and leading raiding parties, usually in response to a request from a big-man or from the relatives of a slain man for whom vengeance was sought. Keesing (1985:237) argues that 'Big Men have held centre stage in the period of ethnographic observation partly because men whose prominence was achieved in warfare and feuding have been forcibly removed from the stage by pacification'. The third type of leader was the priest, who was responsible for maintaining relations

leadership; Solomon Islands is one of the eight nations in the world that has no female representative in the national Parliament at the time of writing—a pattern of under-representation that is almost as extreme in other branches of national and local governance (Corrin 2008). Corrin (2008:172–3) argues that there is considerable continuity between this contemporary under-representation and pre-colonial governance in which women were generally excluded from leadership roles—reinforced by colonial governance that sanctioned indirect rule through headmen, to the exclusion of female leaders.[2] Big-manship is earned by leadership ability, but also through the gift economy of providing feasts and giving away wealth of other kinds to *wantoks*. Under both colonial and post-colonial government, an important part of the leadership that earned big-man status was in mediating the relationship between the state and local communities.

Translation of such big-manship into the parliamentary institution has produced a corrupt and unstable form of parliamentary governance. In the 32 years since independence, there have been 15 governments (Allen and Dinnen 2010). Non-emergence of strong political parties is one of a number of other factors in the parliamentary instability that Jeffery Steeves (1996) has described as 'unbounded politics'. Approximately half the Members of Parliament lose their seat at most elections, thereby accentuating the urgency to accumulate and redistribute within this relatively small window of opportunity. Often losers become losers because they have failed to be generous enough delivering personal wealth to those who voted for them the previous time. This means politicians serve their *wantoks* more than the nation.

It has also had the consequence that politicians who accept bribes from wealthy interests such as loggers and foreign fishing fleets have been better able to survive by passing on a proportion of these payments to those who vote for them. A result is that the politics of development is personalised, simultaneously undermining bureaucratic delivery systems. Ultimately, the problem is driven

---

between a kin group and its ancestors. In parts of western Solomons, such as in the Marovo Lagoon area, there were named leadership roles for women, but these appear to have disappeared entirely as a consequence of the colonial authorities' privileging of men in local leadership positions (that is, as headmen).

2   McDougall (2003:78), however, ponders whether institutional structures that have worked poorly for women and for men would work much better with more women included: 'A better approach might take women's organizations as models to be emulated in new efforts to draw diverse people together for collective action and common purposes.' McDougall found on the island of Ranongga that local women's church networks had bottom-up strengths in enabling collaborative action—strengths that were lacking in both local male social organisation and male-dominated civil society networks in the capital (to which women's groups were being coopted). In her vision, village-level women's collaborations could be the building blocks of more attuned and less aggressive governance. An interesting aspect of this on Ranongga was the use of art—the way mature women engaged their adolescent or adult children in the performance of parodies of young men who disappointed them by migrating to town, supposedly for education or work, but instead indulged in a 'rascal' or 'foreign' lifestyle of drinking, smoking or violence. The male lifestyle they disapproved of was communicated to new generations of young men by culturally attuned clowning using empty beer cans and Rambo attire as props.

both by politicians demanding ever-larger discretionary funds and by citizens of Solomon Islands who drive this political culture. Citizens demand patronage from their elected representatives—often their own kinsmen—in return for their electoral support and in accordance with Melanesian social norms of obligation and reciprocity.

Masta Liu

The post-colonial period has also seen the emergence of what Jourdan (1995a) describes as the 'cultural phenomenon' of the *Masta Liu*, a pejorative term used to refer to the young unemployed men who frequent the streets of Honiara. The *Masta Liu* are very much the product of increasing socioeconomic differentiation, particularly in the urban context (Frazer 1985; Keesing 1992:174, 1994). Their unemployment stems from both low levels of educational attainment and the dearth of employment opportunities. Very few students complete secondary school. Students sit exams at the end of primary school, at the end of form three and at the end of form five. At each stage, large numbers of students are 'pushed out' of the system, often because their parents cannot afford the fees. In 1992, only 2000 of the 8000 students who completed primary school went on to secondary school; and only 25 per cent of those who sat the form three exam were admitted into form four (Jourdan 1995a:221). Furthermore, during the mid-1990s, the education system was producing 1000–1500 secondary school graduates a year, while the number of new jobs, in addition to vacancies produced by retiring workers, was only 700 a year (Fraenkel 2004a:184).

Many, but by no means all, *Masta Liu* engage in petty criminal acts such as theft and extortion. Such acts are motivated not only by economic deprivation and poverty, but also by cultural factors. With regard to deprivation, Jourdan (1995a: 213) finds that hunger is a commonplace occurrence for *Masta Liu* and that petty theft is at its highest at the end of the month when the money has run out and their 'preoccupation with food becomes an obsession'. With regard to the cultural factors motivating delinquent behaviour in town, for Malaitans, particularly the Kwaio, the influence of dead ancestors encourages young men to engage in a range of 'spoiling' behaviours from pig theft to murder (Fifi'i 1989; Keesing 1992:175–8, 1994).[3] There is also an element of what Akin (1999:60) describes as the 'reshaping of *kastom*' to suit the urban environment in ways

---

3   These behaviours are not limited to the Kwaio or to Malaitan pagans. According to Stritecky (2001:71): 'I had conversations about young men's spoiling behaviours with Christians in Catholic, COC [Christian Outreach Centre], SSEC [South Sea Evangelical Church], and SDA [Seventh-Day Adventist] churches, all of whom claim that many young men in town still cultivate ties with deceased male kin, who in turn prompt the young men to steal, drink alcohol, fight and rape women.'

that diminish the control and authority of elders. The prime example of this is the emergence of urbanised forms of compensation demands described by Jourdan (1995a:219; also see Akin 1999:51).

Scholars of the relationships between masculinity and violence in Melanesia have pointed to the importance of foreign, as well as local, influences on the behaviour of young men. Images gleaned from television, videos and pictures have contributed to 'the "Ramboisation" of young Melanesian men' (Jolly 2000:317). Across Melanesia, from Papua New Guinea to Vanuatu, young men 'affect militaristic styles of dress and behaviour that they think convey an aggressive, confident menacing look' (Macintyre 2002:9). Macintyre (2002:10) also observes that the behaviour of militants during the Solomons conflict was strongly reminiscent of the ways in which PNG policemen behaved after returning from 'tours of duty' on Bougainville: 'men…who insisted on swaggering (often drunkenly) around the town wearing their battle fatigues and Rambo-style bandanas, their weapons swung casually over their shoulders.' Other imported cultural influences informing *Masta Liu* behaviours include drug culture (presently limited to marijuana) and American gang culture (transmitted in part via hip-hop and rap music).

Keesing (1985) saw the more traditional Kwaio violence scripts, which these foreign scripts were later seen to complement, as decidedly male. He quotes women as not thinking this way (for example, Keesing 1985:243), when he says:

> Being *nabe*, 'placid, peaceful', is a virtue for a man in some contexts (particularly if he is known to have physical strength and resources to respond aggressively and chooses forbearance); but to be *nabe* when honour demands aggressiveness and anger is a matter of shame, not pride. (Keesing 1985:244)

Adept peacebuilders in a context such as Solomon Islands need to understand in very local ways that there are both peaceful selves and violent selves, and associated scripts, which can be brought to the fore depending on whether one's project is peacemaking or violence. It could be that only peacebuilders from that island will be fully adept at persuading combatants to put their peaceful self forward during reconciliation processes by caressing and cajoling those peaceful identities, and even by poking fun at warlike ones (see Chapter 7, Footnote 2).

'New' and 'old' Chinese identity politics

Chinese identity politics has sometimes been neglected in analyses of the Solomons conflict, when it is in fact important to understanding these conflicts to consider how different Chinese actors see themselves differently one from the other. During the 2006 riots, the Chinese were constituted as folk devils (Cohen 1972), as evidenced by much anti-Chinese graffiti around the capital during our fieldwork in the months after the riots. Even the Commission of Inquiry (2009:5) into the riots went close to collective blaming of the victims: 'The Chinese community needs to take a hard look at itself. It needs to self-regulate its behaviour, clean up its image, the facades of its business houses, become more public-minded, and less rent-seeking.' Old Chinese families, some of whom were spared in the riots because of the respect they enjoyed in Honiara (Moore 2008), separated their identity as 'old Chinese' from that of 'new Chinese' who had arrived more recently from China and allegedly behaved haughtily towards Solomon Islanders in their stores, did not pay fair wages and other alleged petty commercial abuses. New Chinese also persistently corrupt immigration laws by bribing immigration officers for visas and passports. Yet some of the 'old Chinese', as well as Malaysian Chinese who are neither new nor old in Honiara, were at the centre of the politics of king making for cash, and domination of a shadow economy revolving around logging, casinos, other licences and contracts from the government and money laundering.[4] Some 'old Chinese' have been prominent in paying bribes to politicians to induce them to vote for no-confidence motions, in organising prostitution (including for RAMSI personnel) and other abuses. The grievances of those who were angry at the money politics of the election of Snyder Rini as prime minister were directed at the domination of certain 'old Chinese' of the shadow economy as well as at the petty rip-offs of 'new Chinese' store owners.

Identities, reconciliation and transformation

Understandably, RAMSI has found identity issues both too complex and too hot to handle. While this was also true to a degree of the Truce and Peace Monitoring Groups in Bougainville, one of our conclusions was that a strength of peacekeeping in Bougainville was that it targeted leaders on different sides of multiplex divides and urged meetings between them under the security umbrella of the peacekeepers. Their hope was that once the risky business of making the first move was born by the peacekeepers, locals

---

4   The idea of a shadow state cashed by the shadow economy was resonant with the crowd who changed Solomons history on 18 April 2006, as evident in the shouts of 'Waku [Chinese] government' from the mob (Alasia 2008:131).

would take over the diagnosis of the sources of conflict and how they might be reconciled and a new unity might be forged across old divides. This indeed has happened to a much more impressive degree in Bougainville than in the Solomons.

As complex and beyond the nuance comprehension of outsiders identity politics is in Melanesia, one consequence of the big-man phenomenon is that one does not have to be utterly culturally adept to be able to identify the fact that a divide and a knot of grievances coalesce around certain big-men who occupy nearby geographical spaces. What outsiders poorly understand is what makes this identity divide tick and where a great variety of individuals stand in relation to this divide versus various others who have calls on their loyalty. Recognising this seems to have been part of the genius of the Bougainville peace process: being assertive enough to be a catalyst for reconciliation between targeted big-men, with humility enough to then stand back to let locals do all the serious mediation work. Limited willingness of RAMSI to do that, though hardly universal, has been one of its weaknesses.

By 2006, one might have expected RAMSI to be pretty sure on its feet in knowing who the leaders were. But since the burning of Chinatown, we have been unable to identify RAMSI attempts to reconcile Chinese and Malaitans, new and old Chinese or countless other crosscutting conflicts among indigenous Solomon Islanders.[5] In a society of many overlapping layers of identity, it is hard to grasp, harder still to predict, which senses of grievance, relating to which identities, might have sufficient bite to animate violence. Central planning cannot deliver this; only local knowledge can. Yet national institutions such as the Truth and Reconciliation Commission could be crafted to enable pluralised, locally led reconciliation of a variety of hues. So this new institution is a source of new hope—just as the National Peace Council once was a source of that kind of hope before it was dismantled.

---

5   One prominent Chinese business leader said some reconciliations had been undertaken between Chinese victims and their victimisers: 'And Chinese can engage in a Chinese way, which is a comfortable fit with local reconciliation. They kill a pig. We give something back in Chinese custom. In Chinese custom we will bring friends together from both sides over tea. Can be a meal or meal after. The important thing with both indigenous and Chinese ways is that it must come from the heart. In the Chinese way you ask for forgiveness in front of this group of friends from both sides. This involves loss of face, which gives it power, [and] therefore makes it lasting because it is hard to do and comes from the heart.' This gentleman suffered trauma from the events of 2006 for which he sought treatment from a psychologist. He also said: 'The Chinese are easy targets. They have wealth and do not fight back. Victim[s] of envy. "We are poor so that must be because you are rich." Chinese have a stoic philosophy: let the wind pass. This too shall pass.'

Wantoks and big-men as part of the problem and part of the solution

In Chapter 6, we saw how Jimmy Rasta took care of dozens of his boys post-conflict by employing them in his legitimate business. We saw how he and his wife promoted reconciliation with their former enemies while in prison and on release continued to support logistically and financially the Sycamore Tree reconciliation program. Jimmy Rasta's big-manship was part of the problem in the onset and escalation of this conflict, but is also part of its solution. Former prime minister Alebua was a very different kind of figure from the other side to Jimmy Rasta, but this was true of him as well. When we spoke to Alebua for a second time, in January 2010, after he had been released from prison, he was dedicating himself to reconciliation work. It has been a failing of both RAMSI and state elites that they have for the most part stigmatised such men as simply pariahs, or even as 'gangster politicians', as Ken Averre has put it, rather than seeing their stature among the excluded as a resource for good as well as a danger.

In a similar vein, Morgan Brigg (2009) has critiqued Francis Fukuyama's (2008) analysis of *wantokism* as a problem, when it is also a cultural resource for tackling governance challenges. Brigg sees *wantokism* as something insufficiently mobilised to foster emergent national identity building. The form of Brigg's argument is that the only kind of national identity that can be meaningfully constructed must be formed from the clay of starting identities that involve real attachment. One of the promising things about *wantokism* as a resource here is that it has many layers of meaning for Solomon Islanders. In a context in which one's family or clan members are present, family or clan identities will be salient; in other contexts, in which speakers of the same dialect are present, language could be defining, and island or nationality in other contexts. *Wantok* often refers to those who share kinship ties,

> but also includes, on larger scales, those who share the same language, are from the same area, from the same island and the same region of the world. So, in a village context, one's *wantoks* are direct kin, but as one moves further away from local contexts one's pool of *wantoks* expands. (Brigg 2009:153)

Brigg makes his point by arguing that in international settings, all Melanesians can be referred to as *wantoks*; *wantokism* at this level is a resource for constituting a Melanesian Spearhead Group of states that is highly unified in comparative international relations terms. If this is so, why cannot *wantokism* be a resource along the path to forming national identities, rather than simply an obstacle? Some of the strongest national identities are forged in the embrace of difference, as when *pakeha* (white) New Zealanders perform a *haka* that distinguishes them from Australians and unifies their national identity in the context of a rugby test. As we argued earlier, this was Mandela's appeal to South Africa to seize an identity as the nation that transcended apartheid, and Lincoln's to the United States to be the nation that endured an awful struggle to transcend the institution of slavery.

It seems to us that Brigg is right to see that there is no reason why *wantokism* cannot be a cultural resource about difference that, in the hands of deft practitioners of Melanesian identity, can constitute unity. Consider the resilience of *wantokism* after colonial controls were lifted as English civil service leaders departed. Resurgent *wantokism* asserted dominations of political big-men over once proudly independent civil service departments. This post-colonial experience suggests that a post-RAMSI policy of crushing *wantokism* seems an inferior prescription to working with its grain.

A second part of Morgan Brigg's analysis is that *wantokism* is the stuff of a Melanesian resolution to Lord Acton's dictum that 'power corrupts and absolute power corrupts absolutely'. Brigg thinks Melanesians, like South American Indian societies (citing the work of Clastres 2007), early realised that transcendent central power was a mortal risk for the group. The Western solution to this problem was Hobbesian, then republican, to allow the central state to grow stronger and pacify ever-widening spaces within its borders; then to set up democratic checks and balances on central abuse of power. We elaborate somewhat on Brigg's text here. The Melanesian solution to the same problem was to constrain emergent big-men who put together widening coalitions by checking their central power with accountability to local kin obligations, local area obligations via reputation, sorcery and other culturally resonant regulatory mechanisms. As a big-man acquires power by unifying wider networks, all the concentric circles of identity (Smith 1991:24) that he has used as a resource in that constitution of power have claims on him. He has obligations to share wealth he acquires with *wantoks* within each circle, which is a check and balance on him ever becoming supremely wealthy. As a younger man in the process of becoming a power broker, he must be open to being pulled back by his elders, including women, within each circle. Or at least he is obliged to respectfully listen to concerns that *wantok* chiefs and other elders choose to express.

This is what constitutes participatory democratic deliberation as a Melanesian check with a Melanesian form on central abuse of power. To attempt to throw this away in a heroic project of believing that it is possible to replace *wantok* identities with national loyalty could be the worst of both worlds—one in which both Western and Melanesian checks and balances are neutered. This is analogous to the dangers in Melanesian societies of crushing indigenous justice that we have discussed, the danger that neither Western law nor *kastom* delivers freedom and security for citizens. The better path is the search for the hybridities in which formal law and customary law are mutually enabling (Forsyth 2009); just as hybrid economic entrepreneurship that simultaneously strengthens village economies and national market economies is a particularly attractive path to development in societies where local identities are very strong.

Western deliberative-democracy theorists have of course rediscovered the virtues of networked, crosscutting checks and balances in Western contexts as a complement to hierarchical checks and balances. More so in a Melanesian society it is necessary to 'think of possibilities arising from networks for emergent types of checks and balances rather than mechanical forms that operate through hierarchy and administration' (Brigg 2009:159). Mirroring Smith (1991:24), Jenny Job's (Job and Reinhart 2003) research shows that even in a society such as Australia, social capital formation builds like ripples across a pond, expanding primarily from primary groups, family and workgroups, ultimately to trust in the state—more so than Putnam's (1993) Western model of social capital expanding from intermediate groups such as clubs, societies and 'bowling leagues'; though Putnam's model also has a little explanatory power in these data. It does seem a mistake to view, as Fukuyama (2008) does, *wantokism* as a basis for social capital formation that can work only at the local level, as opposed to one that can ripple out to more encompassing circles of trust and obligation.

How often in the course of a year does a wise old man of Solomons society such as Sir Peter Kenilorea, or indeed a wise, respected middle-aged woman such as Joy Kere, take a younger civil service *wantok* aside and counsel them to honour their obligations in the state, to earn the trust the nation has put in them, by fulfilling the duties of their office? In this vein, Brigg (2009) argues that connections facilitated by *wantokism* can be linked with checks and balances in Melanesian social organisation to regulate corruption. This possibility (and emergent reality) becomes more real as 'several decades of marriage across tribal and island groups in modern Solomon Islands has generated a dense countrywide web of relationships' (Brigg 2009:156). Drawing on this web of relationships is what can give the networked governance of corruption that we discuss elsewhere in this book widespread appeal and relevance that can engage growing numbers of citizens. Even when marriage or attending the same school creates weak ties compared with lineage ties, as Granovetter (1974) has shown, there is a strength in weak ties when weak bridging links mobilise a resolve of two strong networks to share a project. Ambitious projects such as strengthening core pillars of governance are best achieved in modern conditions by enrolling (Latour 1986, 1987) networks of pre-existing strength (Castells 1996).

Because big-man accomplishments of power can be accomplished only in a network, big-men are inescapably vulnerable to regulation of their excess by that network. So, Brigg (2009:157) recounts the social fabric that could underwrite his idea of a 'wantoks against corruption' campaign:

> Some Solomon Islanders tell me that the inclusion of *wantoks* from different ethnic groups within a work or project team provides a useful counter to corruption. In other words, *wantoks* might keep each other in check rather than covering for each other when *wantokism* is mobilised for a common goal…Where a closed *wantok* network can provide a way of hiding one's bad practices, a more open network—such as that which would be promoted actively through *wantok* nationalism—could provide mechanisms for transparency and accountability.

A 'wantoks against corruption' campaign opens up prospects of a valued identity emerging that strengthens rather than undermines pillars of the core state. Fundamentalists of pillars of the core state would say *wantokism* will always be hijacked by the greediest politicians and commercial corruptors of the state. Brigg retorts that this is already the case. The question is whether the advocates of good governance will continue to sit back and allow the practitioners of corrupt governance to monopolise the harnessing of the circles of identity that are loosely referred to in this debate as *wantokism*.

Identity as a mask

The quantitative literature on armed conflict does not show that ethnic fractionalisation is a clear predictor of civil war (Collier 2007; Fearon and Laitin 2003). We also do not conclude that the much higher level of identity differentiation in Solomon Islands, compared with Western societies we know, is a root cause of this conflict. We do conclude that entrepreneurs of conflict did mobilise around various concentric identities we have discussed, such as Malaitan. We have seen that resistance and armed violence can be constitutive of identity because when violence begins, people seek refuge by taking sides defined by the entrepreneurs of violence (and therefore of identity). Hence, the source of conflict is not difference per se, but the strategic enrolment of difference to violent projects. To understand the conflict, it is therefore a mistake to see it as an outpouring of an ageless ethnic conflict that has been bottled up, waiting for the cork to blow. This is not to deny that there were underlying structural grievances in this conflict that were constructed around ethnicity. It is to say that our peacebuilding analysis is about focusing on those grievances and the deeper structures that produce them. These include deep structures of inequality that have fallen particularly harshly on the people of the

Weather Coast, for example. Our analyses should not allow identity essentialism to mask the diagnosis of real and perceived inequalities, other grievances and other underlying factors in the conflict that have, sometimes wilfully, become intertwined with identities.

Second, we have sought to argue in this book that success in mounting warlike projects has been based on a manipulation of identity politics and manipulation of outcomes such as compensation payments associated with claims based on respect for identity. This is one line of analysis that has led us to the conclusion that suppression of identities that had been hooked up to violent projects is hardly the way to advance peacebuilding projects. Understanding identity politics is vital to the peacebuilder because we hypothesise that the way to be effective is to be a more skilful entrepreneur of identity politics than the war maker. Instead of crushing identities that have been a problem in the conflict, the astute peacebuilder finds a path to harness those identities to projects of peace. This requires the peacebuilder to be culturally adept, creative and nuanced in a way that would be beyond the capacity of almost all foreigners. It follows that the crucial identity work of peacebuilding must overwhelmingly be crafted by locals.

8. Interpreting the conflict in summary

Table 8.1 summarises some of the key codes we have made in placing the Solomons conflict into the comparative framework of Peacebuilding Compared. This chapter covers all but the last two sections of this table—on peacebuilding strengths and weaknesses, which are discussed in the next chapter. The plan of both chapters is not to work through all the entries in this table, but to draw out some themes. In the rough sequence of Table 8.1, this chapter aggregates topics in the table into a sequence of themes.

Table 8.1 Summary of some codes, Solomon Islands; 650 other variables are coded

Structural factors at root of conflict	Is this a 'consensus' factor among analysts or 'contested but credible' as a possible factor?
Colonialism, World War II and global market forces leave a legacy of uneven development and anti-colonial traditions of resentment over it	Consensus
A divided state without a nation gains independence	Consensus
A first-past-the-post electoral system in a country of wantoks is conductive to instability; corrupt shadow governments seize the resultant opportunities to fund regime changes	Consensus
Emigration from Malaita	Consensus
People of Guadalcanal feel they are not treated with dignity, they feel discriminated against and put down on their own island	Consensus
Malaitans resent the dearth of economic opportunities on Malaita and the difficulties they face when they seize economic opportunities available on Guadalcanal	Consensus
Land tensions in intermarriage between matrilineal and patrilineal peoples; internecine and intergenerational conflict within Gaudalcanal landowning groups	Consensus

Ethnic stereotyping	Consensus
Youth bulge of unemployed young men	Consensus

Proximate factors

Politicians seek political advantage by exploiting grievances over the above structural factors to open ethic divisions	Consensus
History of responding to violence with state compensation for perpetrators	Contested but credible
Vacillation back and forth between responding to violence with a deaf ear combined with police violence and responding with political dialogue about prospects for compensation	Contested but credible
Militant leaders stake a claim as leaders by vowing to overturn grievances; young men join them out of a sense of grievance, for excitement, for loot, to defend the dignity of an identity	Consensus
Opposition politicians see opportunities to change the government by riding to power on a coup enforced by militants	Contested but credible
Logging and other business interests longing for a more captive government fund Members of Parliament who support the coup	Contested but credible
As a result of being released on bail, Harold Keke becomes principal spoiler	Consensus

Key triggering incidents

Premier Alebua's speech of 30 November 1998	Contested but credible

Key war-making actors

Leaders of the IFM, GLF, MEF	Consensus
Malaitan police of the Joint Operation	Consensus
Guadalcanal Premier Alebua	Consensus
Andrew Nori and other political aspirants supportive of a coup	Consensus
The shadow government of business backers of the coup	Contested but credible

Key peacemaking actors

Militants made peace when they concluded they had been used, surrendered weapons, reconciled in prison	Contested but credible
RAMSI	Consensus

Church leaders including Melanesian Brothers, SICA, and many others	Consensus
Women's leaders in churches, Civil Society Network, National Council of Women	Consensus
Sycamore Tree Program, World Vision and other peacebuilding NGOs	Contested but credible
National Peace Council (International Peace Monitoring Group), Peace Monitoring Council	Contested but credible
UNDP	Contested but credible
Guadalcanal Plains Palm Oil Ltd and KFPL Timber, Ringi Cove, showing the way on land resolution	Consensus
Solomon Islands Development Trust, Greenpeace, Oxfam, Kastom Garden and other NGOs struggling for bottom-up development alternatives to dependency on unsustainable logging	Contested but credible
Hopefully, the new Truth and Reconciliation Commission	Contested and remains to be seen

Peacebuilding strengths

Resilience in moving on to new peace processes when one after another failed	Consensus
National Peace Council, Melanesian Brothers, Weapons Free Village Program and other civil society efforts accelerate weapons surrender	Contested but credible
Announcement effect that RAMSI soldiers will arrest those with guns; announcement accelerates effective weapons surrender	Consensus
Arrest of Harold Keke (key spoiler) further accelerates weapons surrender	Consensus
In-line Department of Finance staff quickly stem fiscal haemorrhaging; voluntary tax compliance increases as bar is progressively raised on improved tax administration	Consensus
Winners from gaming compensation, corruption and looting convicted and become losers	Contested but credible
Auditor-General shows true grit in exposing corruption from 2005	Consensus
Sophisticated, graduated, audited exit by RAMSI police	Contested but credible

Peacebuilding weaknesses

Five years delay before RAMSI goes in	Contested but credible

Most refugees have not returned to their homes by 2010; many missed financial assistance for resettlement because of embezzlement by leaders	Consensus
Many thousands of refugees settle in squatter settlements on the fringe of Honiara and are deprived of basic services as a matter of government policy; crime breeds there	Consensus
Corruption at the top is tolerated in the early years of RAMSI; Leadership Code Commission and Ombudsman barely function	Contested but credible
Inaction so far on solving land tensions	Consensus
Gold Ridge mine restart of production still stalled in 2010	Consensus
Combatant reintegration is a disaster; reintegration funds embezzled by their leaders; special constables program further criminalises the police; weak assistance with vocational training and business opportunities for ex-combatants; after excessively dominating peace negotiations at Townsville, combatants excluded from peace processes thereafter; bad faith in implementing legislative intent of Townsville amnesty law	Contested but credible
Police not deployed where people live, where loggers rape, where needed to defuse future rural inter-ethnic conflict	Contested but credible
Weak linkages of village governance up to more encompassing levels of governance	Contested but credible
Reconciliation crowded out by statebuilding and state payments of compensation until 2009	Contested but credible
Bottom-up, participatory village development and education crowded out by top-down statebuilding	Contested but credible
Too much aid funds expatriate consultants who are denizens of Honiara, even denizens of Rove prison after midnight (see Chapter 9, Footnote 9)	Contested but credible
Indigenous institutions insufficiently assert control over foreign-dominated shadow economies; indigenous capacity is crowded out by non-indigenous shadow governments	Contested, credible, but steering networked governance to conquer specific drivers of conflict could be a more productive frame

What structural factors were at the root of this conflict?

Indignity and discrimination

Former prime minister Alebua's analysis during one interview was that the IFM uprising was about frustration because attempts had been made by the people of Guadalcanal in 1978 and 1988 to raise their concerns about being overrun on their own lands before a desperate last attempt in 1998. He saw the uprising as an assertion of dignity by people who had been trodden on and ignored. That is one interpretation of the return to wearing traditional bark loincloths by IFM warriors to assert a shared Guale identity with a symbolic marker of difference.[1] It was an assertion of the dignity of who Guadalcanal fighters were. In colonial times, the people had a problem with outsiders putting themselves above Guales, and in recent decades they similarly had a problem with Malaitans doing this. They found it disrespectful for Malaitains to change place names on their island of Guadalcanal. They looked at a cabinet and a civil service in which a majority of those in the top jobs were Malaitans and felt discriminated against. 'There is a promotion network among people from the same ethnic group. It's who you know' (Guadalcanal political leader). The other side of this is a Malaitan view that because they are more economically and bureaucratically successful, their children are discriminated against in the education system:

> To obtain a place in secondary school a Malaitan child has to pass the national examination with very high marks, and placement is not guaranteed. This form of discrimination was set up to prevent Malaitans—who are the largest ethnic minority in the Solomons—from 'dominating' other groups in the professions and government service. (Gegeo 2001:500)

Land disputation

From the Malaitan side, one root cause might be seen as a failure of land law combined with rapid population growth putting pressure on land. In practical terms, thousands of Malaitans were driven off land they had paid for, from houses they had worked hard to build and farms and businesses they had laboured to develop, on Guadalcanal. Theirs was a legitimate grievance, too, which justified for them resort to arms—a grievance rooted in the failure of Solomons land law to give them certainty of tenure on leased land. An interesting aspect of the

---

1 Sometimes this bare-bodied warrior dress was complemented with bits of khaki uniform they could lay their hands on and Rambo-style headbands (Carter 2006:42).

reconciliations that occurred in Rove prison between IFM and MEF militants was that they shared sympathy for each others' predicament in that they had grievances over land matters that 'fell on the deaf ears of government'. Each side genuinely understood the anger of the other at grievances being ignored by government, because they deeply felt a sense of being dismissed as well.[2]

This uncertainty also slowed the recovery of Guadalcanal. The Gold Ridge mine has still not moved into production at the time of writing in 2010 because no agreement had been secured with landowners on resumption of the lease for the mine. For cultural reasons, Solomons democracy since independence has consistently favoured retention of a land law under which only indigenous owners can hold title to land in perpetuity. Eighty-five per cent of the nation's land is covered by traditional tenure. This need not preclude guarantees of secure long-term leases that enable investment to occur by foreigners or indigenes from other islands. The UNDP (2004:10) makes the point that 'narrow land-focused initiatives' can make conflict worse because in conditions in which customary non-violent dispute resolution has broken down any change is risky. On this analysis, the fundamental problem is not land law per se, but a want of dispute-resolution processes that are granted legitimacy by all parties to settle land disputes with dispatch and certainty. One interesting response to this on Malaita has been a family-tree program in which villagers are assisted to draw their family trees back a number of generations. This helps them to reframe the claims of those they are in dispute with over land, by seeing their adversaries in many cases as ultimately their relatives. Genealogies can also simply clarify what is in dispute for the disputants to discuss. AusAID's Solomon Islands Strengthening of Land Administration Project and Community Sector Program and the National Peace Council have provided some support for this work.

Even such basic clarifying initiatives are not a good thing in all contexts. The problem is not just that Solomons land law can be predictable and knowable only at a local (as opposed to a national) level. It is that land is subject to crosscutting claims at the local level that are mostly not ownership claims, and therefore Western legal virtues such as predictability, knowability to outsiders and commensurability are unattainable. Debra McDougall (2005) has written an instructive piece on the 'unintended consequences of clarification' of land law on the island of Ranongga (New Georgia Group). McDougall's (2005:82) analysis begins by conceding that

---

2   Allen (2008:189–91) has developed this point: 'Whilst the Guale ex-militants point to cultural differences with Malaitan settlers as one of their grievances, it is the government that is held responsible for creating the situation in the first place. Similarly, whilst Malaitans state that the Guale militants went "too far" with the use of violence during the land evictions, they also place ultimate responsibility on the government for not responding adequately to the Guale uprising and for creating the economic conditions which originally forced Malaitans to settle in Honiara and north Guadalcanal.' 'In this manner, Guales do not blame Malaitans for being there in the first place, and Malaitans do not blame Guales for wanting to evict them. Each side places the moral culpability upon the government' (p. 189).

[m]any Solomon Islanders of all walks of life would like to use legal means to secure customary rights to property and land—sometimes because they hope to start projects that will tap into translocal flows of cash, but sometimes because they worry that their children and grandchildren will have no garden land.

While they might want to make land rights permanent and secure, they also understand that the process of doing so can endanger the value they place on an ethical way of living together. On Ranongga, McDougall found that islanders would, for example, accept gifts of food from the son of a man during that man's funeral ritual to signify that they as members of a lineage with a claim on the land acknowledged that the son could continue to farm the land his father had cleared. Some might not accept money, however, lest this signify too much about sharing of the land that privileged the son's usage. Material exchange at such rituals consolidates property usage rights, yet the speeches made during the rituals explicitly deny those very rights, or at least any exclusionary interpretation of them.

> For those claiming to own land, cutting off other people in this way is not only politically risky—it is also counter to the ethics of landownership. In a Ranonggan variation on a pan-Pacific theme, the people of the land ought to be loving and generous to those other people who live under their care. I was often told that only usurpers fight about land in courts, because the real landowners are happy to welcome foreigners and would not aggressively assert social hierarchy. (McDougall 2005:83)

Land disputes in McDougall's data mostly did not turn on objections over the way land was used, but over failure to ask permission of the right people in the right way. Hence, it was common for winners in land disputes to then invite the loser to engage in the very land usage that the loser had fought for. 'Rather than attempting to *exclude* others, Ranonggan disputants saw themselves as fighting for the right to *invite* others to share in their property. The right to invite others implies the power to cut them off, but I take the difference in emphasis as significant' (McDougall 2005:86). The transfer of goods at ritual moments of vindication of certain property uses is not meant to signify alienation of property from recipients, but signifies appreciation, regard and kindness at moments of formally ratified sharing. 'When differential property rights are articulated via exchange, very little is explicitly stated about who is who and who owns what. Such differentiation is accomplished implicitly, through the poetics of ritual exchange' (McDougall 2005:90).

It follows that a problem that Ranonggans have with any codification of traditional land law is that codification cannot leave enough room to articulate land claims without cutting people off. The double move of verbally denying property rights at the very moment they are ritually affirmed is a foundation of Ranonggan peacebuilding via the affirmation of sharing as the basis of unity and harmony. In such a ritual context, codification of customary land law can be a threat to peace (see also Scott 2000:73–4, 2007).

In light of these insights, there is virtue in the Ministry of Justice and Legal Affairs consulting on a Tribal Land Disputes Resolution Panels Bill. It would replace the courts and legal practitioners with local panels of chiefs and leaders to resolve land disputes. This is part of a Justice Delivered Locally initiative of the ministry (Parliamentary Inquiry 2009:176). One way forward is flexibly creating space for local land-dispute resolution that can eschew rights to exclude in favour of rights to decide how to include foreigners in the sharing of land. Such an approach informed by McDougall's insights might allow land law to be something that reinforces nation building rather than endangers it.

Infrastructure and inequality

Uncertain land tenure is just one cause of the poor long-term economic performance of Solomon Islands. The 2008 People's Survey suggests that 72 per cent of Solomon Islanders still do not have electricity (from either mains electricity, solar power or generator) (McMurray 2008:8), and even fewer own a telephone (though since 2008 mobile telephony has begun to take off). Seventy-eight per cent of the population do not have water piped into their house (IMF 2007:12). Resentments over the scramble between different ethnic groups for very limited employment opportunities in the formal economy were a root cause of the conflict. A road to the Weather Coast would help them to sell some of what they grow, especially as their produce diversifies with the support of local NGOs such as Kastom Garden. Investment targeting Malaita and access for ambitious Malaitans to Pacific temporary labour migration schemes in Australia and New Zealand would take some of the pressure off their migration to Guadalcanal (ironically, given the history of blackbirding).

It was the unequal distribution of economic opportunities that drove the conflict. A governor of the Central Bank argued that it was significant that the conflict was not led by people from the north of Guadalcanal 'because they had economic opportunities'; rather it was led from the Weather Coast where poverty was desperate. In fact, *all* the Guale militant leaders were from the Weather Coast (Allen and Dinnen 2010). Grievance over regional poverty came out in Harold Keke's trial when he lamented the lack of health centres and hospitals on the Weather Coast as causing unjust suffering.[3] On this, it would be good to listen to Keke and build some health centres in more cut-off parts of the Weather Coast.

---

3   *Regina v Keke* [2005] SBHC 48; HCSI-CRAC 254 of 2004 (18 March 2004). *Regina v Harold Keke, Ronnie Cawa and Francis Lela*, Criminal Case No. 254 of 2004, High Court of Solomon Islands. '*Father Geve Case*'.

The shadow economy of logs

The next structural issue that arises in Table 8.1 goes to the ideas of the shadow economy and the shadow state, particularly as manifest through the market for logs. There are 2.8 million hectares of forests in Solomon Islands, covering 85 per cent of the land area, though only one-fifth of these forests are suitable for commercial logging (Greenpeace 2008:4). The governments of Prime Minister Mamaloni in the 1980s, but particularly between 1994 and 1997, were captured by Asian logging interests. Yet Mamaloni and his successors also used the multinational loggers; the capture was mutual and mutually beneficial. The 1993 election saw the defeat of the Mamaloni government by a Francis Billy Hilly-led coalition committed to regulation of the logging industry's trail of destruction. A Timber Control Unit was established, local processing encouraged in order to phase out whole-log exports and export duties were imposed (Fraenkel 2004a:40). These were exactly the reforms needed to strengthen the nation's economy and environment then, as now. Within a year, Billy Hilly's government had fallen, allegedly as a result of the logger Marving Brothers bribing five ministers to desert the government (Kubutaulaka 1998:145) (see also Bennett 2000:345 on the alleged role of Robert Goh in passing logger payments to achieve the demise of Billy Hilly). Those who crossed the floor to desert him were well rewarded and timber exports accelerated sharply (Dauvergne 1998:534). From 1997, another reformist prime minister, Bart Ulufa'alu, also sought to restore integrity to forestry regulation, only to be ousted in the coup of 2000. The Ulufa'alu Forestry Bill was passed in 1999, but was never gazetted.

The patron–client relationships between indigenous politicians and Asian loggers that were strengthened by the demise of these two reforming prime ministers are distinguished from Indonesia's crony capitalism by the fact that Solomons cronies had little interest in the Solomons beyond logs, whereas in Indonesia the cronies were also engaged in controlling banks and industrial capitalism. There were the same patterns of bribery of politicians to bypass regulatory controls, to grant logging concessions and to evade taxes and export duties. In Chapter 9, we discuss in more detail whether William Reno's (1998, 2000) concept of a shadow state dependent on a shadow economy, developed in certain African societies, is apt to describe the Solomons' shadow economy of logs.

Another difference was that President Suharto, like President Ferdinand Marcos under his crony capitalism of logs in the Philippines (Dauvergne 1998), was the constant centre of power in Indonesia who controlled cronies such as his ethnically Chinese logging magnates. During the 1990s, Suharto played them off against each other. In Solomon Islands, it was the ethnically Chinese logging interests, particularly from Malaysia, who were more constant and the politicians more fungible. This should be qualified by saying that there was a small core of Solomons politicians who always positioned themselves above the fray during the Tension and other times of crisis; these men, such as Sir Peter Kenilorea, were not fungible as political leaders, though of course they were still fungible as prime ministers. Melanesian big-man traditions meant a stable party system did not evolve in the British parliamentary institutions the Solomons inherited. Political big-men who survived by giving out largesse always wanted to be on the side that controlled the budget. They were routinely open to the highest bidder among foreign commercial interests willing to bribe them. So they changed sides regularly and lost office regularly when they lacked a patron who would provide cash to dispense to supporters below them. All of the six former prime ministers we interviewed said governments, including their own, lived in constant fear of defections lured by bribes; in the 1990s, one said that believe it or not there were Members of Parliament whose vote could be bought for as little as S$1000–2000. When we recounted this to a leading Chinese business identity, he said that various prime ministers who complained about their MPs allowing money from loggers to influence their loyalty themselves took money from loggers. In the most recent vote-buying allegation over a vote of no confidence in the prime minister, the former opposition leader was charged over an alleged bribe of S$50 000 to a government minister, Severino Nuaiasi, to change sides (O'Connor 2007a).

One business leader said that there was less business bribery since RAMSI was in town, as RAMSI enforcement concerns made business more cautious. Nevertheless, the 'new Chinese' who had arrived recently were quite aggressive in paying bribes and, for all business people,

> you don't say no to requests. You give as little as possible. For their part, politicians are trapped in the political culture. They can't say no to requests for school fees, etc. If businesses do not help enough, politicians say, 'I will mark you when I come to power and harm your company.' So the businessmen are damned if they do, damned if they don't.

When unregulated logging boomed in the periods when politicians beholden to logging interests took over, the Solomons economy boomed. Cubic metres of log production increased more than twentyfold between the early 1960s and the early 1990s (Moore 2008:73). It was not a sustainable boom because once an area was logged out, the area not only stopped booming as the boom moved on to the next island, logged-out areas also left rivers and streams polluted, soil for agriculture eroded and ecosystems that supported wildlife for hunting and fishing devastated. Future opportunities for sustainable logging and eco-tourism were often lost. Many sacred sites were destroyed. The first boom was followed by the bust of the Asian financial crisis, which greatly reduced demand from Asian loggers. Then when political instability passed a certain threshold, many loggers disappeared for a few years after the Asian financial crisis. This evidence of boom and bust matters because international comparative research suggests that economic volatility is a source of both violence as warfare (N. Ferguson 2006) and violence as crime (Fischer 1999:Appendix N). Figures 8.1, 8.2 and 8.3 suggest that the boom enabled by RAMSI security after 2004 was even steeper than the Mamaloni boom of the 1990s. This boom before the final bust of forest exhaustion was only temporarily restrained by the global financial crisis of 2009.

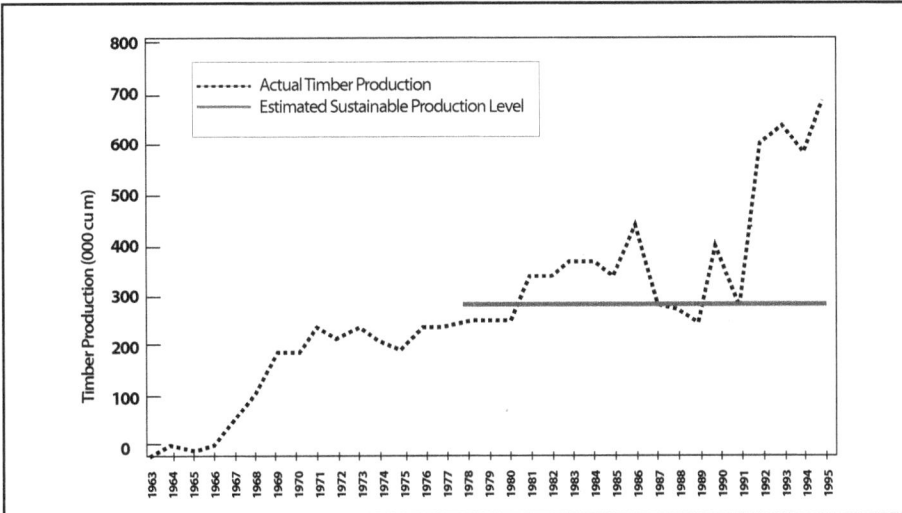

Figure 8.1 Solomon Islands annual timber production, 1963–95 ('000 cu m)

Source: Frazer (1997:47)

Notes: Frazer's data sources are as follows: Solomon Islands Statistics Office *Statistical Bulletins*, 9/85, 15/88, 22/93; Central Bank of Solomon Islands *Annual Reports*, 1993–95; Solomon Islands Ministry of Natural Resources 1994 (reproduced from Allen forthcoming).

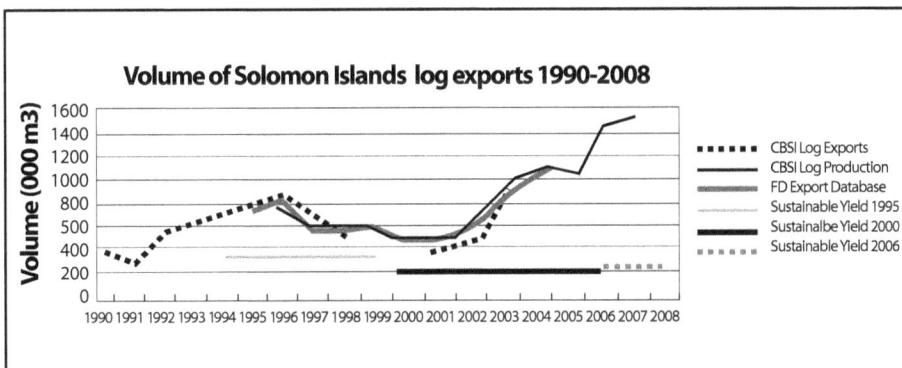

Figure 8.2 Solomon Islands log production and exports, 1990–2008 ('000 cu m)

Sources: Central Bank of Solomon Islands (CBSI) *Quarterly Reviews*, 15(1)/2003, 16(4)/2004, 17(1)/2005, 17(2)/2005, 20(1)/2008, 20(3)/2008, 21(1)/2009; Forestry Department Export Database; URS 2006 (reproduced from Allen forthcoming).

Notes: CBSI log-export data are derived from the Customs Division via the National Statistics Office. According to an officer of the Economic Department of CBSI, the National Statistics Office did not report log-export data for 1998 and 1999 and has not reported such data since 2004 (D. Kiriau, Personal communication, August 2009). CBSI log-production data are derived from the Forestry Department and can include a very small volume of logs that are consumed domestically. The Forestry Department Export Database data were reported in URS Sustainable Development (2006:10). Sustainable yield estimates made in 1995, 2000 and 2006 are also reported in URS Sustainable Development (2006).

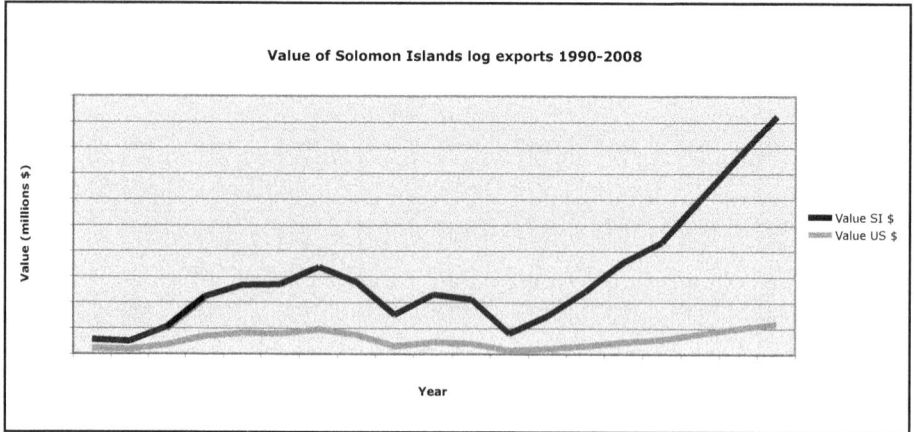

Figure 8.3 Value of Solomon Islands log exports, 1990–2008 (S$ and US$)

Sources: Central Bank of Solomon Islands (CBSI) *Quarterly Reviews*, 15(1)/2003, 16(4)/2004, 17(4)/2005, 20(3)/2008, 21(1)/2009 (reproduced from Allen forthcoming).

Logging not only engenders a macroeconomic instability of boom and bust. We have also seen that it worsened micro-instabilities of internal and inter-communal conflicts over who had the right to profit from selling logging rights. Many local people and landowners have been complicit in driving an unsustainable logging industry and opening up local divisions and conflicts over logs.

The lowest of many low points in logging policy was in 2007 when votes were being bought for a no-confidence motion in the Parliament. Six million dollars in donor funds allocated in the budget for tree replanting was raided to fund an announcement that each of the 50 electorates would have a sawmill built with the replanting monies. It was said that the approved mill only eventuated in the electorates of those who voted the right way. In an era of global warming, where Melanesia finds itself custodian of one of the three great remaining areas of tropical forest on the planet, Solomon Islands undermines donor confidence in its potential for donor support for forestry or carbon offsets with such reckless opportunism. Carbon offset cash will flow only to places where the risk assessment is strong that replanting undertakings will stick.[4] The Solomons is not one of those places.

The Forest Resources and Timber Regulations have some exemplary provisions that require any timber company that negotiates with a community to 'meet with

---

4   In current practice it is common, according to one Malaysian Chinese logging investor we interviewed, for paperwork to exist indicating that replanting is occurring when it is not.

the chosen representatives of the landowners in public' and that such meetings must occur in the presence of the landowners' legal advisor, representatives of the province and of the national government's Forestry Division (Aqorau 2008:250). The challenge is to transcend the culture of corruption and inaction in forestry regulation to allow such provisions to actually be implemented.

Greenpeace (2008) produced a fine report, *Securing the Future: An alternative plan for Solomon Island forests and economy*, arguing for a sustainable government revenue by reducing boom harvest levels to an estimated 'sustained yield' level. By shifting to local processing rather than round-log export, by strengthening tax and customs compliance, cracking down both on blatant evasion and on double invoicing (Dauvergne 1999:537) transfer pricing, sound management of logging and replanting could give Solomon Islands a solid core to its economy in perpetuity. Just as its fishing stock could be a sustainably managed resource that increases in value as the world's population increases and the global supply of fish declines, so tropical timber, sustainably managed, can be an increasingly valuable resource as the crisis of climate change deepens. The Greenpeace argument is for local community forestry producing sawn timber for export gradually supplanting multinational logging corporations.[5] This means village-based portable sawmilling from natural forest. Greenpeace's report shows community eco-forestry is 58 per cent more profitable to landowners and governments than round logs for export. Greenpeace (2008:3) recommends an immediate moratorium on new logging licences and cancellation of existing licences whose holders are breaching their conditions or are not in compliance with the law. As Hviding (2003) warns, however, success can be extremely elusive for such projects; chiefs who Western environmentalists thought were allies can suddenly accept a lucrative deal with Asian logging corporations. Sustainability is most likely when green NGOs are led by Solomon Islanders 'steeped in the organisational frameworks of indigenous landholding groups' (Hviding 2003:552; see also McDougall 2005).

An alternative policy analysis is that calls for moratoriums have been ignored for too many years now. The best technical estimates are of exhaustion of the forests by 2014 (URS Sustainable Development 2006). Hence, one argument is that it is best for the government to focus on sustainable plantation models, especially village-owned plantations, at this late stage of forestry decline. That might deliver a huge national investment in tree replanting. One promising model has been the Forest Stewardship Council-certified KFPL Timber plantation at Ringi Cove in Western Province. It has a memorandum of understanding with each village in the plantation area that guarantees sustainability through replanting and a secure flow of royalties income, employment opportunities and

---

5   In the 1990s, Dauvergne (1998:529) warned that exports from small Solomons sawmills were often of such poor quality that importers re-sawed it, reducing prices.

maintenance of infrastructure such as roads, electricity and water in perpetuity. At Ringi Cove, the company's community relations department is effectively the government—or at least the level of government above village-level government that works and delivers something to citizens. KFPL Timber also provided a form of governance that, far from disenfranchising villages, enabled community building. As a result, Ringi Cove is one of the most harmonious and flourishing places one can visit in the Solomons. KFPL Timber is one of the largest employers in the country, with 1000 employees.

Figure 8.4 Children of the Lobi Community sit on a newly cut tree from the Greenpeace-supported eco-forestry project in their village, Lobi Community, Marovo Lagoon, Solomon Islands, 9 September 2004

Photo: Greenpeace/Natalie Behring-Chisolm

Carbon finance incentive payments could assist with funding the enforcement institutions needed to make either policy approach work. International pressure on the Solomon Islands Government to ensure it did not nobble forestry law enforcement could be built from the profound regional threat climate change poses to the Pacific. Two kinds of law enforcement capability transformations are needed here: one is corruption of politics and the bureaucracy by multinational loggers (see pp. 70–74, 117–18); the other is shifting the focus of policing from towns to village constables who have authority to launch enforcement actions on breaches of conditions of logging licences (see pp. 68–70). In the past, local anti-logging activists have allegedly been murdered after they opposed Asian logging corporations (Greenpeace 2008:6). Clearly, there is also a need for police to be active in remote villages protecting the local agents of environmental change on whom reform depends.

The Greenpeace vision for sustainable logging in Solomon Islands is instructive in terms of the tactical shift from which it has issued. In years past, Greenpeace campaigned by targeting specific multinational logging corporations and exposing their abuses. Inside the Solomons, this had minimal impact because the capture of national elites by logging interests was so widespread. Local elites were also getting some dollars in their pockets from the loggers as well as some non-elite landowners who became a grassroots constituency in support of unsustainable logging.[6] Greenpeace realised it had to demonstrate to local elites and the ordinary villagers from whom they draw their authority that they could all be much better off by running their own community eco-forestry and that this could be a benefit their grandchildren would continue to enjoy. Greenpeace is now developing eco-forestry in 60 communities. The Solomon Islands Development Trust and Greenpeace have worked together on community eco-forestry since 1995. In contrast with the returns from community eco-forestry, trickle-down from the multinational loggers does not last, causes internal divisions in the community between haves who were bought off and have-nots who missed out and devastates the environment that sustains their agriculture, hunting and fishing (WWF 2005:3.5).

Forest certification has made little progress in the Solomons; all but one of the schemes that were getting under way in the late 1990s were shut down by the conflict (Wairiu 2004). By far the largest importer of Solomons log exports is China, where forest certification has no market visibility or traction. The Solomon Islands Forest Industry Association developed a Logging Code of Practice in 1996, which achieved little because 'most loggers do not obey compulsory environmental regulations, let alone voluntary ones' (Dauvergne 1999:527).

Forestry has overall a gloomy history in the Solomons, with only small numbers of bright spots such as the Ringi Cove plantation and scattered community eco-forestry projects. Nevertheless, in many tropical contexts, regrowth can be fast and opportunities for carbon financing are bound to escalate in decades ahead

---

6   Allen (2009a) and Dauvergne (1999:535–6) point out that there is some scattered evidence of resistance as well, such as women and children forming 'human shields' to prevent logging machinery entering their land on Makira (*Solomon Star*, 13 January 2006).

in ways we cannot yet foresee. Once it has a credible forestry enforcement infrastructure, the Solomons must position itself to grasp these opportunities. It is never too late to seize the agenda of improved forestry enforcement even if all it accomplishes is to reduce the extent to which reckless extraction of the last large trees destroys small trees and ground cover (see Dauvergne 1999).

Gold Ridge

A secondary, but nevertheless important, resource conflict that was part of the complex of disputes at issue was Gold Ridge, an Australian mine opened only in 1998, the year conflict escalated. Guadalcanal people felt aggrieved that only a small proportion of the profits from the mine would go to the people of Guadalcanal. Locals had exaggerated views of the magnitude of those profits. A mine executive told us how a local leader had said to him that the mine was so important to the world economy that if the people of Guadalcanal kept the mine closed, this would push up the price of gold. They saw the mine as 'financing an increasingly Malaitan dominated government and public sector' (Carter 2004:2). The mine was the primary reason for a new demand in the 1999 version of the 'Demands by the Bona Fide and Indigenous People of Guadalcanal'. This was for 50 per cent of all revenue generated from investments on Guadalcanal.

A new Australian operator, Australian Solomons Gold Limited, took over the site in 2005. But at the time of writing it had not been able to reach agreement with landowners on terms for reopening. The workforce at the site in mid-2009 to prepare the mine for opening included no Malaitans. Local women told the new operator that they had been pleased at first that the mine would create new employment opportunities. But then most women were glad when the conflict closed the mine. This was because the mine caused brother to fight brother over money and job opportunities.[7] There was jealousy when the mine provided one village with a school ahead of another village. The women also blamed the mine for increasing access to alcohol and resultant domestic violence. Many men also do not want the mine to reopen. Among those who do, many have the commercially unrealistic view that because the gold is on their land, 100 per cent of the benefit from exploiting it should go to locals. Conversely, many Malaitans in the government believe that too much of the benefit from the

---

7   Filer and Macintyre (2006:224) have discussed, on the one hand, the dilemma in Melanesia that 'mining, in spite of the problems it generates, appears to be a sure way that local people can gain employment, business opportunities, roads, hospitals and schools—the development that the government has been unable to deliver…[so they] construct their interests and attempt to manage their engagement with others to ensure they reap the benefits of development'. On the other hand, locals can quickly turn against mining because of the form that the 'resource curse' takes in Melanesia: 1) in political terms, competition on the national stage for resource rents (Banks 2005); 2) in cultural terms, unrealistic hopes and expectations (Guddemi 1997); and 3) in environmental terms, destruction of the agriculture/fishing/hunting environment that sustains the majority in order to deliver mining benefits to a minority (Filer 1990).

mine in 1998 was given to local landowners, who squandered it and wrecked the houses, the cars and the electricity lines that Gold Ridge delivered to their community. As lessees of the mine land, who then lease it on to the Australian operator, the government, or many within it, resist giving a larger share of royalties to landowners than the government receives. The mine operator expects the government to take responsibility for reconciling the tensions that persist around the mine; the government expects the operator to do so. Guadalcanal Plains Palm Oil shows an alternative path to government, business and indigenous society sharing responsibility for creating a better future.

Figure 8.5 IFM members on 3 November 2003 occupying the Gold Ridge mine site displaying weapons they said they had acquired since the Townsville Peace Agreement

Photo: Angela Wylie, *The Age*

Guadalcanal Plains Palm Oil Limited

The only private employer on Guadalcanal bigger than Gold Ridge was the foreign-owned oil-palm plantation on the plains 40 minutes from Honiara. The majority of its workforce was Malaitan. This was a focus of resentment. All these Malaitan workers and their families were driven out in the conflict and have not returned. The oil-palm plantation stood alongside Gold Ridge and the city of Honiara itself as a large development that had disintegrative impacts in opening up intergenerational and internecine conflicts over money for land, rents and royalties, which were nominated by Solomon Islander scholars Tarcisius Kabutaulaka (2001) and John Naitoro (2000, 2003) as causes of the Guale uprising.

This business has reopened on the basis of a willingness to negotiate a completely different business model with the Guadalcanal landowners. In 2005, the Solomon Islands Government called for expressions of interest to rehabilitate the ransacked oil-palm business. New Britain Palm Oil Limited (the largest PNG producer), in turn owned by Malaysian interests, registered an interest. Separately, it took chiefs and women's leaders from the plantation area on a tour of its New Britain plantation to see how it operated and how it collaborated with indigenous landowners. They liked what they saw and heard.

Previously, the land had been leased long-term by the government from the landowners, with the government in turn leasing it to the palm-oil company. The new operator and the landowners agreed to insist that the commercial relationship be simplified by cutting out the government. The government was persuaded to grant the land back to the landowners who then directly leased it for 50 years to the company under new terms that included an option for a 20-year extension. The agreement was for the company to pay a quarterly rent of S$100/ha. Second, a monthly royalty of 10 per cent of the value of fresh fruit is paid, after deductions for shipment and storage. Third, landowners have 20 per cent equity in the company. Formerly, the royalty was 2 per cent (Fraenkel et al. 2010). A preference for hiring from the landowning community of 10 000–15 000 people, followed by a preference for hiring from elsewhere in Guadalcanal, was the third part of the agreement. Many locals have other jobs or do not want plantation work, so approximately 30 per cent of the 1800 workers have been hired from other islands. None to date has come from Malaita, apart from a few who are married to local women. But now with all local demand for jobs on the plantation effectively satisfied and with the interest landowners now have in helping the business to flourish in the royalties returned to them, there is a debate about allowing limited numbers of Malaitans to return to the business. They would be highly respected Malaitan families at first with excellent plantation skills, to build confidence in gradual reintegration. High workforce turnover is a huge problem and a core of workers committed to the industry would help with this.

The new operation is based on the nucleus-estate model that has been extremely successful in West New Britain. The centralised commercial estate is surrounded by out-growers—in this case, landowners producing palm-oil on both registered and customary land—who piggyback on the company's processing facilities, infrastructure and technical support. The company has ambitious plans to expand both commercial and out-grower areas. But not all landowners are happy, as evidenced by two arson attacks on the company's office in the past five years, allegedly by disgruntled landowners.

The company funds scholarships for landowners' children to attend university and high school as well as vocational training in the workplace. The landowners have also decided to invest half their royalty payments mainly to fund scholarships; the fund has S$6 million already. The ANZ Bank, which is keen to attract funds and support a big, stable peacebuilding business, was paying 10 per cent interest long term on the trust fund through the 2008–09 global financial crisis. The operator sees trustee education on transparency, deliberative agreement on how to invest royalties and responsible trusteeship for the future of their children as corporate citizenship obligations.

New Britain Palm Oil Limited has been a leader in establishing an international organisation to continuously improve the sustainability of palm-oil production, with 260 members representing producers, consumers, the food and chemical industries and 12 NGO members: the Roundtable on Sustainable Palm Oil (<www.RSPO.org>). The company's head of research is vice-president of the roundtable. It hopes to be one of the first organisations to reach the certification standards. The Guadalcanal plantation has not yet achieved that certification. The company is committed to carbon-footprint reduction by eschewing planting that replaces primary forest or in any area having one or more High Conservation Values (a position it has been seeking to persuade the roundtable to in collaboration with WWF). They are considering plans to plant tropical trees on the perimeters of their plantations. They consult with WWF, the Nature Conservancy and Oxfam on their environmental planning.

Youth bulge

The extreme youthfulness of the Solomon Islands population interacted with inter-island migration to Guadalcanal to create a youth bulge on Guadalcanal. Young men were separated from the discipline of village authority (including on the IFM side, where a core of Weather Coast militants roamed across Guadalcanal, and beyond) and separated from the discipline of employment after the economy crashed under the weight of the Tension. While there has been some semblance of a semi-organised gang phenomenon that has been used by politicians post-conflict in places such as Burns Creek and White River on the fringes of Honiara, this problem is nowhere near as deep and structured as it is in Port Moresby and certain other towns in both Papua New Guinea and Indonesia (Braithwaite et al. 2010a).

The militant youth gang problem during the Tension had something in common with the Bougainvillean armed Raskols posing as BRA who in fact were semi-organised youth crime groups. Another common feature between Solomon Islands and Bougainville is that they did not persist as semi-organised criminal youth gangs in the way martial arts groups and former militias persisted for many years in Timor-Leste, Aceh and other former conflict areas in Indonesia as criminal organisations (Braithwaite et al. 2010a). Former militia leaders such as Jimmy Rasta, George Gray, Harold Keke and Andrew Te'e for different reasons are not organised-crime leaders in Solomon Islands today. There are no large heroin, marijuana and other illicit drug markets, illicit gambling or prostitution markets that have attracted organised crime groups. The Tension was an era of organised crime in extortion, protection rackets and armed robbery. But that era of organised crime effectively ended with the arrival of RAMSI. This is a fundamental reason why RAMSI is so highly valued by ordinary people. And indeed it has been a great contribution of RAMSI that a society that had a virulent problem of violent organised criminal gangs does not have this problem today. This is not to downplay the significance of the disorganised and semi-organised crime we have described as perpetrated by gatherings of disenchanted youth. These youth seek a collective solution to their marginalisation by asserting the dignity of some layer of identity that is important to them and that they perceive as having been disrespected.

What have been the proximate factors in the conflict?

We interpret proximate factors in this conflict to be the actions of certain politicians who, recognising how deep were the structural factors we have just summarised, and how deeply felt were the grievances associated with them, sought political advantage by encouraging a politics of ethnic resentment. We conclude it to be a contested but credible interpretation that Ezekiel Alebua, as Harold Keke alleged, recruited Keke and other Weather Coast militant leaders to stir up anger across all of Guadalcanal. This interpretation is contested by a number of the Guale militants interviewed by Matthew Allen; they played down the role of Alebua and attributed much greater agency to themselves. Indeed, Alebua contests this interpretation himself. It could be that discontent spun out of control in a way Alebua did not approve of, and when it did Alebua worked hard with other leaders to try to calm the violence. But at the very beginning, the limited evidence is consistent with Alebua encouraging the mobilisation of mobs of young men as a ploy to shore up his precarious hold on the premiership of Guadalcanal, partly as a result of his earlier failure as prime minister to back the 'Demands by the Bona Fide and Indigenous People of Guadalcanal'. We also conclude that the agency of many local big-men was a proximate factor. Yet so were many very young men railing against the authority of both their elders and the government, mobilising their followers around many more local identities than the master Guadalcanal and Malaita identities of the conflict's height.

Conflict escalated to coup with the mobilisation of the MEF. That mobilisation happened largely because leaders such as Jimmy Rasta took a stand, saying Malaitans had been too patient waiting for the government to defend them; Malaitans must defend themselves. Young men spontaneously rallied to them in large numbers once they did that. They mostly joined up to defend their people, but prospects of excitement and loot for unemployed youth were probably in the mix. That having happened, ambitious men such as Andrew Nori became involved as strategists to steer the volatile political force that was the MEF. And multinational logging and other business interests became involved by bankrolling Members of Parliament who would install a new prime minister to replace Bart Ulufa'alu.

A history—including a very recent history—of compensation payouts by the state to those who threatened violence based on ethnic grievance possibly made both mobilisations more attractive ploys than they otherwise might have been. The state vacillated back and forth, at one moment responding to violence with a deaf ear and with police violence; at the next moment, responding with political dialogue that entailed prospects of compensation. This vacillation was not responsive and was not a fair and firm way of dealing with violence.

What were the key triggering incidents?

The IFM often referred to the murders by Malaitans at Mt Austin as a precipitating grievance, but these murders were not a triggering incident because the Tension was not something triggered immediately in their aftermath. Both sides reported as precipitating incidents particular meetings with Prime Minister Ulufa'alu at which he did not seem to them to listen or respond empathically to their grievances. But again we cannot code these as triggering incidents because militants did not take to arms immediately after them. On the other hand, an inflammatory speech delivered by Premier Alebua on 30 November 1998 did spawn violence immediately afterwards, so this is coded as a triggering incident.

In retrospect, some interpret Premier Alebua posting bail for Harold Keke at the beginning of 1999 as a triggering incident because Keke then organised an escalation of the violence, and from then on was the largest individual obstacle to peace. But this was an escalation only after the conflict was well under way. This is therefore coded as a proximate factor in escalation rather than as a trigger.

Figure 8.6 Harold Keke praying in July 2003 with one of the Melanesian Brothers whom he was holding captive on the Weather Coast

Photo: Ben Bohane

Who were the key actors who fuelled the conflict?

It follows from the previous section that the key actors in starting the conflict were

- Premier Alebua, who influenced his relative Harold Keke and other IFM leaders, each of whom did their own enrolling of young militants
- Jimmy Rasta, Alex Bartlett and other MEF leaders and politicians such as Andrew Nori, Manasseh Sogavare and Sir Allan Kemakeza, who made themselves available to be enrolled by the MEF militants to overthrow Prime Minister Ulufa'alu
- senior Malaitan police who defied the Constitution to stage the coup
- business interests (mainly in logging) who certain informants rumoured bankrolled the parliamentary votes for the overthrow of Ulufa'alu (though it is impossible to be certain about these allegations).

Who were the key peacebuilding actors?

Many of the key war-making actors subsequently became key peacebuilding actors. In prison, most of the militant leaders on both sides, along with Ezekiel Alebua, became leaders of reconciliation through the Sycamore Tree Program. The sincerity of some of these leading war makers turned peacemakers is contested, including by one of the leading Chinese powerbrokers of the Solomons:

> Reconciliation is not coming from the heart from these former militants clutching their Bibles. They are not sincere. They will be doing the same thing as soon as RAMSI leaves. There is no hope for this generation. We have to wait until they grow old and put our hope in a new generation.

It was the militants themselves, along with Andrew Nori and scholar Tarcisius Tara Kabutaulaka, who were the key brokers of the (albeit flawed) Townsville peace, though the premiers of Guadalcanal and Malaita provinces also played their roles, and Sir Peter Kenilorea (2008) was also important. Sir Allan Kemakeza played the decisive role in inviting RAMSI in with a strong mandate that allowed RAMSI to become a singularly important peacebuilding actor. But it is hard to think of Sir Allan as unequivocally a 'peacemaker' when he embezzled so much of the money intended to support the peace!

Female and male church leaders were the most consistently important peacebuilding actors, with the Melanesian Brothers especially important in terms of reconciliatory practice and weapons collection, and the Solomon Islands Christian Association was especially important in policy development and networking for peace.

At the height of the power of the crowd in Solomon Islands history, when Snyder Rini was displaced as prime minister in April 2006, the two key nodes of practical power after Parliament House were the Governor-General's residence and the Honiara Hotel, where its owner, Sir Thomas Chan, pulled the strings of the largest parliamentary faction, the one that anointed Rini and had supported Kemakeza before him. The second two sites of power were approached by the mob, but, unlike Parliament, were not stoned by it—not because of the protection of the police or military (national or international), but because of the protection of the Melanesian Brothers, who made peace with the angry citizens who approached.[8] Even earlier, Qantas asked for the presence of Melanesian Brothers as a condition for it landing in Honiara during the Tension (Carter 2004:6). The Melanesian Brothers also did more effective

---

8   In the case of the Honiara Hotel, a healthy number of Malaitan security personnel were also stationed to guard the premises.

peacemaking than the police or the state in moving between the bunkers of both sides during the Tension to prevent more escalation than there might otherwise have been. The brothers had four semi-permanent camps between the bunkers where the machine guns of the two armies were positioned. The brothers themselves in our interviews believed that the most effective thing they did was to persuade both sides on many occasions to carry back bodies of enemies they had killed to their families. The brothers orchestrated this so fighters would meet those families and see the pain, especially of the women, as they thanked the fighters for returning their men. The Peace Monitoring Council (PMC) collected more weapons than RAMSI and it has been argued that most of the PMC weapons collection was actually accomplished by the Melanesian Brothers (Carter 2006:74–5). In fact, many church organisations played peacemaking roles to prevent the larger catastrophe that might have been on Guadalcanal.

At the height of the Tension, a Civil Society Network emerged that coordinated energetic networking for peace from many organisations in civil society. Matthew Wale was one of many important leaders in that network. The National Council of Women was important for networking women's organisations into peacebuilding—work that continued into 2010 with the conduct of restorative justice training, among other initiatives.

We have argued that the Peace Monitoring Council and its successor, the National Peace Council (supported initially by the International Peace Monitoring Team), played undervalued and highly multidimensional roles in promoting peace and reconciliation. World Vision and Oxfam played significant roles in reconciliation, trauma counselling and redevelopment, as did many other international NGOs and the donor community of nations. The Solomon Islands Development Trust has been the most important of many important local NGOs and has been one of the local NGOs that has worked effectively with Greenpeace in confronting the drivers of conflict in the money politics of logging. Not all was rosy in the NGO sector, however, and at the height of the conflict it was greatly divided against itself.

The United Nations played a much smaller part here than in most international peace operations. Nevertheless, the UNDP and other agencies have made some important contributions that have come up in our text. Major powers—the United States, China, the European Union, the United Kingdom and Japan (the former imperial masters)—did not play major roles. Australia and New Zealand had the trust of these powers to show regional leadership.

Guadalcanal Plains Palm Oil showed a path for restarting peace through development by taking active responsibility with chiefs and the government for untangling the land disputation that was holding back economic opportunities.

KFPL Timber at Ringi Cove similarly pioneered a strong model of collaborative economic development with chiefs based on sustainable management and long-term land leases.

As usual, there were many others beyond those we have singled out; it takes more strategic actors to make peace than to make war. In the Solomons, there were many unsung peacemakers. In the next chapter, we consider the strengths that these actors at different levels of society had available to them to mobilise, and the peacebuilding weaknesses they had to transcend.

9. Peacebuilding strengths and weaknesses

In this chapter, we move under a set of themes through the strengths and weaknesses entries in the final section of Table 8.1. The Solomons' was a conflict that could have become a major war, but was successfully contained. Unlike the story of Timor-Leste, in the next Peacebuilding Compared volume, where every village in the nation suffered death and devastation, the overwhelming majority of the Solomon Islands population stayed out of the conflict and concentrated on sustaining their village economies and taking care of the vulnerable members of their own villages. In spite of the fact that the country is very poor, disintegrated, poorly and corruptly governed and even though basics such as refugee and combatant reintegration were exceptionally poorly managed, Solomon Islands has experienced the loss of only one peacekeeper, in an ambush, and really no other armed conflict deaths since 2003. One reason for this has been RAMSI.

RAMSI: safe but sometimes aloof hands

A weakness of the RAMSI intervention was its poor timing. If Australia, New Zealand and other South Pacific countries were going to send peacekeepers in, it would have been more effective to do so when they were first asked, in 1998. This would have saved most of the loss of life that subsequently occurred and prevented the looting of institutions and the total collapse of the economy between 2000 and 2002.

A strength is that when RAMSI did arrive, it quickly re-established law and order. Violence fell immediately and weapons surrender was quick and successful by any international comparative standard. This success in re-establishing safety in conflict areas seems to be the key to why, in spite of various frequently voiced criticisms of RAMSI that we will consider, 90 per cent of Solomon Islanders in 2007 and 89 per cent in 2008 continued to support the presence of RAMSI (McMurray 2008:10; for a discussion of similar results of earlier surveys, see Anderson 2008:7). One worry is that confidence in RAMSI engendered dependency on RAMSI that has held back the rebuilding of confidence in Solomon Islands institutions. The real test of RAMSI's success should be less confidence in itself than confidence in the institutions it leaves behind.

Ninety per cent confidence is perhaps particularly surprising given that, unlike the peacekeepers in Bougainville, in the Solomons, 'some of the early RAMSI military personnel transgressed local cultural codes by involvement with prostitutes and local women' (Moore 2004:178). RAMSI personnel attracted much more criticism from locals than the Truce and Peace Monitoring Groups in Bougainville. Bougainville's peacekeepers were seen as much closer to the local community. The decision to locate most RAMSI staff in a segregated compound well out of town and most of the rest in white enclaves in prestigious suburbs did not help (compared with the situation in Bougainville, where most peacekeepers were spending most of their time in the villages). Out of and about town as well, locals saw too little of expatriates walking about with locals at the market and too much of them driving with other expatriates in airconditioned cars or sitting together in airconditioned restaurants (such as the Lime Lounge, with its almost exclusively white clientele, as in the extract from our fieldnotes below) (see also Allen 2006):

> RAMSI from Australia are an embarrassment when they holiday in Gizo. Skinnydipping in front of the main street. Lewd behaviour with girls in the swimming pool. They stick together and do not mix with local people. They don't go around and introduce themselves to businesses. So how would they find out where homebrew is sold? They suffer from 'Lime Lounge Syndrome'. (Interview with Western Province businessman, 2006)

Fiscal strengthening and economic reform

Another great achievement of RAMSI from 2003 on was stemming the haemorrhaging of revenue into the pockets of militants and their business cronies. The rapid movement to fiscal balance after 2003 encouraged donors to return in a generous fashion—so generous that now donor dependency is a problem, with 60 per cent of the national budget coming from that quarter (Fukuyama 2008:27). Francis Fukuyama (2008) also sees credible commitment on long-term land leases as an obstacle to development. The problem, as he sees it, is that both investors and traditional landowners do not trust Solomon Islands institutions of land law. The Solomon Islands Government has continued to shy away from tackling the land issues at the heart of the conflict. It has established a Commission of Inquiry into Land Dealings in Guadalcanal and is consulting on a Tribal Land Disputes Resolution Panels Bill, but to date, one post-conflict government after another has found land reform too hard.

Poor-quality commercial institutions generally inhibit investment and deliver low returns to those who have invested; these include the cost of corruption and political instability, unreliable and costly utilities, poor and expensive transportation, burdensome business procedures and uncertain rule of law, particularly insecure contract enforcement (IMF 2007:14). Beyond land law, Fukuyama sees *wantokism* as one of the things that holds back trust in and commitment to national institutions. As Brigg (2009) has countered, however, *wantokism*, wisely harnessed, can also be, and already is to some degree, a resource for trust building (see Chapter 7). Fukuyama regards national secondary schools for the best students from different ethnic groups as something that has worked in the past in Melanesia for forging a national identity among students who share an educational experience together that is oriented to future national leadership. This attracted much interest from Australia when advanced by the famous American scholar but not when advanced earlier by the National Peace Council (NPC 2004:Appendix 8): 'Validate the role of boarding schools to bring children from different islands together to live together, work together and play together.'

An exacting challenge for a peace operation such as RAMSI, which aspires to great national change and a new national discipline, is its vulnerability to charges of hypocrisy. Roughan et al. (2006:2) charge it with demanding austerity while 'practicing profligacy' and remaining 'opaque' while preaching 'transparency'. One might add that while urging de-politicisation of the criminal justice system, it used that system in a highly politicised fashion on many fronts (Averre 2008; Goldsmith and Dinnen 2007). Short peace operations such as in Bougainville keep the internationals out of murky waters that induce such resentment. This indeed was the diagnosis of a number of Bougainville old hands—that RAMSI was at risk of overstaying its welcome. Yet the survey data show that despite a formidable list of criticisms that range from the use of tear gas on 18 April 2006 to RAMSI military and police importing all their food from Australia instead of buying fresh fish and fruit from local markets, RAMSI is popular enough for citizens to want it to stay.

For all the problems, RAMSI made a wonderfully supportive contribution in helping an insolvent nation to solvency, in enabling it to move from a nation that could not pay its civil servants to one that could. Simple improvements to tax and customs administration and an in-line RAMSI accountant-general who immediately put a stop to the release of unauthorised expenditure for corrupt public officials were profoundly important contributions to restoring public services. These measures quickly ended a period in which there were no clear rules of the game of public spending.

Justice strengths and weaknesses

The criminal justice system has been both a strength and a weakness post-conflict. It would be hard to find another peace operation that has secured more convictions for conflict cases, and particularly such a high success rate among the most senior militants on both sides. While RAMSI was much slower to move against the most kleptocratic members of the elite, particularly Prime Minister Kemakeza, in the end it sent him, another former prime minister and half a dozen former cabinet members to prison. Corruption is being better exposed by a reinvigorated Office of the Auditor-General and a multidimensional anti-corruption policy that has a long way to go, but is making headway. The policy is still too timid and too bereft of investigators with the training to mount sting operations that result in bribe-paying foreign loggers losing their licences.

By any comparative standard of post-conflict justice, the Tension trials and the corruption trials were pretty fair.[1] After considering allegations of ethnic bias by RAMSI in-line justice officials, the Parliamentary Inquiry (2009:140) into RAMSI was not persuaded there was any such ethnic bias. On the debit side, there was inevitable selectivity that at times approached the determination of another coalition of the willing in Iraq to convict the 52 leaders who had their photos on those famous playing cards. Indeed, in 2009, RAMSI had a list of the top-10 fugitives that it still sought to capture. Former prime minister and Opposition Leader, Manasseh Sogavare, accused RAMSI of 'pursuing selective justice' in the Tension trials (Parliamentary Inquiry 2009:135). Convicted militants felt aggrieved at the lack of interest of the police in investigating earlier murders of close relatives of theirs. Some in Rove and Tetere prisons said they were political prisoners; some had a significant understanding of the laws of war and argued they had not breached them—it was not murder to kill an enemy soldier in battle. Great though the number of prosecutions was, most of the serious crimes of the conflict could not be pursued for want of resources. Militants were entitled to feel conned by the amnesty agreement at Townsville. The Solomon Islands Parliament was entitled to feel that its will in voting for the

---

1 We should not underestimate what an accomplishment this was. Judges were not allowed to sit on conflict cases involving their *wantoks*. A senior Malaitan judge explained that this was necessary because people like him thought militants such as Jimmy Rasta had saved Malaitans in Honiara: 'He was protecting property and life including myself…We appreciated what they did, the MEF. We provided them with food free…The police were doing nothing to protect us.' One might say that when this judge gives this as a reason why he could not sit on the trial of his *wantoks*, does it also mean he could not justly try IFM militants? Having sat in on one of this judge's trials and read transcripts of his cases, we think they were mostly fair and resulted in just convictions in these difficult post-conflict circumstances where no justice is perfect. We appreciated the openness with which both he as a judge and the prosecutors and defence (from the Office of the Public Solicitor) who appeared before him were willing to be open with us about the biases and conflicts that were inevitable in such a context, and that run through Solomon Islands society in a way one does not find in more legally homogenous settings where the 'rule of law' is well established.

amnesty was disrespected when 'RAMSI did not consider whether to support any amnesty proposal but rather put its resources into trying to make sure that any such claims were defeated' (Averre 2008:10).

In the trials of Harold Keke for murdering Father Geve and of militants for murdering Brother Sado, the court found police failed to accord defendants their full constitutional rights when they were arrested (Averre 2008:11). Australian lawyer, Gary Scott, publicly alleged blatant legal violations by Australian police that frustrated his defence of Jimmy Rasta Lusibaea (Marshall 2004). In the trial of MEF leader Alex Bartlett, a defence subpoena forced revelation of a written agreement between the Australian Federal Police-funded Solomon Islands Police Commissioner, Shane Castles, and two crucial witnesses whereby the witnesses received 'significant financial and other assistance on the condition they kept the agreements secret and gave evidence in Court only in accordance with their police statements' (Averre 2008:11; see also O'Connor 2007a).[2] Such unlawful behaviour in Australia would have had disastrous consequences for the career of a police commissioner.

The most crucial weakness of the justice system, as revealed in the work of the National Peace Council and the Parliamentary Inquiry into RAMSI (2009), has been the failure to enable and support conflict prevention by chiefs and churches at the village level. This was the form of justice that the People's Surveys showed 90 per cent of citizens value most highly (see Chapter 4, Footnote 3).

Weaknesses of governance linkages

RAMSI has focused its governance capacity building very much on Honiara and national institutions based there. Yet Scales et al. (2002:7) argue that perhaps the more important weaknesses of governance are in the quality and clarity of linkages between village government—the level that matters most to most citizens—and more encompassing levels of government at the provincial and national levels. In a village society, strengthened national institutions that do not connect in an effective way to village governance have truncated traction. Provincial government capacity is even less than national governmental capacity—much less. Provincial government is remote from most villages and there is no system of local government. Only a few regions of the nation are linked together by councils of chiefs—an institution commonly used in other parts of Melanesia for linking villages into more encompassing governance systems.

---

2 See, in addition, Chapter 5, Footnote 9 on the substantial payments made by the Australian Federal Police to family members of the alleged victim of sexual abuse by former Solomon Islands attorney-general Julian Moti. Justice Debbie Mullins of the Supreme Court of Queensland found them 'an affront to the public conscience' that called the integrity of the administration of justice into question—an interpretation later rejected by the Queensland Court of Appeal (*R v Moti* [2010] QCA 178).

Churches do perform this function to a degree, at least where denominational schisms are not deep. Church building predates colonial statebuilding by decades in the Solomons (Joseph and Browne Beu 2008:2). Though as Joseph and Browne Beu (2008:1) also point out, in some ways more recent civil society institutions—notably, the Solomon Islands Football Federation—have done more effective integrative institution building across the length and breadth of the nation than has the state.

Unlinking the power of shadow governments

We have seen that one governance linkage that has worked since the Mamaloni governments came to power is between Members of Parliament and a shadow government, or competing shadow governments,[3] of business leaders with investments in logging, hotels, casinos, prostitution and fishing. The arrival of RAMSI saw a second shadow government of advisors operating alongside the electorally accountable government (Dinnen 2008a:68). The first shadow government is mostly ethnically Asian; the second mostly Caucasian.

As indigenous Solomon Islanders see the linkages of their village governance to national and provincial government languish, they sometimes lament the strong linkages they can see whereby shadow governments of foreigners at times make puppets of those they elect. That interpretation was important to understanding the sentiments manifest in the April 2006 riots and to understanding the ethos of resistance to foreign domination of the Sogavare government that came to power in its aftermath. A third, also ethnically Asian, foreign shadow network is constituted by Taiwanese funding, especially of the Rural Constituency Development Fund of S$1 million per parliamentarian per annum to spend more or less as they wish. In addition, in 2006, Taiwan was alleged to have a 'secret slush fund', for 'influence peddling…worth well over $10 million, provided by the back door to the Prime Minister's office' (Skelton 2006). Taiwan is seen as a more benign source of foreign cash by indigenous Solomon Islanders partly because it makes much fewer demands on what government policies should prevail than the other two types of shadow governments. The one policy demand that counts for Taiwan is hard edged, but matters little to the average Solomon Islander: continuing diplomatic recognition of Taiwan. Beyond that, Taiwan mostly exercises only soft power. Yet one prominent Chinese powerbroker in Solomon Islands posited the Taiwanese funding as the most important reason for the nation's poor economic prospects:

---

3   For example, in April 2006, one we have seen was ensconced at the Honiara Hotel supporting Syder Rini's candidature for the prime ministership with backers organised by Sir Thomas Chan. And a competing shadow government in waiting was camped with their Asian business sponsors at the Iron Bottom Sound Hotel.

It prevents Solomon Island politics from maturing and learning to stand on its own feet. Getting elected to Parliament is like winning a $1 million Taiwanese lottery ticket. It's the only way to milk the cow. It's different from Australia where you can have wealthy men like Kevin Rudd and Malcolm Turnbull contesting politics.[4]

But largesse from all the shadow governments of foreigners interacts with first-past-the-post electoral politics and *wantokism* in a way that effectively disenfranchises most citizens—just as it empowers foreign shadows. The foreign shadows provide the largesse to politicians; the favoured politicians use it to reward those who vote for them (mostly *wantoks*). First past the post with many candidates, each with narrow ethnic power bases, means candidates have only to pay off a small proportion of the electorate to win. The rest of the electorate gets little back from the government. So you get government of the few, by the few, for the few foreign shadows.

In this section and throughout the book, we have described the workings of three types of shadow states[5] of foreigners as described in our interviews: first, RAMSI as a neo-colonial shadow government; second, competing factions of predominantly Asian, predominantly logging, business interests that pool funds to bankroll ballots for the prime ministership and votes of no confidence in incumbent prime ministers; and third, the generous development funding Taiwan puts directly into the hands of MPs. A fourth type of shadow state rather closer to William Reno's (1995) original formulation of the concept in Sierra Leone existed between the 2000 coup and the arrival of RAMSI. In this period, the unelected shadows were powerbrokers of the MEF, such as Andrew Nori and Jimmy Rasta. The idea of the shadow state (Reno 1998, 2000) is not that elected governments are puppets of their shadows. Those with formal state power use those with shadow economy and warlord power, just as the latter use the politicians to deliver their specific interests. In the application of the idea of a shadow government (of towns and provinces) by Van Klinken (2007; see also Braithwaite et al. 2010a) to explain the onset of armed conflict in certain provinces of Indonesia, the most common form of payoff sought by members of the shadow government was government contracts. This has been much less important to the shadow governments we have described in the Solomons compared with favourable treatment for logging, fishing, land and casino deals, extravagant and unaccountable compensation and diplomatic leverage.

---

4   He then went on to lament why a comparatively wealthy Solomon Islander, former Central Bank governor Rick Hou, who in his view would make the most talented prime minister for the nation, would never be motivated to play the money politics involved in being prime minister. During the conflict, Hou was threatened at the point of a gun by militants demanding money. A year later, in 2010, he was in fact elected to the Parliament but not to the ministry.

5   In Reno's (1995, 2000) formulation, the shadow state is distinguished from the formal state conceived in conventional Weberian terms as: 1) secure in a monopoly over the legitimate use of force; 2) an administrative order regulated by law; and 3) sovereign in authority within a set of geographical borders.

Sinclair Dinnen, in commenting on an earlier draft of this section, queried whether we had so many shadow governments in play here and so many differences from William Reno's shadow states in Africa that we must question the analytical value of the concept for the Solomons. It could indeed be that as Peacebuilding Compared progresses we find that it is more analytically strategic to deploy the more generic framework of networked governance (Bevir and Rhodes 2003; Castells 1996; Rhodes 1997) that does not connote any particular form of exchange between politicians and network partners. Networked governance also does not necessarily impute anything dark or shadowy about networking between politicians and others. Networked governance analysis allows a dissection of specific forms of linkages—some normatively healthy, some unhealthy. We have introduced another reason for pondering whether networked governance might have been a more productive frame than the shadow government frame we have infused into our analysis at times. This is that the absence of certain types of linkage is a problem of peacebuilding in the Solomons—most importantly, linkages between village governance and more encompassing levels of government. On the other hand, all four of the types of shadow government we posit in this section do have their sinister side. Between them they have 'sucked out' (Ignatieff 2003:162) and corrupted much indigenous capacity, making the capacity that is available rather more at the service of powerful foreign and criminal interests than at the service of powerless villagers and the institutions that should sustain them.

William Reno's conceptualisation of a shadow state connects to a much older literature in economics on the shadow economy. The Solomons certainly became one of those societies in which very little of the economy, including the big international trade items of logs and fish, was recorded in the formal economy of the national accounts and taxed. Key aspects of Reno's shadow state certainly apply to the past two decades of Solomons history. These are the ideas of a shadow state as something 'constructed behind the façade of laws and government institutions' that establishes 'a form of personal rule' (Reno 2000:434). People such as prime ministers Mamaloni, Kenilorea and Rini, MEF leaders such as Jimmy Rasta and Andrew Nori and a cast of envelope-stuffing Asian business leaders all bear considerable similarities to the practitioners of the shadow state, as a form of personal rule, which Reno found in parts of Africa. As in such African states, the Solomons has seen clandestine circuits, particularly linked to a shadow economy of logging, systematically corrupt the Public Service and institutions for its accountability. As in Africa, in the Solomons, accountability institutions, such as the Public Service Commission, the Auditor-General's office, the Ombudsman and the Leadership Code Commission, were progressively dismantled and de-fanged because they were potential obstacles to personal rule and to the ability of rulers to capture rents.

RAMSI is a 'shadow government' that reverses this latter feature; it has been dedicated to strengthening these very institutions, even if it did in practice sometimes 'suck out' Solomons civil service capacity.[6] It shadowed the commanding heights of the state with foreign advisors in a manner more like the influence of the International Monetary Fund (IMF) and the World Bank in Africa. Taiwan's influence has different points of commonality and difference again. One could say that Taiwanese aid has been directed to strengthening the hands of patrimonial personal rule (against the rule of institutions), in this respect more consistently with the shadow state analysis. The clandestine circuits that link Taiwanese diplomats to Solomons political leaders fit the idea of a shadow state operating as personal rule by a mix of state and non-state actors operating behind the façade of a formal state structure.

All of the shadow governments we discuss here are *in part* 'clandestine circuits' wielding power behind a 'façade of formal sovereignty' (Reno 2000:437). Reno (2000:442) speaks of 'the existence of a Shadow State [as]…a matter of degree, rather than an all-or-nothing proposition'. On this continuum, the Solomons of the 1990s could have been closer to what Le Billon (2000:785) has described as the shadow state of the 'commodification of Cambodian forests' than to 1990s Sierra Leone.[7] Reno (2002) has discussed the similarities between what some describe as the shadow state controls of the Russian *mafiya* of the 1990s and shadow states in Africa. Reno sees the critical difference as being that the

---

6 John Wood commented here that in respect of these three accountability institutions, there indeed seems to be more evidence of sucking in of Solomons civil service capacity by RAMSI than sucking out. The Auditor-General's office, for example, has been transformed from an office of three people who did almost nothing, failing to complete an audit in 20 years, to 'an office of 30 local Solomon Islanders and a small number of RAMSI personnel who regularly make reports to Parliament' (Parliamentary Inquiry 2009:155).

7 In some senses, Cambodia and Solomon Islands are both cases where an 'abundance of shadows' (J. Ferguson 2006:15) apply, wherein rulers borrow '"the shadow, not the substance" of a Western capitalist economy'. Cambodia is an interesting case in that international pressure for 'good governance' resulted in a 'legalizing [of] shadow state politics' in the aftermath of a period in which the following logic expressed by a prime ministerial aide had kept economic activity in the shadows: 'To provide revenues to the Public Treasury is not the norm. Now, we make a lot of money. If we inject this money in the Ministry of Finance what will be the use? And who will benefit from this money? We don't know! If I do not steal this money, somebody else will do it and will kill me with the weapons bought with it' (interview with senior official conducted by Le Billon 2000:799). In the post-conflict period after this, '[t]he "shadow state" is thus a domestic response to the political challenges and opportunities posed by multi-party democratic governance and the neo-liberal perspective of "government by the market", in which "the market is viewed not merely as a means of allocating goods and services but as a form of social regulation" (Graf 1995:141). Rather than opposing such a dominant paradigm, state actors seek to co-opt it, thereby benefiting from its financial opportunities, including access to aid, while simultaneously reshaping it into an instrument of power' (Le Billon 2000:799). 'Good governance' influences delivered a biased legal framework in Cambodia that gave exclusive rights of forest exploitation to a favoured few. This was an effect not totally dissimilar to the insipid impact of RAMSI on forest exploitation. The co-prime ministers of Cambodia were able to mimic a green, democratic, accountable discourse of transition 'while integrating forests into their own power bases' (Le Billon 2000:802). 'Under "anarchy", marginalized segments of society were able to manoeuvre to gain some access to forest resources and to integrate themselves into the growing monetised economy, thereby counterbalancing somewhat unequal power relationships. Under "order", this room for manoeuvre gave way to an *exclusionary* form of capitalism, embodied in the take-over of forest access rights by large transnational companies' (Le Billon 2000:802).

Russian state was quite capable of controlling the Russian *mafiya*, including through the use of force, whereas it was beyond the capacity of many weak African states to control the warlords who were the key figures in their shadow states (just as it was impossible for Solomons prime ministers between 2000 and 2003 to control the MEF or Harold Keke).

Comparative projects such as Peacebuilding Compared that progressively add cases over a long period of research might do best to remain open minded about the similarities and differences of accumulating cases to extant conceptualisations in the literature. This is the way we feel about the shadow state concept as we have deployed it in this case and our Indonesian cases (Braithwaite et al. 2010a). There are ways in which it fits quite evocatively with the Solomons experience, especially when we leave ourselves open to the idea of competition among a variety of different kinds of shadow states. Other cases invoke even more variety in 'shadow networks' (Duffield 2002), as in our Bougainville case study, which could be conceived as one in which the 'shadow armies' of private security forces (Sandline) backed by shadowy international mining interests were in play, and were decidedly shadowy players (J. Ferguson 2006:15). The 'shadow' metaphor is not only about darkness, deviousness and non-transparency; it is also about a parallel economy, parallel government or parallel military that sticks with the formal economy/government/military like a shadow sticks to a person. But governance in the Solomons is also importantly shaped by civil society networks that are not at all clandestine and not very corrupt. Pre-eminently, we are thinking of the church here. So we do wonder whether there might be more comparative purchase in diagnosing networks of governance, some of which hide in shadows, others that do not; some of which are a form of state/economy parallel to the formal ones, others that are simply on a different plane (a 'higher' one in the case of the church!). Just as individuals simultaneously identify with different layers of identity (Chapter 7), so they can move among multiple overlapping and fluid networks.

Reasserting control by Solomons institutions over foreign interests in a shadow economy

It could be argued that the Solomons is a case study of how the World Bank good governance agenda of statebuilding and its predecessor, the neo-liberal, small government agenda, have fared equally badly (Carroll and Hameiri 2007). An alternative analysis is that the institutional change most needed is a dismantling of the shadow state(s), at least where it involves payment of foreign cash to advance commercial or foreign diplomatic interests rather than national interests. Second, the institution building most needed is not top-down from

Honiara, but strengthening linkages bottom-up from village governance. It is not police cars in Honiara, but village constables on foot in remote areas where logging tensions bubble up. Many Solomon Islanders focus on corruption and shadow governments as the key challenges, rather than statebuilding, when they commonly say: 'It's not the car we need to change, it's the driver.'

The Centre for Independent Studies (Sodhi 2008:5) was unfortunate enough to release a paper just before the global financial crisis in which it drew lessons from Iceland—a country no more endowed with natural resources than the Solomons, but blessed with institutions that had delivered it prosperity. By the end of that year, the list of nations that were dramatically less solvent than Solomon Islands was a short one, but it included Iceland. Fishing, logging and tourism present the most important, sustainable economic futures for Solomon Islands. They would actually develop better if they were more uncoupled from foreign control (if foreign shadow governments could be put back in their boxes) and better linked to the local governance of the nation's 900 islands. Before the Tension, fishing was better supported for local economic development by dispersed fish-collection centres with refrigeration (Aqorau 2001). These were looted or destroyed by young men during the period of chaos. In the case of logging, Greenpeace (2008) and the Solomon Islands Development Trust have long made the case for progressive elimination of logging licences for foreign investors in favour of community eco-forestry linked to international markets. With fishing, the most strategic thinkers in the Solomon Islands Government favour the elimination of all licences for foreign fishing fleets in favour of developing indigenous capacity, where necessary in partnership with foreign technology and skill transfer.[8] In tourism, the need is to connect the already strong skill sets of the Honiara and Gizo hotel and hospitality industries to village hospitality development, and inter-island transport to tourist paradises on culturally enriching and environmentally pristine remote islands.

This is not to say that there are not also important areas such as minerals exploration (for example, nickel on Isabel Island) in which direct foreign investment that is collaboratively linked to village governance around mine sites is the best development model. It is just to say that the sites where uncoupling from foreign economic development agenda setting is needed are more important sites than those where more foreign involvement would be a benefit. Where foreign help is most needed is with education investment to help Solomon Islanders become more sophisticated in choosing economic development options with bottom-up and top-down linkages that actually deliver development benefits to

---

8   Sustainable fishing is becoming more possible for Pacific countries because of increasingly effective cooperation through the Tuna Commission since 2004 and compliance becoming easier to monitor because of international cooperation in monitoring, NGO participation, satellite monitoring and paper trails for tracing the catch that make it hard to sell fish in Europe and Japan without documentation of where the fish was caught and processed. The effect is that a catch unsupported by a paper trail attracts a lower price.

the country's citizens. Australia's aid program since 2003 has been spending 15 times as much on law and justice as on education (AusAID 2007:2). New Zealand has been concentrating its assistance much more on education. The education budget remains badly skewed towards funding for the children of the elite to participate in higher education. There has been a great deal of fraud in this program, with students continuing to receive scholarship payments for years after they have dropped out of their course, for example.

Where the Centre for Independent Studies' analysis (Sodhi 2008) seems right is that too much of the aid to Solomon Islands is 'boomerang funding' into the pockets of Australian consultants and companies[9] and that in spite of higher levels of foreign aid support than can be found almost anywhere in the world (67 per cent of GDP in 2005) (Anderson 2008:13), Solomon Islanders in the past decade have been considerably worse off economically than they were in the 1970s, with still only a small minority having access to electricity and telephony. For the moment, they are much better off in health, particularly with respect to malaria, thanks to foreign assistance, though globalisation could ultimately reverse its health benefits through HIV/AIDS.

Resilient civil society that can heal itself

One element in common between Solomon Islands and Bougainville is that Moore (2007:171) concludes that there were attempts to mediate the peace through 'more than twenty-five peace negotiations and forums'. As in Bougainville, in the Solomon Islands, there were many more failed peace talks than successful ones. A peacebuilding strength of Solomon Islands civil society was to have the resilience to push on from failed talks, using the tiny accomplishments that had been secured at the early talks as a slight foundation on which to build ultimate agreement for quite a successful disarmament process.

Even though RAMSI has not empowered civil society as strongly as it might have and although the Solomons' state institutions are top-down in ways that fail to foster bottom-up linkages, Solomon Islands civil society has proven resilient. Most of the reconciliation work that has mattered has been local in civil society, led by chiefs, women, churches and militants from inside their prison cells. The Solomon Islands Development Trust and the Solomon Islands Christian

---

9   Sixty-two per cent of total Australian assistance to Solomon Islands in 2006–07 was spent on expert technical assistance compared with an OECD average of 24 per cent (Hayward-Jones (2008a:5). One extreme example of profligacy was a peak of 53 expatriate staff in corrections that continued through 2006. Even on the night shift, when prisoners were locked down, high-priced expatriates were being paid to sit in Rove prison. As one of the Australian corrections staff said, 'I can't imagine what they do all night' to earn the higher salaries they are paid compared with locals. By mid-2009, the number had more than halved to about 20, but still one would have thought this an expensive and peculiar aid priority.

Association have been particularly strong indigenous NGOs with a bottom-up philosophy. This philosophy has also captured the imagination of many of the international NGOs, who have been large investors in Solomons civil society. Oxfam is one such NGO; a good example of the indigenous organisations it supported is Kastom Garden. Kastom Garden works with unemployed rural youth to reconnect them to productive garden-based work. Not all disenchanted youth who are being destroyed by *kwaso* (homebrew) are open to reconnection to their land and culture in this way, but for those who are it provides a path back to agricultural economic development. Kastom Garden also helps rural communities diversify the output from their gardens, improves their gardening techniques and provides more productive seed varieties and strains resistant to common crop diseases.

Unfettered media

Table 8.1 lists a media comparatively not dominated by the government as a strength in comparative terms, even though it faced repeated threats and demands for compensation from thugs operating at the behest of powerful interests and has practised self-censorship of reporting high-level corruption. Some would say the media elites are part of Malaitan elite networks. We, however, saw nothing like the fragmentation of the media into separate Muslim and Christian media that occurred in Ambon, for example (Braithwaite et al. 2010a:Chapter 3). The news pages, editorials and letters columns of the *Solomon Star* newspaper are engaging and diverse in opinion. The Solomon Islands Broadcasting Corporation has some outstanding programming, some of it replete with florid criticisms of the government and RAMSI alike. Public interest activists such as John Roughan of the Solomon Islands Development Trust and his son, Paul Roughan, when he led Transparency Solomon Islands, were never really muzzled for the want of a media outlet for their critiques. Special mention must be made of the world-class contribution of Mary-Louise O'Callaghan in getting the Solomons' story into the international media via her columns in *The Australian*.

The compensation roadblock to truth and reconciliation

A distinctive perversity of peacebuilding in Solomon Islands is that perpetrators have little interest in apologising for their violence. Instead, they managed a backstage identity as combatants and a front-stage identity as victims, so as to maximise large compensation payments from the government. Successive governments have served the nation poorly by paying them.

While we have seen that compensation has deep historical roots in Solomon Islands societies, a government compensation culture has evolved as a shallow and quick fix for teetering governments focused on surviving the next vote of no confidence. We have seen that this government compensation culture increases long-run risks of violence (Chand 2002). It becomes possible for leaders of both sides to win (and taxpayers to lose) when both sides ignite violence confident of a state payout to desist. The scam is even better for leaders when they skim payouts intended for combatants and refugees into their own pockets, as happened on both sides in the Solomons. Once that kind of iterated gaming of state compensation has set in, the best way to turn winners into losers is to convict them in criminal courts. Hence, in the context of the distinctive Solomons history of government compensation to major criminals, RAMSI's robust law enforcement was needed.

A challenge for the Truth and Reconciliation Commission is to tell the truth of the damage that the government compensation culture has done and to convince the society that government compensation has encouraged violence more than ended it. A good starting decision has been legislation that precludes the commission from getting involved in compensation. The Truth and Reconciliation Commission will be worthwhile if it achieves nothing more than persuading the nation that government compensation for horizontal disputes must end, and has ended. Courts are the places where such compensation can be pursued against perpetrators. That of course does not preclude suits against the government where the government is the perpetrator. Reintegration support for refugees and rank-and-file fighters who hand in their guns is best funded directly to them by international donors, precisely so such funds cannot be extorted from governments—and so they cannot be embezzled by ministers and provincial premiers for that matter! Even international donors that fund reintegration payments to ex-combatants must make clear that they are one-off donors who cannot be gamed repeatedly with compensation demands.

The Truth and Reconciliation Commission needs to reconnect citizens to thinking about reconciliation as something people do between one another, and communities do with each other. Competition for state compensation crushes reconciliation as something that can build peace by touching people's hearts. Solomon Islanders already understand this. They just need to see new institutions of reconciliation working well in a new spirit of national healing, forgiveness and rebuilding for the next generation. The reason why the Sycamore Tree restorative justice program discussed in Chapter 6 has had success in bringing combatants together is that the combatants in a sense own the program. Because the state has nothing to do with it, compensation bids to the state do not crowd out the genuine interpersonal and inter-group work of reconciliation.

In the end, crime did not pay

As in most of the conflicts we have so far considered in Peacebuilding Compared, in the Solomons, the most important leaders who started the conflict fared poorly out of it. Harold Keke, tortured by mental illness, serving several life sentences in Rove prison, is the most dramatic instance. He has little freedom of movement even about the prison during his long confinement and is severely disturbed. Part of this problem could be a bullet that struck his brain. But many lesser militant leaders were either killed or ended up in prison. Some of the political masterminds of the conflict have not gone to prison, but their influence and reputations ended up in tatters. Guadalcanal Premier Alebua rapidly lost political support during 2001 and the former prime minister would never be a major force in Solomons politics again. In June 2001, he was lucky to survive gunshot wounds to the eye, chest and arm after an attempt by disgruntled militants from his own side to assassinate him. Later in the decade, he had to take his wounded body into prison.

Andrew Nori's law firm was allegedly paid S$517 549 in 'legal fees' by the government for his negotiations on behalf of the MEF/Joint Operation. Once this became public, he was deeply discredited, particularly in the eyes of MEF combatants who felt they received so little for their sacrifices in defending their people. One MEF member burnt down Nori's law offices in protest, was captured by the police and died after attacks on him in the police cells. In February 2001, the Registrar of the High Court initially refused to renew Nori's practising certificate—a decision Nori eventually had overturned. Nori has so far been clever enough to avoid any legal sanction for his central role in an alleged coup. But Nori told John Braithwaite that his reputation had been damaged 'irreparably' and that some things he had done in representing MEF demands to the government had been 'a personal and professional mistake' for which he was sorry. Another informant said that there had been a suicide in Nori's family as a result of his travails. As far as the police leaders of the Joint Operation were concerned, their police careers have ended and so have those of hundreds of police who worked for them. Dozens of former officers up to deputy commissioner level did prison time over the coup. Jimmy Rasta and his wife gave years of their lives to Rove prison and he faces another attempted murder trial starting in November 2010, notwithstanding his landslide election victory. The hopeful thing is that they continue to give to the prison's reconciliation work today, and to released combatants whom they employ in their business.

10. Statebuilding that contained conflict but shelved specifics that fuelled conflict

Diagnosing specificities or templates for pillars?

In Chapter 9, we argued that a necessary ingredient for peace was to end gaming the state with compensation claims by replacing it with a rule of law. As always, the rule of law turned out to be a beautiful theory that ushered in some ugly practices by RAMSI and the post-conflict state. But it was a fairer rule of law than that which preceded it. When the bar has been progressively raised on some critical barriers to enduring peace—including ending the culture of gaming government compensation, the culture of corruption and harassment on the streets—perhaps we should count a peace operation as a success.

Solomon Islands is still a state riddled with corruption, but today it has an auditor-general and media that expose this publicly, an admirably multidimensional anti-corruption strategy and some of the very worst kleptocrats, even former prime ministers, have been convicted. Zero tolerance of corruption would mean no-one left standing to run the nation. Determination to prosecute the most seriously corrupt at every future point in the nation's history, however mighty, can gradually reduce the heights of corruption to which one must jump before being sanctioned. Commitment to progressively lowering the bar to cut down the worst few cases can mean that future generations come to look back with shock at the corruption tolerated by their forebears.

Where there has not been continuous improvement is in bottom-up reconciliation and bottom-up development. A challenge for the Truth and Reconciliation Commission is to signal the need to reverse this. Certainly, there were short-term statebuilding imperatives for RAMSI centred on Honiara. But the retreat from AusAID's previous village-up civil society development strategy should not have gone as far as it did. Primary and secondary education are in desperate need of restoration to a higher proportion of donor support for Solomon Islands. Inferior access to health centres on the Weather Coast is an injustice at the root of this conflict that can be fixed.

RAMSI support to keep combatants secure in prison could now be pruned right back. Indeed it might be time to consider the proposals of ex-MEF leaders for a Forgiveness Bill that might pardon most ex-combatants in 2012 (as discussed in Chapter 6). It might be time for Sir Peter Kenilorea's agenda of upending policing, so that village constables become key personnel in preventing rural unrest from spreading to the capital in future (see Chapter 5).

Prosecution of foreign loggers who pay bribes to chiefs or cabinet ministers, who make sexual slaves of children in remote parts of the archipelago, who assassinate environmental activists, is overdue. Perhaps the most disappointing thing about RAMSI is that its law enforcement emphasis has not extended to international commercial interests who corrupted the Solomons tax system and its customs administration, who funded the buying of votes of no confidence in the Parliament and, worst of all, who destroyed regulation of the sustainability of the export industries—logging and fishing—that are the Solomons' greatest hope. What a tragedy it is that Australian Prime Minister Howard missed the opportunity to insist in 2003 that independent law enforcement against those who corrupt the regulation of logging and fishing be a condition of going in to save the prime ministership, and possibly the life, of Sir Allan Kemakeza.

Sustainable trees and sustainable fish stocks are keys to the future of Solomon Islands. These are areas where the nation does not need more foreign investment, but less. Strong leaders are needed to transcend the shadow governments of foreigners to make these assets work for the villagers of all the nation's islands. These indigenous leaders already exist; their formidable capacity can be drawn back into Solomon Islands institutions as expatriates exit.

Allen and Dinnen (2010) have discussed the 'often neglected' importance in the onset of political instability and the tensions of 'the disruption to political patronage networks engendered by the combined impact, in the late 1990s, of declining demand for Solomons log exports due to the Asian financial crisis and the reform agenda of the Ulufa'alu government' (see Hameiri 2007, 2009a). This government instability has been a key weakness of the state that has undermined effectiveness in nipping violence in the bud and has fostered profligate resort to state compensation payouts to criminals in desperate attempts to buy political survival. Political instability has led to even more desperate resort to playing the ethnic violence card in politics.

Designing an architecture of politics to render it more stable is no simple challenge. We share Jon Fraenkel's doubts about imported electoral engineering solutions from other parts of Melanesia that have not worked well there, or have been counterproductive (Fraenkel 2004b, 2006; Fraenkel et al. 2008). Indigenous innovation is needed to craft more stable versions of Solomon Islands political culture. That will best emerge from a rich, open, creative, plural discussion of options, as opposed to deals among extant elites, which risk elite gaming and positioning to preserve privilege. The Working Committee on Political Party Integrity Reform has shown some promise, as indicated by a Lowy Institute report (Hayward-Jones 2008b) on what seemed a constructive, imaginative dialogue. In common with Fraenkel et al. (2008), that dialogue makes a good case for the dissolution of Parliament when a motion of no confidence succeeds. Because such a large proportion of sitting members loses their seat in every Solomon Islands election, members might be reluctant in no confidence motions if their success would require dissolution of Parliament. The other remedy advanced in this book is targeted prosecution of the most serious political corruption cases. Passing plain envelopes stuffed with cash to buy votes to unseat a prime minister through a vote of no confidence is clearly the kind of serious corruption that would be caught by a policy of gradually lowering the prosecutorial bar on anti-corruption enforcement. Like Fraenkel et al. (2008:9), we suspect that 'one or two convictions of would be lobbyists offering cash in the run up to a Prime Ministerial election' would help greatly to chill the practice.

Other peace processes have been much more successful than the Solomons' in securing the return of refugees chased from their homes and rebuilding those homes when they have been demolished. The nettle of improving land-dispute resolution has not really been grasped. While it is encouraging to see Guadalcanal Plains Palm Oil Limited and Gold Ridge return to becoming the huge employers and exporters they once were (more painfully in the case of Gold Ridge), and while it is hoped that one day Malaitans might work in some of the jobs they were chased from, it is disappointing that for now Malaitans are unwelcome to apply for the jobs and that areas around these key economic projects are no-go zones for Malaitans. A national capital in which most of the population are squatters is a risky upshot, especially with high-violence areas such as Burns Creek where governments discourage further squatting by refusing to provide basic services such as running water. Where can they go, these Malaitans with a long, proud history of labour migration from their island, with so few employment opportunities? One response to this knotty dilemma could be a formidable opening of Australian and New Zealand labour markets to Solomon Islanders.

There is little sense in which the planners of RAMSI in Canberra in 2003 designed a mission that was attuned to helping with the specific structural and proximate factors listed in Table 8.1 as implicated in the onset of this conflict (Allen and Dinnen 2010). There is also no sufficient sense in which RAMSI attuned its 2003 strategy, or subsequently retuned it, in light of the peacebuilding weaknesses specified in Table 8.1 and Chapter 9, most of which had already been identified by the National Peace Council and subsequently listed in its 2004–09 strategic plan (NPC 2004).

This is not to deny that RAMSI did not very quickly turn around some critical risk factors: guns, unsafe streets in the capital and fiscal insolvency. And we will list in the next section some ways that RAMSI did learn to craft peace by creating spaces in which locals could diagnose specificities of reform. Some of the challenges listed in Table 8.1 were viewed by RAMSI as matters of national sovereignty. Included in this category were the challenges of reconciliation that heals indignities felt by people, fixing the dysfunctional culture of state compensation, fixing land law and land administration, fixing forest and fisheries administration, repatriating refugees and reintegrating combatants, rebalancing uneven development, constitutional reform to improve linkages of governance down to and up from villages, Gold Ridge, youth unemployment and alcohol abuse, internal migration, building health centres on the Weather Coast and a good number of others. At the same time, improving all elements of the criminal justice system, tax and customs administration and various other state functions we have discussed, in which RAMSI was highly interventionist, were somehow not in the category of matters to be left to national sovereignty.

One interpretation is that instead of diagnosing Solomon Islands' problems RAMSI might help fix, RAMSI went in with fairly standard World Bank good governance objectives and templates for fixing them. A slightly different interpretation is that RAMSI's planners in 2003 did have an analysis of what were the root causes of the conflict that RAMSI should seek to remedy.[1] But it was an analysis that was short on specificity. What RAMSI's planners hoped to do was re-establish the rule of law and rebuild a weak or failed state. Yes, the Solomons was a weak state and had suffered a collapse of rule of law. But not all aspects of state performance in critical areas were weak. Few countries have had a larger malaria problem than the Solomons and few countries have fared as

---

1   When Susan Woodward (2007) argues that planning interventions with the aim of fixing root causes of war can make things worse, she is mainly targeting the kind of analysis of root causes that RAMSI did engage with to a degree—one that draws on general empirical lessons that when states are failing and there is widespread poverty and the like, war is more probable. 'First, policies currently designed to address the root causes are based on research in the 1990s that has largely been discredited or superseded, but the policy world has not adjusted to the criticisms and newer scholarship. If the analysis is wrong, it may be better not to address "causes" at all' (Woodward 2007:64). Other aspects of her analysis, however, are relevant to even the most contextually attuned attentiveness to root causes. In particular, she argues that the changes wrought by the war itself can so transform the situation on the ground that addressing original root causes can be off point. More generally, for any problem, addressing its original causes is not always as cost effective a cure as some conceptually quite different approach, as we know from what works when we are ill. In spite of all of this, it seems to us a sound methodology to always ask what were the structural, proximate and triggering factors in a particular conflict and to consider whether there are important things peacebuilders might consider doing about any of these in the cause of future prevention. We could be wrong, however, and the Peacebuilding Compared project will examine whether peace is more sustained after wars where more of the (a) consensus and (b) contested, structural and proximate factors in the conflict are addressed.

well in programs to reduce it. Few developing countries have courts of law in their capital as professional and independent as the Solomons' and few have as professional and independent a central bank.

A diagnosis that correctly yet sweepingly says that a large part of the problem was a weak state does not help. It does not help because all states have their weaknesses and many of those weaknesses are irrelevant to the onset of armed conflict. A mostly strong state that has specific weaknesses, such as Saddam Hussein's Iraq and George W. Bush's United States, can get itself into needlessly nasty conflicts because of those weaknesses. The question is which specific state weaknesses that drive conflict are fixable. Then the need is to work with locals to help to fix them. And one might add that there is a need to diagnose which specific non-state institutions encourage violence and to work with locals to help reform them—a whole-of-society as opposed to whole-of-government approach.

RAMSI was slow and limited in learning to conduct that kind of diagnosis. In its early years, it was not responsive to the specificities of the weaknesses it found—nor did it respond to the identification of strengths by building out from them. It did not follow a responsive strategy of 'pick problems and fix them; pick strengths and expand them' (Braithwaite 2008:115–26). First, it had a statebuilding mind-set, so that assisting with village development, for example, was not in its sights. Its diagnosis being that a weak state was the problem, it instead set out to strengthen what it saw as the core institutions of the state: the institutions of law and order, the finance ministry, state accountability institutions and the institutions of the Public Service (including administration of the Parliament). The names of the RAMSI pillars capture this core-of-the-state ethos: 'law and justice', 'economic governance' and 'machinery of government'. Yet leaving the Solomons with a prison administration with much improved security professionalism is a less valuable legacy than helping to leave it with an improved land administration would have been. By this we mean a land administration that solves some of the problems of land injustice that fuelled the conflict or that resolves the insecurity of land tenure that shackles economic development (Fitzpatrick and Monson 2009). 'Registration of customary land by tribes/clans' has been on the list of the 'Demands by the Bona Fide and Indigenous People of Guadalcanal' from 1988 to this day (Parliamentary Inquiry 2009:198). Malaitans have different perspectives on the land law and administration solutions needed, but agree with their adversaries that this was a root case that must be addressed. It was not part of the RAMSI methodology to go back to the Bona Fide Demands to consider which of them should be picked up as peacebuilding priorities.[2]

---

2   This is not to deny that some of the Bona Fide Demands were implausibly tall orders—such as relocating the national capital.

At one level, it was reasonable of RAMSI planners to believe that they could not fix everything and that it was best to concentrate on a finite set of challenges and tackle them well. But a more attuned, limited set of challenges might have been the specificities with the best chance of preventing recurrence. For almost none of these challenges are internationals the most effective players (one exception being deployment of soldiers). The question is where internationals can best add value to local efforts to fix the problems that matter most. That is not the question the planners of RAMSI asked. It was also not the way Prime Minister Howard and Foreign Minister Downer of Australia framed their intervention strategy.

A positive development in terms of a return to the kind of specificity of peacebuilding analysis that we found the National Peace Council to be doing before it was closed has occurred with the recent Solomon Islands Parliamentary Inquiry (2009) into RAMSI. Its report focused in quite a systematic way—on the basis of an impressive body of testimony from across the archipelago—on what it concluded were root causes of the conflict that should be addressed. The Special Coordinator of RAMSI and the high commissioners of Australia and New Zealand all testified that they did not see it as their responsibility to address the root causes (Parliamentary Inquiry 2009:205), which the inquiry accepted. The members of the inquiry agreed that it was the responsibility of the Solomon Islands Government to do so. They concluded that the first step of the way forward is for the Truth and Reconciliation Commission to recommend an approach to tackling root causes and other conflict-prevention priorities. Then, the next step is for the Solomon Islands Government to assert leadership in its response to the commission's findings. This does indeed seem a way forward at the time of writing. Once that Solomon Islands government leadership to tackle key risks and build on key peacebuilding strengths has been grasped, one might hope for a policy shift to supporting those Solomons priorities on the part of Australia and New Zealand. Persevering with core pillars of statebuilding as donor priorities would then surely be inferior to that responsiveness.

Learning the craft of peace

RAMSI started work in 2003 with a clarity of focus on three core pillars of the state that many modern statebuilders would find admirable. RAMSI was not monolithic, however. Many within the mission lost sight of that clarity of focus. In the jargon of the field, those who lauded the initial RAMSI template of statebuilding pillars would say 'mission creep' set in. We suggest it was mission learning that set in among those who broke ranks with statebuilding templates and that RAMSI's non-monolithic qualities were its saving grace. Actually, one of the things many RAMSI personnel learnt was how to constrict the mission's involvement in certain areas and allow local actors to expand their peacebuilding ambitions.

A key example is the establishment of the Truth and Reconciliation Commission in 2009. For years this had been government policy, and even before RAMSI it had been a bottom-up priority of the church and civil society networks. Before 2009, RAMSI put considerable energy into resisting a Truth and Reconciliation Commission so as to maintain focus on building its three pillars. Australian thinking was that a Truth and Reconciliation Commission would give 'mixed messages' concerning the core criminal enforcement, rule-of-law focus of the mission. An officer of the Commonwealth Secretariat recalled that 'we received repeated requests, starting around 2003 [from the Solomon Islands Government], for advice on comparative models of truth and reconciliation processes from other Commonwealth countries'. When the secretariat dropped into Canberra on the way to offer such assistance,

> Canberra had expressed alarm at the idea of a formal truth commission...I was left in no uncertain mind by Canberra and the High Commissioner in Honiara, and the head of RAMSI, that I should let the request from Solomons for comparative TRC ideas just bubble along. This was considerable pressure...given Australia is an important Commonwealth country too.

By 2009, Australia and RAMSI had stopped all resistance to a Truth and Reconciliation Commission and were even offering support. Does this mean RAMSI had lost its way, drifting dangerously into mission creep? We would rather say that RAMSI had learned to listen. The learning diffused RAMSI's focus little because locals asserted the leadership over the Truth and Reconciliation Commission model they wanted and called in most of the outside help from the UNDP and the International Centre for Transitional Justice, not from RAMSI. Other examples from the pages of our book of how RAMSI learned to be responsive to peacebuilding specificities articulated by local voices include the following.

- RAMSI withdrew from the police posts where local voices said they were least needed. It did so in a way that left behind the physical assets that local police said they needed to remain effective, also learning lessons from policing failures that RAMSI police leaders had experienced in Timor-Leste on this matter.

- RAMSI had a defensible point of view on the dangers of federalism reform as something that might fragment the cost-effectiveness and accountability of a small state, and compound opportunities for corruption. Belatedly, RAMSI leaders recognised that this might be their view, but they could not keep the lid on a federalism debate that most Solomon Islands leaders wanted. So it eased its resistance to that federalism conversation.

- RAMSI listened to the community critique that its law enforcement had been excessively focused on visible militants and insufficiently focused on shadowy 'big fish'. Some quite big fish were put behind bars after 2006 and this critique diminished somewhat.

- RAMSI listened to the critique of Sir Peter Kenilorea, and indeed of the nation's two most recent prime ministers, that policing was becoming too Western and too Honiara centred, supporting the development of a part-time village constable program with advice from a Bougainvillean with experience of their village auxiliary police program. Or at least some key players in RAMSI listened.

- When something positive was accomplished in policing, RAMSI public relations shifted away from publicising RAMSI's contribution to praising the Solomon Islands Police Force in order to build community confidence and trust in their own policing institution (as opposed to public relations for RAMSI).

- AusAID staff within RAMSI have supported a renewed shift to village-based development assistance informed by village voices.

- RAMSI police—or some of them—learned that they had mismanaged the riots outside Parliament and on the streets of Honiara in 2006. They realised there were things they needed to learn from the wisdom of indigenous policing practices that had many times in the past prevented that kind of rioting from spinning out of control. They also learned lessons from formed police units in nations with wider experience of riot control than Australia and New Zealand.

How did this learning happen? RAMSI leaders could be as defensive as those of any peace operation. And many were so defensive that they learnt little from their own mistakes, blaming them on local incompetence. Yet a strength from quite early on was that RAMSI built in a commitment to evaluation modalities that would allow it to learn from its internal and external critics. The result was a culture of grudging, if sometimes slow, responsiveness to critique. This was evident at a conference organised by The Australian National University in Canberra in 2006. Mary-Louise O'Callaghan, an Australian journalist married to a Solomon Islander who had lived in the country for many years, delivered a scathing account of RAMSI's unresponsiveness to local voices at the conference. RAMSI police leaders were furious after her presentation, asking pointed questions about who had the bright idea of inviting such an unfair critic. Within days of follow-up conversations with those police leaders and then others in the Australian Government, RAMSI had made one of its best personnel decisions:

hiring O'Callaghan as a communications adviser. From that office, she helped push RAMSI into countless community relations listening projects touring the villages over the next four years.

One of the criticisms O'Callaghan made of RAMSI police that day was of inadequate training in the culture and languages of the countries to which Australian police were deployed. That situation has greatly improved since 2006, with Pacific islander trainers working at the Majura International Deployment Group headquarters of the Australian Federal Police, more apt scenario training, improved post-rotation debriefing and sharing of lessons with the next rotation of personnel. Past antagonisms and mutual misunderstandings between AusAID, police, military and non-Australian components of RAMSI have been partially remedied by extended placements of AusAID, military and foreign trainers at Majura and placements of AFP officers in AusAID and at Australia's military peacekeeper training centre. Both high-level and low-level committee structures within RAMSI on the ground have also been adapted to foster cross-cultural learning not only between foreigners and Solomon Islanders but also to foster police responsiveness to the culture of development agencies and vice versa. Many Australian RAMSI officers do not learn from Pacific island and New Zealand contingents, but most return from RAMSI enriched by what they have learnt not only from Solomon Islanders but also from the inhabitants of other Pacific islands.

This learning has also been institutionalised at a higher level by continuous Pacific Islands Forum reviews of RAMSI.[3] Even more important have been reviews conducted by the Parliament of the Solomon Islands (especially the one in 2009), which incorporated televised engagements with citizens on all the main islands of the nation. The People's Surveys (McMurray 2008) that were part of RAMSI's performance indicator reviews also generated more systematic public opinion feedback on where citizens were more and less disappointed with what RAMSI was doing. The lively local mass media also pushed productively for greater RAMSI responsiveness. We hypothesise that it has been RAMSI's learning to be more responsive that has maintained the high public support for it in those surveys.

In sum, a feedback and responsiveness culture was gradually institutionalised within RAMSI and by the Solomon Islands state and civil society. On all fronts, the most important way responsiveness took more steps forward than backwards was by creating spaces in which RAMSI leaders could leave their Honiara compound to enter dialogue in villages and towns. There were, however, certainly

---

3 These occurred from 2007 under the auspices of the Enhanced Consultative Mechanism among RAMSI, the Solomon Islands Government and the Pacific Islands Forum. See: <http://www.encyclopedia.com/doc/1G1-165067373.html> (viewed 29 June 2010).

backward steps, such as cutting funding from the National Peace Council. The result of this dialogue is the 'peacebuilding creep' we are describing in this conclusion as something different from 'mission creep'. In these spaces where dialogue was enabled, RAMSI became responsive to suggestions as to who would be best able to do what. Perhaps it was the church rather than RAMSI which should advance this agenda; perhaps it was chiefs who should be given modest resources to support that agenda rather than national or foreign elites in the capital; perhaps a Truth and Reconciliation Commission supported by the UNDP could take on another, and so on. There were also timing issues in such collaborative dialogue: 'Last year [a particular group] was my most appropriate partner on this challenge, next year you will be the better partner; can we work together as partners on this next year?' Rather than mission creep, this was mission creativity. In part, it allowed societal creep onto RAMSI's agenda and far beyond, including onto some of the neglected specificities and needed diagnostics of contextual peacebuilding.

Figure 10.1 RAMSI Special Coordinator James Batley receives a gift of betel-nut from a community elder of Chief Moro's village on the Weather Coast in August 2005 as other Solomon Islands and foreign dignitaries look on

Photo: David Jones

Responsiveness to local context and local voices was a slow, sometimes backtracking process for RAMSI. We think there might be some inevitability about this. We wonder if the reason policing of the colonial era seemed more responsive to the realities of Solomon Islands societies than policing of the RAMSI era was simply that colonial policing had been making mistakes, evolving and learning from local context for longer. We do not have historical data from the evolution of colonial policing in Solomon Islands to support this inference. We simply find it an interesting hypothesis to support our future empirical work on this question.

We do not know of examples of weak states progressing in a linear fashion to become strong states in matters of years, as opposed to decades or centuries. The durations of international peace operations are measured not in decades or centuries, sometimes not even years, but in months. So we might simply say that the experience of history at this stage of Peacebuilding Compared is that learning how to be a strong state is always a slow dawn. So we must be humble in what we expect in a few years. Some of the kinds of responsiveness on which we have lamented slowness could be challenges we might never expect a peace operation to meet. Consider responsiveness to the criticism of locking up lots of bit players while letting the 'big fish' off. Even the most commercially sophisticated economies that have extremely strong states—the United States, the United Kingdom, Japan and Germany—take long years to build cases for criminal prosecutions against 'big fish'. And then their prosecutions frequently fail. Hence, it seems unrealistic to expect a struggling transitional justice system with limited technical support from donors to have this capacity during the short life of a peace operation. RAMSI was an unusual mission in lasting more than a few years; and it was only after a few years that it locked up some really big fish. Hence, even though most of the big fish about which Solomon Islanders remain concerned roam free, we might still regard RAMSI as extraordinarily successful in its responsiveness on this matter. Certainly, RAMSI achieved some prosecutorial results against major targets more quickly than the International Criminal Court has done, or could do.

The kinds of learning we have been describing are inevitably slow and perhaps would be possible only with a persistent and well-resourced intervention such as RAMSI. For a less well-resourced peace operation of shorter duration than RAMSI, the 'slow-food' (Boege 2006; Bowden et al. 2009) approach of the 'light intervention' in Bougainville (Regan 2010) has considerable advantages in its different approach to learning. Bougainville saw countless waves of patient bottom-up reconciliation built on previous waves, expanding the geographical reach of the peace and the breadth and depth of renewal across society. The architecture of the top-down peace settlement was also sequenced, with linkages that required one side to meet a commitment before the other side would deliver their next undertaking in an agreed sequence (Regan 2008; Wolfers 2006). This sequenced architecture was a slow creation of Bougainvilleans themselves, with drafting assistance from a tiny clique of foreign advisors. It only began as a successful peace process on the ashes of a number of previous peace agreements that had failed. The contribution of the international peacekeepers was a small fraction of RAMSI in numbers, duration, budget and scope of operations (see Braithwaite et al. 2010b). There was in Bougainville nothing approaching the ambition John Howard and Alexander Downer took into Solomon Islands—as revealed in our interviews—of staying until a credible state was built to replace a failed state.

The role of peacekeepers was nevertheless extremely important in enabling the slow cooking of peace by and for the people of Bougainville. It became slow food that filled their stomachs with *wan bel* ('one belly', actually meaning harmonised relationships) that they savoured and secured because they, rather than the foreign peacemakers, owned it. The peacekeepers gave confidence to combatants who were afraid to meet to reconcile before they arrived; they created safe spaces at crucial times in which the peace could mature.

We do see one choice for internationals, then, as a slow-food approach, in which peacekeepers keep guns and spoilers out of the kitchen. And another choice is a slow-learning approach in which a multidimensional peace operation gradually comes to terms with the challenges of statebuilding over many years. When the latter path is taken, our analysis internal to the Solomon Islands case supports the comparative conclusion of Howard (2008) that the responsiveness and mission learning that we call 'peacebuilding creep' is the key factor that turns failing aspects of the mission into more successful ones. But we also conclude RAMSI could have adapted to the contextual challenges faster had it gone in with a radically different initial framing of the mission.

Reframing for faster, fuller responsiveness

We have argued that a strength of RAMSI is that it created spaces for dialogue where it could learn to be responsive to local agenda setting. It falteringly, yet increasingly, became a learning organisation, partly because of some good early design work on continuous reviews and performance evaluation that was responsive to feedback from Solomon Islanders.

We have also concluded that RAMSI's fundamental weakness was that at first it framed the intervention with the wrong question. This was: how do we build the fundamental pillars of a state that has failed? Alexander Downer framed it even more counterproductively in our interview as staying until the intervention had 're-engineered' the Solomon Islands state. Our argument has been that there were many dimensions to this error. We also note as an aside that it follows from our analysis that it is possible for a mission to be motivated by an even more counterproductive framing question than the one RAMSI had—for example: 'How do we achieve regime change?' The most important two errors of the RAMSI framing were, first, that it was blind to the strengths of the Solomon Islands state and society as manifest in village institutions, churches, women's networks, sporting organisations and much more that delivered human security to most villages even at the height of the conflict. Second, it did not take as a starting point a diagnosis of the specificities of the root causes of the conflict. So what might have been a sensible framing? We suggest three questions that might have formed a better starting frame for a collaborative peace process.

1. What is currently working to provide most people in Solomon Islands a high level of community safety and human security, and how might these strengths be supported?
2. What were structural and proximate factors that contributed to the conflict (as in Table 8.1) and how might these be remedied?
3. What new risks to the peace do locally knowledgeable people fear (such as revenue collapse as a result of ending log exports)? What can be done to hedge these risks?

Assiduously and collaboratively working at answering these questions cannot secure fast and full responsiveness in peacebuilding. Yet we contend they are simpler questions that could have delivered quicker specificity of targeting than the more abstract ambition of building core pillars of a state stigmatised as having failed. Or worse, regime change followed by who knows what?

We construe successful peacebuiding as a craft. A craftsperson does not follow a template. That is what factories do when they make a piece of furniture, for example. When a craftsperson makes furniture, there is no recipe that says do this much planing, this much sawing, gluing, sanding. The craft is a creative, evolutionary practice rather than a templated one. Furniture making as craft is about looking at how the piece is evolving in the process of the craft, how to go with the grain by now planing some more here but not there. As Sparrow (2000:201), from whom we have adapted the furniture metaphor, puts it, being a craft means resisting the idea of work being organised around tools; tools are organised around work. Furniture making is a solitary craft, though one learnt in communities of practice, and through apprenticeship, just as peacebuilding is. Peacebuilding is, however, a collaborative rather than a solitary craft. A richer analogy might be to the craft of the musician in an orchestra. The first violin is collaborating up to the conductor, down to the other violins, laterally to the woodwind section and last, but far from least, she is profoundly attuned to the emotional effects of the music in causing the audience to gasp, laugh, cry or lapse to serenity. A collaborative craft is not about following a fixed mandate because creative success turns on hearing and seeing opportunities to connect creation to positive human emotions. 'We would not have great symphony orchestras if conductors focused only on keeping musicians from playing out of tune' (Heimer 1997).

But is the sheet of music played by a musician a template? Well, yes; neither the craft of peacebuilding nor the musical craft is a template-free zone. In this volume, we have referred to many templates: the software in the Solomon Islands Customs Division that makes it impossible to change certain fields on the customs valuation without leaving behind your electronic signature, and completely impossible to change other fields, is a nice example of a sharply prescriptive template. What our conclusion resists is an international template that is an overarching constraint on where a mission cannot go and must go on questions of governance development. A mission needs a mandate that empowers and sets limits on how and why peacekeepers can arrest people, use different levels of force and take over certain functions from a sovereign government for an agreed period. It need not be a mandate that rules out forms of development assistance agreed in local dialogues and falling within the competence and budgetary capability of the mission to support with other partners. Accountability of a peace operation is not best assessed as compliance with the letter of a prescriptive mandate, but more in the way that some accountability was achieved for RAMSI, with Pacific Islands Forum and Solomon Islands Parliament hearings and reports, community surveys, measurement and reporting of good and bad outcomes and robust debate in local media. So perhaps we learn to see elements of the peacebuilding craft from the solitary furniture maker, and other elements from the symphony metaphor, but we get closer to the craft mentality by pondering jazz improvisation. Musical scripts are used and adapted continuously, but in ways generated by interactive learning from the moves of other musicians in an ensemble and from audience reactions. That is not to say there are no limits to the mandate of the jazz musician; however good you are, you cannot jump on the stage and take over someone else's gig!

The craft of peacebuilding is one of collaborative learning, of getting the timing right, deciding which different sets of collaborators should be assembled at different times to work sequentially on new problems. It is the craft of not playing the grand finale to the concert before the audience has begun to warm to the music, of not being mandated to stage an election until citizens have begun to believe in democracy. It is an uncharted social process engaging many actors. We must expect it to be slow.

Pillars and shadows

The pillars of great public buildings in capitals of the West symbolise the solidity of the state. It is an odd kind of learning from ancient Greek and Roman statebuilding that the West sent architects to Athens and Rome to draw templates of the only residues of those republics that stood: the pillars that once held up the rubble around them. Of course, the pillars were a misleading symbol of how the architectures of ancient states and more modern ones were gradually cobbled together over centuries.

Part of our analysis in this book has been that developing states need to pay attention not just to building neat pillars but also to the messy business of managing shadow states (Reno 1995) that fracture and corrupt those pillars. In the Solomons case, the shadow economy of logging and a complex of relationships among foreign business and diplomatic interests and local politicians and militants have shadowed and recurrently opened cracks in the architecture of the state. We have concluded that RAMSI's contribution to improving that kind of management has been modest.

The particular way RAMSI set about repairing and constructing pillars of the Solomons state was by shadowing each key functionary of the pillar with an expatriate—a dual-desk approach. At first, RAMSI officers directly operated core organs of government, especially the security and finance sectors. This was necessary and successful in stabilising the society. Then the strategy was for these in-line expatriates gradually to build the capacity of their counterpart at their dual desk until they were ready to take over completely. We have concluded this was mostly not successful because outstanding operational police and operational finance bureaucrats were not always good trainers of their counterparts. They were often prone to frustration at the inferior education or experience of those they shadowed and to taking over again as soon as something was done badly. RAMSI frequently did not apply the basic lesson of peacebuilding that something done tolerably well by locals is always better than something done extremely well by outsiders.

In any case, as Bayley and Perito (2010) and Wilson (2010) have argued in relation to police building, it is better for operational peacekeepers to be replaced by management consultants experienced in building police institutions and police academy experts who set up training for local trainers who do the in-line training in the language, and using the cultural scripts, familiar to those who are trained. It is an odd theory of how to build an institution to train all members of the institution one by one before there is an architecture those individuals can inhabit. Much more than training is needed in a police force to build logistical capability, personnel and promotion systems, transport and communication systems, data processing, police accommodation, secure armouries and many other management systems. So we suggest it was a flawed conception of how to build the pillars of the state to put outsiders in to run them in their way and then to rely so heavily on those same individuals to remake themselves as trainers of counterparts to run those pillars in ways that locals felt would be sustainable. As Bu Wilson has said to us, quoting Ed Rees, '[w]e would not think it sensible to build a health system by flying a thousand doctors into a country, so why would we think that was the way to build a police service?' (see further Wilson 2010:185).

The Solomons case reinforces the lesson from previous research that a boom-and-bust economy is a threat to peace (N. Ferguson 2006) and increases the risk of crime waves (Fischer 1999:Appendix N). Extreme poverty is a structural driver of armed conflict (Collier 2007), but even rich countries suffer more wars during periods of history punctuated by extreme boom and bust (like the period from the 1890s to 1939). Boom and bust in an economy in which the dominant exports—logs and fish—have been more in the shadow economy than in the formal economy of taxpaying have cashed up both foreign and indigenous corruption, contributing to unusually unstable government coalitions.

The current boom that took off after 2003 is not just a logging boom; it is also a boom in donor funding triggered by RAMSI. What a double tragedy it will be if, just as RAMSI created the security that amplified the 2004–10 logging boom, it amplifies the bust of a final collapse of logging stocks when that bust coincides with RAMSI's exit. RAMSI succeeded with locals in getting guns off the street and in securing macroeconomic stability in the short term. But prospects for long-run peace and political stability are slim if there is not long-run macroeconomic stability, no matter how well statebuilding and incarceration of militants are executed. Shadow governments could unravel the state again if the specific grievances that led to conflict continue to be swept under the carpet.

Appendix

Numbers and types of people interviewed, Solomon Islands case

Elected official	15
Civil servant/judge	26
Political leader of oppositional group	1
IFM/GRA combatant	5
MEF combatant	10
Police Joint Operation coup participant	2
Other Solomon Islands Police Force	4
RAMSI military—Australia	7
RAMSI military—New Zealand	7
RAMSI military—Fiji	3
RAMSI military—Papua New Guinea	2
RAMSI police—Australia	25
RAMSI police—New Zealand	5
RAMSI police—Vanuatu	4
RAMSI police—Papua New Guinea	3
RAMSI police—Fiji	1
RAMSI police—Marshall Islands	1
RAMSI civilian	29
Chief/indigenous/village leader	4
Church leader	9
Women's NGO	6
Environmental NGO	2
Development NGO	8
Human rights/peacebuilding NGO	19
Other NGO	2
Journalist	3
Business leader	20
Student/youth leader	5
Foreign government (ambassador, foreign minister of another country, AusAID, and so on)	18

International organisations (United Nations, World Bank, and so on)	8
Researcher/university academic	2
Victim/refugee (dozens in other categories are refugees)	2
Other	0
Total interviews	240
Total people interviewed	258

References

Akin, David 1999 'Compensation and the Melanesian state: why the Kwaio keep claiming', *The Contemporary Pacific* 11(1), 35–67.

Alasia, Sam 2008 'Rainbows across the mountains: the first post-RAMSI general elections', in Sinclair Dinnen and Stewart Firth (eds), *Politics and State Building in Solomon Islands*, Canberra: ANU E Press.

Allen, Matthew 2006 'Dissenting voices: local perspectives on the Regional Assistance Mission to Solomon Islands', *Pacific Economic Bulletin* 21(2), 194–201.

Allen, Matthew 2007 Greed and grievance in the conflict in Solomon Islands 1998–2003, PhD dissertation, The Australian National University, Canberra.

Allen, Matthew 2008 'Politics of disorder: the social unrest in Honiara', in Sinclair Dinnen and Steward Firth (eds), *Politics and State Building in Solomon Islands*, Canberra: ANU E Press and Asia Pacific Press.

Allen, Matthew 2009a Research proposal: the political economy of logging in Solomon Islands, Canberra: The Australian National University.

Allen, Matthew 2009b 'Resisting RAMSI: intervention, identity and symbolism in Solomon Islands, *Oceania* 79(1), 1–17.

Allen, Matthew (forthcoming) 'The political economy of logging in Solomon Islands', in R. Duncan and S. Pollard (eds), *Strengthening Pacific Economic Analysis*, Manila and Canberra: Asian Development Bank and The Australian National University.

Allen, Matthew and Sinclair Dinnen 2010, 'The North down under: antinomies of conflict and intervention in Solomon Islands', *Conflict,Security & Development* 10(3), 299–327.

Amnesty International 2000 *Solomon Islands: A forgotten conflict*, London: Amnesty International.

Amnesty International 2004 *Solomon Islands Women Confronting Violence*, London: Amnesty International, <http://www.amnesty.org/en/library/info/ASA43/001/2004>

Amnesty International 2009 Solomon Islands: the truth and reconciliation commission cannot work in isolation, Public statement, Amnesty International, London, viewed 29 April 2009, <http://www.amnesty.org/en/library/info/ASA43/001/2009/en>

Anderson, Tim 2008 *The Limits of RAMSI*, Sydney: AID Watch.

Aqorau, Transform 2001 'Sustainable management and development of Solomon Islands fishery resources: new directions in fisheries policy', *Pacific Economic Bulletin* 16(2), 120–6.

Aqorau, Transform 2008 'Crisis in Solomon Islands: foraging for new direction', in Sinclair Dinnen and Stewart Firth (eds), *Politics and State Building in Solomon Islands*, Canberra: ANU E Press and Asia Pacific Press.

Australian Agency for International Development (AusAID) 2007 *Aid Activities in Solomon Islands*, Canberra: Australian Agency for International Development, viewed 16 April 2007, <http://www.ausaid.gov.au/country/cbrief.cfm?DCon=5714_5074_8646_2331_4632andCountryID=16andRegion=SouthAsia>

Australian Agency for International Development (AusAID) 2008 *Violence Against Women in Melanesia and East Timor: Building on global and regional promising approaches*, Canberra: Australian Agency for International Development.

Averre, Kenneth Hall 2006 Pre-trial incarceration in Solomon Islands and the reasonableness of its length: a post conflict intervention context, Paper presented to the 20th International Conference of the International Society for the Reform of Criminal Law, Brisbane, 2–6 June 2006.

Averre, Kenneth Hall 2008 *The Tension Trials—A defence lawyer's perspective of post conflict intervention in Solomon Islands*, Canberra: State, Society and Governance in Melanesia Project, The Australian National University.

Banks, Glenn 2005 'Linking resources and conflict the Melanesian way', *Pacific Economic Bulletin* 20(1), 185–91.

Batten, Aaron and Satish Chand 2008 'Rolling RAMSI forward: some ideas from the literature', *Pacific Economic Bulletin* 23(1), 128–46.

Bayley, David H. and Robert M. Perito 2010 *The Police in War: Fighting insurgency, terrorism, and violent crime*, Boulder, Colo.: Lynne Rienner.

Bennett, Judith A. 1987 *Wealth of the Solomons: A history of a Pacific archipelago, 1800–1978*, Pacific Islands Monographs Series, No. 3, Honolulu: University of Hawai'i Press.

Bennett, Judith A. 1993 '"We do not come here to be beaten": resistance and the plantation system in Solomon Islands to World War II', in Brij V. Lal, Doug Munro and Edward D. Beechert (eds), *Plantation Workers: Resistance and accommodation*, Honolulu: University of Hawai'i Press.

Bennett, Judith A. 2000 *Pacific Forest: A history of resource control and contest in Solomon Islands, c. 1800–1997*, Cambridge and Leiden: The White Horse Press and Brill Academic Publishers.

Berman, Bruce J. 1998 'Ethnicity, patronage and the African state: the politics of uncivil nationalism', *African Affairs* 97, 305–41.

Bevir, Mark and R. Rhodes 2003 *Interpreting British Governance*, London: Routledge.

Boege, Volker 2006 *Bougainville and the discovery of slowness: an unhurried approach to state-building in the Pacific*, Occasional Paper Series No. 3, Brisbane: The Australian Centre for Peace and Conflict Studies.

Bowden, Brett, Hilary Charlesworth and Jeremy Farrall 2009 'Introduction', in B. Bowden, H. Charlesworth and J. Farrall (eds), *The Role of International Law in Rebuilding Societies after Conflict*, Cambridge: Cambridge University Press.

Braithwaite, John 2005 *Markets in Vice, Markets in Virtue*, New York: Oxford University Press.

Braithwaite, John 2008 *Regulatory Capitalism: How it works, ideas for making it work better*, Cheltenham, UK: Edward Elgar.

Braithwaite, John, Valerie Braithwaite, Michael Cookson and Leah Dunn 2010a *Anomie and Violence: Non-truth and reconciliation in Indonesian peacebuilding*, Canberra: ANU E Press.

Braithwaite, John, Hilary Charlesworth, Peter Reddy and Leah Dunn 2010b *Reconciliation and Architectures of Commitment: Sequencing peace in Bougainville*, Canberra: ANU E Press.

Brigg, Morgan 2009 'Wantokism and state building in Solomon Islands: a response to Fukuyama', *Pacific Economic Bulletin* 24(3), 148–61.

Bureau of Democracy, Human Rights and Labor 2006 *Country Report on Human Rights Practices in Solomon Islands*, Washington, DC: US Department of State, viewed 17 August 2006, <www.state.gov/g/drl/rls/hrrpt/2005/61627.htm>

Butler, A. 2006 'An Australian government perspective', in Sinclair Dinnen and Stewart Firth (eds), *Politics and State-Building in Solomon Islands*, Canberra: ANU E Press and Asia Pacific Press.

Carroll, Toby and Shahar Hameiri 2007 'Good governance and security: the limits of Australia's new aid programme', *Journal of Contemporary Asia* 37(4), 410–30.

Carter, Richard 2004 Lessons learnt from indigenous methods of peacemaking in Solomon Islands, with particular reference to the role of the Melanesian Brotherhood and the religious communities, Unpublished document, Christian Peacemaking, Honiara.

Carter, Richard 2006 *In Search of the Lost: The death and life of seven peacemakers of the Melanesian Brotherhood*, Norwich, UK: Canterbury Press.

Castells, Manuel 1996, *The Information Age: Economy, society and culture. Volume 1: The rise of the network society*, Oxford: Blackwell.

Chabal, Patrick and Jean-Pascal Daloz 1999 *Africa Works—Disorder as a political instrument*, Oxford: James Currey and Indiana University Press.

Chand, Satish 2002 'Conflict to crisis in Solomon Islands', *Pacific Economic Bulletin* 17(1), 154–9.

Clastres, P. 2007 *Society Against the State: Essays in political anthropology*, New York: Zone Books.

Cohen, Stanley 1972 *Folk Devils and Moral Panics: The creation of the Mods and Rockers*, St Albans, Hertfordshire: Paladin.

Collier, Paul 2007 *The Bottom Billion: Why the poorest countries are failing and what can be done about it*, Oxford: Oxford University Press.

Commission of Inquiry 2007 *Commission of Inquiry into the April 2006 Civil Unrest in Honiara*, Second Interim Report, Honiara: Department of the Prime Minister, Government of Solomon Islands.

Commission of Inquiry 2009 *Commission of Inquiry into the April 2006 Honiara Civil Unrest in Honiara: Recommendations, conclusions and findings*, Honiara: Government of Solomon Islands.

Corrin, Jennifer 2008 'Ples bilong mere: law, gender and peace-building in Solomon Islands', *Feminist Legal Studies* 16, 169–94.

Corris, Peter 1973 *Passage, Port and Plantation: A history of Solomon Islands labour migration, 1870–1914*, Carlton, Vic.: Melbourne University Press.

Cullen, Francis T. 1994 'Social support as an organizing concept for criminology: presidential address to the Academy of Criminal Justice Sciences', *Justice Quarterly* 11(4), 527–59.

Dauvergne, Peter 1998 'Globalisation and deforestation in the Asia-Pacific', *Environmental Politics* 7(4), 114–35.

Dauvergne, Peter 1999 'Corporate power in the forests of the Solomon Islands', *Pacific Affairs* 71(4), 524–46.

Department of Foreign Affairs and Trade 2004 *Solomon Islands: Rebuilding an island economy*, Canberra: Department of Foreign Affairs and Trade, Commonwealth of Australia.

Diamond, Jared 1997 *Guns, Germs and Steel: A short history of everybody for the last 13,000 years*, London: Vintage.

Dinnen, Sinclair 2002 'Winners and losers: politics and disorder in the Solomon Islands 2000–2002, *Journal of Pacific History* 37(3), 285–98.

Dinnen, Sinclair 2007a 'A comment on state-building in Solomon Islands', *Journal of Pacific History* 42(2), 255–63.

Dinnen, Sinclair 2007b The politics of unrest—external intervention and the challenges of state-building in Solomon Islands, Paper presented to Solomon Islands: Where to Now?, State, Society and Governance in Melanesia Project, The Australian National University, Canberra, 5 May 2006.

Dinnen, Sinclair 2008a 'State-building in a post-colonial society: the case of Solomon Islands', *Chicago Journal of International Law* 9(1), 51–78.

Dinnen, Sinclair 2008b 'Dilemmas of intervention and the building of state and nation', in Sinclair Dinnen and Stewart Firth (eds), *Politics and State Building in Solomon Islands*, Canberra: ANU E Press and Asia Pacific Press.

Dinnen, Sinclair and John Braithwaite 2009 'Reinventing policing through the prism of the colonial kiap', in Peter Grabosky (ed.), *Community Policing and Peacekeeping*, Boca Raton, Fla: CRC Press.

Duffield, Mark 2002 'War as a network enterprise: the new security terrain and its implications', *Journal of Cultural Research* 6, 153–65.

Ellison, Graham and Conor O'Reilly 2008 'From empire to Iraq and the "war on terror"', *Police Quarterly* 11(4), 395–425.

Fearon, James D. and David D. Laitin 2003, 'Ethnicity, insurgency, and civil war', *American Political Science Review* 97(1), 75–90.

Ferguson, James 2006 *Global Shadows: Africa in the neoliberal world order*, Durham, NC: Duke University Press.

Ferguson, Niall 2006 *The War of the World: Twentieth-century conflict and the descent of the West*, New York: Penguin.

Fifi'i, J. 1989 *From Pig-Theft to Parliament: My life between two worlds*, Translated and edited by Roger M. Keesing, Honiara: Solomon Islands College of Higher Education and University of the South Pacific.

Filer, Colin 1990 'The Bougainville rebellion, the mining industry and the process of social disorganization in Papua New Guinea', *Canberra Anthropology* 13(1), 1–39.

Filer, Colin and Martha Macintyre 2006 'Grass roots and deep holes: community responses to mining in Melanesia', *The Contemporary Pacific* 18(2), 215–31.

Fischer, David Hackett 1999 *The Great Wave: Price revolutions and the rhythm of history*, Oxford and New York: Oxford University Press.

Fitzpatrick, Daniel and Rebecca Monson 2009 'Balancing rights and norms: property programming in East Timor, the Solomon Islands and Bougainville', in Scott Leckie (ed.), *Housing, Land and Property Rights in Post-Conflict United Nations and Other Peace Operations*, Cambridge: Cambridge University Press, 124–52.

Forsyth, Miranda 2009 *A Bird that Flies with Two Wings: Kastom and state justice systems in Vanuatu*, Canberra: ANU E Press.

Fraenkel, Jon 2004a *The Manipulation of Custom: From uprising to intervention in the Solomon Islands*, Wellington: Victoria University Press.

Fraenkel, Jon 2004b 'Electoral engineering in Papua New Guinea: lessons from Fiji and elsewhere', *Pacific Economic Bulletin* 19(1), 122–32.

Fraenkel, Jon 2006 'Political consequences of Pacific island electoral laws', *Demetrius*, Canberra: The Australian National University, viewed 5 January 2009, <http://dspace.anu.edu.au/handle/1885/43135>

Fraenkel, Jon, Matthew Allen and Harry Brock 2010 'The resumption of palm-oil production on Guadalcanal's northern plains', *Pacific Economic Bulletin* 25(1), 64–75.

Fraenkel, Jon, Anthony Regan and David Hegarty 2008 *The dangers of political party strengthening legislation in Solomon Islands*, SSGM Working Paper 2008/2, Canberra: State, Society and Governance in Melanesia Project, The Australian National University.

Frazer, Ian 1985 'Circulation and the growth of urban employment amongst the To'ambaita, Solomon Islands', in M. Chapman and R. M. Prothero (eds), *Circulation in Population Movement: Substance and concepts from the Melanesian case*, London: Routledge and Kegan Paul.

Frazer, Ian 1997 'The struggle for control of Solomon Island forests', *The Contemporary Pacific* 9(1), 39–72.

Fry, Greg and Tarcisius Kabutaulaka 2008 'Political legitimacy and state-building intervention in the Pacific', in G. Fry and T. T. Kabutaulaka (eds), *Intervention and State-Building in the Pacific: The legitimacy of 'co-operative intervention'*, Manchester: Manchester University Press.

Fukuyama, Francis 2008 'State building in Solomon Islands', *Pacific Economic Bulletin* 23(3), 18–34.

Gegeo, David Welchman 2001 'Cultural rupture and indigeneity: the challenge of (re)visioning "place" in the Pacific', *The Contemporary Pacific* 13(2) (Fall), 491–507.

Goldsmith, Andrew and Sinclair Dinnen 2007 'Transnational police building: critical lessons from Timor-Leste and Solomon Islands', *Third World Quarterly* 28(6), 1091–109.

Gordon, Robert J. 1983 'The decline of Kiapdom and the resurgence of "tribal fighting" in Enga', *Oceania* 53, 205–23.

Government of Solomon Islands 2002 *Solomon Islands Human Development Report 2002: Building a nation*, Queensland: Mark Otter.

Graf, William 1995 'The state in the third world', *The Socialist Register* 31, 140–62.

Granovetter, Mark S. 1974 'The strength of weak ties', *American Journal of Sociology* 78(6), 1360–79.

Gray, George 2002 *Habuna Momoruqu (the blood of my island): violence and the Gudalcanal uprising in Solomon Islands*, SSGM Working Paper, Canberra: State, Society and Governance in Melanesia Project, The Australian National University, <http://rspas.anu.edu.au/papers/melanesia/working_papers/Tanis-Gray.rtf>

Greenpeace 2008 *Securing the Future: An alternative plan for Solomon Island forests and economy*, Honiara: Greenpeace.

Guddemi, Philip 1997 'Continuities, contexts, complexities and transformations: local land concepts of a Sepik people affected by mining exploration', *Anthropological Forum* 7(4), 629–48.

Hameiri, Shahar 2007 'The trouble with RAMSI: reexamining the roots of conflict in Solomon Islands', *The Contemporary Pacific* 19(2), 409–41.

Hameiri, Shahar 2009a 'State building or crisis management? A critical analysis of the social and political implications of the Regional Assistance Mission to Solomon Islands', *Third World Quarterly* 30(1), 35–52.

Hameiri, Shahar 2009b 'Governing disorder: the Australian Federal Police and Australia's new regional frontier', *The Pacific Review* 22(5), 549–74.

Harris Rimmer, Susan 2010 *Building Democracy After Conflict. Case study: the Solomon Islands truth commission*, Canberra: Centre for International Justice and Governance, The Australian National University.

Hayward-Jones, Jenny 2008a *Beyond good governance: shifting the paradigm for Australian aid to the Pacific islands region*, Policy Brief, September 2008, Sydney: Lowy Institute.

Hayward-Jones, Jenny 2008b *Engineering Political Stability in Solomon Islands: Outcomes report*, Sydney: Lowy Institute.

Hegarty, David 2003 *Peace interventions in the South Pacific: lessons from Bougainville and Solomon Islands*, Working Paper 2003/4, Canberra: State, Society and Governance in Melanesia Project, The Australian National University.

Hegarty, David, Ron May, Anthony Regan, Sinclair Dinnen, Hank Nelson and Ron Duncan 2004a *Monitoring peace in Solomon Islands*, Working Paper 01/04, Canberra: State, Society and Governance in Melanesia Project, The Australian National University.

Hegarty, David, Ron May, Anthony Regan, Sinclair Dinnen, Hank Nelson and Ron Duncan 2004b *Rebuilding state and nation in Solomon Islands: policy options for the Regional Assistance Mission*, Working Paper 2004/2, Canberra: State, Society and Governance in Melanesia Project, The Australian National University.

Heimer, Carol 1997 *Legislating responsibility*, American Bar Foundation Working Paper No. 9711, Chicago: American Bar Foundation.

Herbert, Tania 2007 *Commercial Sexual Exploitation of Children in the Solomon Islands: A report focusing on the presence of the logging industry in a remote region*, Solomon Islands: Christian Care Centre, Church of Melanesia.

Howard, John 2003 Ministerial statement to Parliament on the Regional Assistance Mission to Solomon Islands (RAMSI) by the Prime Minister of Australia, Parliament House, Canberra, viewed 29 November 2005, <www.pm.gov.au/news/speeches/speech422.html>

Howard, Lise Morjé 2008 *UN Peacekeeping in Civil Wars*, Cambridge: Cambridge University Press.

Hviding, Edvard 1996 *Guardians of Marovo Lagoon: Practice, place, and politics in maritime Melanesia*, Honolulu: University of Hawai'i Press.

Hviding, Edvard 2003 'Contested rainforests, NGOs, and projects of desire in Solomon Islands', *International Social Science Journal* 178, 539–53.

Ignatieff, Michael 2003 'The burden', *The New York Times Magazine*, 5 January, 1, 62.

International Monetary Fund (IMF) 2007 *IMF country report*, No. 07/304, Washington, DC: International Monetary Fund.

Job, Jenny and Monika Reinhart 2003 'Trusting the tax office: does Putnam's thesis relate to tax?', *Australian Journal of Social Issues* 38(3), 307–34.

Jolly, Margaret 2000 'Epilogue: further reflections of violence in Melanesia. Violence and governance in Melanesia—an introduction', in Sinclair Dinnen and Allison Ley (eds), *Reflections on Violence in Melanesia*, Sydney and Canberra: Hawkins and Asia Pacific Press.

Joseph, Keith and Charles Browne Beu 2008 *Church and state in Solomon Islands*, Discussion Paper 2008/11, Canberra: State, Society and Governance in Melanesia Project, The Australian National University.

Jourdan, Christine 1995a 'Masta Liu', in V. Amit-Talai and H. Wulff (eds), *Youth Cultures: A cross-cultural perspective*, London: Routledge.

Jourdan, Christine 1995b 'Stepping-stones to national consciousness: the Solomon Islands case', in Robert J. Foster (ed.), *Nation Making: Emergent identities in postcolonial Melanesia*, Ann Arbor: University of Michigan Press.

Kabutaulaka, Tarcisius Tara 1998 'Deforestation and politics in Solomon Islands', in Peter Larmour (ed.), *Governance and Reform in the South Pacific*, Canberra: National Centre for Development Studies.

Kabutaulaka, Tarcisius Tara 2001 *Beyond ethnicity: the political economy of the Guadalcanal crisis in the Solomon Islands*, Working Paper 01/01, Canberra: State, Society and Governance in Melanesia Project, The Australian National University.

Kabutaulaka, Tarcisius Tara 2004 'Solomon Islands', *The Contemporary Pacific: Political Reviews, Melanesia*, (Fall), 393–401.

Kabutaulaka, Tarcisius Tara 2006 'Crowded stage: actors, actions and issues in post-conflict Solomon Islands', in John Henderson and Greg Watson (eds), *Securing a Peaceful Pacific*, Christchurch: University of Canterbury Press.

Kabutaulaka, Tarcisius Tara 2008 'Westminister meets Solomons in the Honiara riots', in Sinclair Dinnen and Stewart Firth (eds), *Politics and State Building in Solomon Islands*, Canberra: ANU E Press and Asia Pacific Press.

Karle, Warren 2004 *Conflict in the 'Happy Isles': The role of ethnicity in the outbreak of violence in Solomon Islands*, Monograph Series, No. 5, Canberra: Australian Defence College.

Keesing, Roger M. 1985 'Killers, big men, and priests on Malaita: reflections on a Melanesian troika system', *Ethnology* 24(4), 237–52.

Keesing, Roger M. 1992 *Custom and Confrontation: The Kwaio struggle for cultural autonomy*, Chicago and London: University of Chicago Press.

Keesing, Roger M. 1994 'Foraging in the urban jungle: notes from the Kwaio underground', *Societe des Oceanistes* 99, 167–75.

Kenilorea, Peter and Clive Moore (eds) 2008 *Tell It As It Is*, Taipei: Centre for Asia-Pacific Area Studies, RCHSS.

Latour, Bruno 1986 'The powers of association', in J. Law (ed.), *Power, Action, and Belief: A new sociology of knowledge?*, Sociological Review Monograph 32, London, Boston and Henley: Routledge and Kegan Paul.

Latour, Bruno 1987 *Science in Action: How to follow engineers and scientists through society*, Milton Keynes, UK: Open University Press.

Le Billon 2000 'The political ecology of transition in Cambodia 1989–1999: war, peace and forest exploitation', *Development and Change* 31, 785–805.

Leslie, Helen 2002 'Gendering conflict and conflict management in the Solomon Islands', *Development Bulletin* 60, 13–16.

McDougall, Debra 2003 'Fellowship and citizenship as models of national community: United Church Women's Fellowship in Ranongga, Solomon Islands', *Oceania* 74(1/2), 61–80.

McDougall, Debra 2005 'The unintended consequences of clarification: development, disputing, and the dynamics of community in Ranongga, Solomon Islands', *Ethnohistory* 52(1), 81–109.

Macintyre, Martha 2002 On masculinity and the use of violence in contemporary Melanesia, Paper presented to Australian Anthropological Society Annual Conference, The Australian National University, Canberra, 3–5 October 2002.

McLeod, Abby 2009 'Police capacity development in the Pacific: the challenge of local context', *Policing and Society* 19(2), 147–60.

McMurray, Christine 2008 *People's Survey 2008*, Canberra: ANU Enterprise.

Maley, William 2009 'Democracy and legitimation: challenges in the reconstitution of political processes in Afghanistan', in Brett Bowden, Hilary Charlesworth and Jeremy Farrall (eds), *The Role of International Law in Rebuilding Societies after Conflict: Great expectations*, Cambridge: Cambridge University Press.

Mamdani, Mahmood 1996 *Citizen and Subject: Contemporary Africa and the legacy of late colonialism*, Princeton, NJ: Princeton University Press.

Mamdani, Mahmood 1999 'Historicizing power and responses to power: indirect rule and its reform', *Social Research* 66(3), 859–86.

Marshall, Will 2004 'Australian lawyer condemns lack of legal rights in the Solomon Islands', World Socialist website, 3 February 2004, viewed 2 August 2009, <www.wsws.org/articles/2004/>

Meister, Robert 1999 'Forgiving and forgetting: Lincoln and the politics of national recovery', in Carla Hesse and Robert Post (eds), *Human Rights in Political Transitions: Gettysburg to Bosnia*, New York: Zone Books.

Moore, Clive 2004 *Happy Isles in Crisis*, Canberra: Asia Pacific Press.

Moore, Clive 2007 'External intervention: the Solomon Islands beyond RAMSI', in M. Anne Brown (ed.), *Security and Development in the Pacific Islands: Social resilience in emerging states*, London: Lynne Rienner Publishers.

Moore, Clive 2008 'No more walkabout long Chinatown: Asian involvement in the economic and political process', in Sinclair Dinnen and Stewart Firth (eds), *Politics and State Building in Solomon Islands*, Canberra: ANU E Press and Asia Pacific Press.

Morgan, Michael 2005 *Cultures of dominance: institutional and cultural influences on parliamentary politics in Melanesia*, Discussion Paper, Canberra: State, Society and Governance in Melanesia Project, The Australian National University.

Muggah Robert 2004 *Diagnosing demand: assessing the motivations and means for firearms acquisition in the Solomon Islands and Papua New Guinea*, Discussion Paper, Canberra: State, Society and Governance in Melanesia Project, The Australian National University.

Naitoro, John 2000 *Solomon Islands conflict: demands for historical rectification and restorative justice*, Update Papers, Canberra: Asia Pacific School of Economics and Management, The Australian National University.

Naitoro, John 2003 Articulating kin groups and mines: the case of the Gold Ridge project in the Solomon Islands, PhD dissertation, The Australian National University, Canberra.

National Peace Council (NPC) 2004 *Strategic Plan, July 2004 to December 2009*, Honiara: National Peace Council.

National Peace Council (NPC) 2006 *To Build Lasting Peace in Solomon Islands*, Honiara: National Peace Council.

O'Connor, Patrick 2007a Solomon Islands Government defeats no-confidence motion, World Socialist Web Site, viewed 2 August 2009, <www.wsws.org/articles/2007/aug2007/solo-a25.shtml>

O'Connor, Patrick 2007b Solomon Islands Government rebuts Canberra's child sex allegations against Attorney-General, World Socialist Web Site, viewed 2 October 2009, <http://www.wsws.org/articles/2009/oct2009/moti-o17.shtml>

O'Connor, Patrick 2009a Evidence backs Julian Moti's allegation of politically motivated charges, World Socialist Web Site, viewed 2 October 2009, <http://www.wsws.org/articles/2009/oct2009/moti-o17.shtml>

O'Connor, Patrick 2009b Australian Federal Police disclose 1,500 pages of documents in Julian Moti case, World Socialist Web Site, viewed 2 October 2009, <http://www.wsws.org/articles/2009/oct2009/moti-o17.shtml>

Office of the Auditor-General 2007 *An auditor-general's insight into corruption in Solomon Islands government*, National Parliament Paper No. 48, Honiara: Government of Solomon Islands.

Office of the Special Coordinator 2004 *Helpem Fren: RAMSI, a partnership with the people of Solomon Islands*, Honiara: Office of the Special Coordinator.

Organisation for Economic Cooperation and Development (OECD) 2005 *Security System Reform and Governance*, Paris: OECD Publishing.

Oxfam 2003 *Australian Intervention in the Solomons: Beyond operation Helpem Fren. An agenda for development in the Solomon Islands*, Melbourne: Oxfam.

Pacific Islands Forum 2004 *Social Impact Assessment of Peace Restoration Initiatives in Solomon Islands*, Suva: Pacific Islands Forum Secretariat.

Parliamentary Inquiry 2009 *Parliamentary Inquiry into the Facilitation of International Assistance Notice 2003 and RAMSI Intervention*, (Chairman Hon. Peter Boyers), Honiara: Parliament of Solomon Islands.

Patrick, Stewart and Kaysie Brown 2007 *Greater Than the Sum of its Parts— Assessing 'whole of government' approaches to fragile states*, New York: International Peace Academy.

Plunkett, Mark 2003 *Stress-Testing Solomon Islands Peace Operation Scenarios*, Queensland: Griffith University.

Pollard, Alice A. 2000 'Resolving conflict in Solomon Islands: the women for peace approach', *Development Bulletin* 53, 44–6.

Ponzio, Richard 2005 'The Solomon Islands: the UN and intervention by coalitions of the willing', *International Peacekeeping* 12(2) (Summer), 173–88.

Putnam, Robert D. 1993 *Making Democracy Work: Civic traditions in modern Italy*, Princeton, NJ: Princeton University Press.

Rawlings, Gregory 2006 *Regulating Responsively for Oversight Agencies in the Pacific*, Canberra: State, Society and Governance in Melanesia Project, The Australian National University.

Regan, Anthony 2008 'Sustainability of international peace-building interventions—the Bougavinville experience, 1997–2006', in Greg Fry and Tarcisius Tara Kabutaulaka (eds), *Intervention and State-Building in the Pacific*, Manchester: Manchester University Press.

Regan, Anthony 2010 *Light Intervention: Lessons from Bougainville*, Washington, DC: United States Institute of Peace Press.

Reno, William 1995 *Corruption and State Politics in Sierra Leone*, Cambridge: Cambridge University Press.

Reno, William 1998 *Warlord Politics and African States*, Boulder, Colo.: Lynne Rienner.

Reno, William 2000 'Clandestine economies, violence and states in Africa', *Journal of International Affairs* 53(2), 433–59.

Reno, William 2002 'Mafiya troubles, warlord crises', in Mark R. Beisinger and Crawford Young (eds), *Beyond State Crisis?*, Baltimore: Johns Hopkins University Press.

Rhodes, Roderick 1997 *Understanding Governance*, Buckingham and Philadelphia: Open University Press.

Roughan, Paul 2004 *National Integrity Systems Transparency International Country Study Report: Solomon Islands 2004*, Vic., Australia: Transparency International.

Roughan, Paul, B. K. Greener-Barcham and Manuhuia Barcham 2006 *Where to now for RAMSI?*, CIGAD Briefing Note 1/2006, Palmerston North, NZ: Centre for Indigenous Governance and Development, Massey University.

Rudé, George 1981 *The Crowd in History: A study of popular disturbances in France and England, 1730–1848*, (Revised edition), London: Lawrence and Wishart.

Salisbury, R. F. 1962 *From Stone to Steel: Economic consequences of technological change in New Guinea*, Carlton, Vic.: Melbourne University Press.

Scales, Ian, Sinclair Dinnen and David Hegarty 2002 *Governance at the Grassroots:Workshop on participation beyond the centre in Solomon Islands 15–16 April 2002*, Canberra: State, Society and Governance in Melanesia Project, The Australian National University.

Scott, James C. 1985 *Weapons of the Weak: Everyday forms of peasant resistance*, New Haven, Conn.: Yale University Press.

Scott, Michael W. 2000 'Ignorance is cosmos; knowledge is chaos: articulating a cosmological polarity in the Solomon Islands', *Social Analysis* 44(2), 56–83.

Scott, Michael W. 2007 *The Severed Snake: Matrilineages, making place, and a Melanesian Christianity in southeast Solomon Islands*, Durham, NC: Carolina Academic Press.

Shearing, Clifford and Les Johnston 2005 'Justice in the risk society', *The Australian and New Zealand Journal of Criminology* 38(1), 25–38.

Skelton, Russell 2006 'The hard graft behind the riots', *The Age*, 29 April, 1–3.

Smith, Anthony D. 1991 *National Identity*, Harmondsworth, UK: Penguin.

Sodhi, Gaurav 2008 'Five out of ten: a performance report on the Regional Assistance Mission to the Solomon Islands (RAMSI)', *Issues Analysis* 92, 31 January 2008.

Solomon Star 2006 'Detainees win PM's heart', *Solomon Star*, 28 December 2006.

Sparrow, Malcolm 2000 *The Regulatory Craft: Controlling risks, managing problems and managing compliance*, Washington, DC: The Brookings Institution.

Steeves, Jeffrey 1996 'Unbounded politics in the Solomon Islands: leadership and party alignments', *Pacific Studies* 19(1), 115–38.

Stritecky, J. M. 2001 Looking through a moral lens: morality, violence and empathy in Solomon Islands, PhD dissertation, University of Iowa.

Tryon, Darrell T. and Brian D. Hackman 1983 *Solomon Island Languages: An internal classification*, Canberra: The Australian National University.

United Nations Development Programme (UNDP) 2004 *Emerging Priorities in Preventing Future Violent Conflict*, New York: United Nations Development Programme.

United Nations Development Programme (UNDP) 2005 *Solomon Islands Country Program*, New York: United Nations Development Program, viewed 20 March 2010 <http://www.unddr.org/countryprogrammes.php?c=180>

URS Sustainable Development 2006 Solomon Islands national forest resource assessment update 2006, Prepared for AusAID and the Department of Forests, Environment and Conservation.

Van Klinken, Gerry 2007 *Communal Violence and Democratization in Indonesia: Small town wars*, London: Routledge.

Wainwright, Elsina 2003 *Our Failing Neighbour: Australia and the future of the Solomon Islands*, Barton, ACT: Australian Strategic Policy Institute.

Wairiu, Morgan 2004 Forest certification in Solomon Islands, Paper presented to Forest Certification in Developing and Transiting Societies Symposium, Yale School of Forestry and Environmental Studies, New Haven, Conn., 10–11 June 2004.

Waiwori, Christopher 2006 'Quest for political power', *Solomon Star*, 10 May 2006.

Weber, Eugen 1976 *Peasants into Frenchmen*, Stanford, Calif.: Stanford University Press.

White, Geoffrey 2007 *Indigenous governance in Melanesia*, Discussion Paper 2007/5, Canberra: State, Society and Governance in Melanesia Project, The Australian National University.

Wielders, Iris 2008 'The regional assistance mission to Solomon Islands in global perspective', in Greg Fry and Tarcisius Tara Kabutaulaka (eds), *Intervention and State-Building in the Pacific: The legitimacy of 'cooperative intervention'*, Manchester and New York: Manchester University Press.

Wilson, Bu V. E. 2010 Smoke and mirrors: the development of the East Timorese police 1999–2009, PhD dissertation, The Australian National University, Canberra.

Wolfers, Edward 1983 'Centralisation and decentralisation until independence', in Peter Larmour and Sue Tarua (eds), *Solomon Islands: Politics and government*, Suva: Institute of Pacific Studies, University of the South Pacific.

Wolfers, Edward P. 2006 *Bougainville autonomy—implications for governance and decentralisation*, Public Policy in Papua New Guinea Discussion Paper Series, No. 5, Canberra: The Australian National University.

Wood Report 2005 *Report of a Review of Accountability Institutions of Solomon Islands by John T. D. Wood*, Honiara: Technical Assistance Governance Facility for Solomon Islands.

Woodward, Susan L. 2007 'Do the root causes of civil war matter? On using knowledge to improve peacebuilding interventions', *Journal of Intervention and Statebuilding* 1(2), 143–70.

World Wide Fund for Nature (WWF) 2005 *A Forest Strategy for Solomon Islands 2006–2011: Final report from WWF SI forests strategy planning workshop*, Honiara: World Wide Fund for Nature.

Index

www.ingramcontent.com/pod-product-compliance
Lightning Source LLC
Chambersburg PA
CBHW061240270326
41927CB00035B/3449